Jonathan Tucker is a former associate director of the Indian and Southeast Asian department at Spink and Son and has operated a gallery in St James's, London, with his wife Antonia Tozer since 2000. He is also a consultant for Bonhams and is a recognised authority in the field of Indian and Southeast Asian art, particularly in sculpture. He lived in Asia for eleven years and spent many years exploring the ancient trade routes between China and Europe, travelling the entire length of the Silk Road with the exception of Iraq. He is the author of *The Silk Road: Art and History* (Philip Wilson Publishers), an illustrated and annotated map of the Silk Road for Odyssey Travel Guides; *The Silk Road: Central Asia, Afghanistan and Iran* (I.B. Tauris); and *The Troublesome Priest: Harold Davidson, Rector of Stiffkey.*

The SILK ROAD

China and the Karakorum Highway

A TRAVEL COMPANION

Jonathan Tucker

I.B. TAURIS

LONDON · NEW YORK

First published in 2015 by
I.B.Tauris & Co Ltd
London • New York
www.ibtauris.com

ISBN: 978 1 78076 356 9
eISBN: 978 0 85773 933 9

A full CIP record for this book is available from the British Library
A full CIP record is available from the Library of Congress

Library of Congress Catalog Card Number: available

Printed and bound by Page Bros, Norwich, UK

For Antonia

Contents

Illustrations

Figures

Maps
(all drawn by the author)

Foreword
by Paul Theroux

What is extraordinary about the lavish and loosely ravelled anfractuosities of thoroughfare that go under the name 'The Silk Road' – winding across half the globe, over deserts and rivers and mountain ranges – is that almost 2,000 years ago the Pacific Ocean was connected culturally with the Mediterranean. And the Mediterranean gave access to the whole of Europe. So, as Jonathan Tucker writes in this exhaustive and enjoyable book, the twain really did meet, East and West, in mutually satisfied curiosity, commerce, romance, swapping inventions, treasures and ideas.

And this is also why Tucker relates that an Asiatic parrot in an ivory cage might be found in ancient Athens, and 'an Egyptian Pharaoh mask found in the thirteenth-century grave of a Mongol woman at Genghis Khan's capital of Karakorum'. And it is, by the way, the reason that, with the benefit of Chinese technology, Europe had rudders (rather than steering oars) and compasses on their ships, and stirrups and bridles on their horses (thus allowing Europe the Age of Chivalry), and movable type (the Chinese preceded Gutenberg), and much else. Consider the 'angels of Miran' – European-style winged male figures carved on a Buddhist shrine in Asia. 'The "angels of Miran" are nothing short of amazing,' Mr Tucker writes, 'and no one was more surprised at their discovery than [the archeologist Aurel] Stein himself: "How could I have expected by the desolate shores of Lop-nor, in the very heart of innermost Asia, to come upon such classical representations of cherubim?"'

And of course there was the silk – one of the earliest and rarest commodities that China exported to the West. Tucker tells the amazing story of sericulture; how Chinese silk was sought by Romans who could afford it; how the rearing of silkworms and the cultivation of mulberry trees remained China's greatest secret, from the earliest times, until the widespread deforestation – and that included mulberry trees – of Mao's Cultural Revolution.

The Silk Road was the reason that China had Persian dancers, and lute players and 'Sogdian dancing girls' from the West; and why, in one of the happiest convergences on earth, Greco-Persian artisans were making their own versions of Buddhist images and bas-reliefs and temple carvings at Taxila – Buddha had a new somewhat Grecian face and robes; and why so too did the *bodhisattvas*, in the singular beauty of Gandharan art.

'A famous visitor to Taxila during the Parthian era [first century AD] was St Thomas who, according to Christian legend, was commissioned by King Gondophares (r.c.AD 20–50) to build him a palace.' Like St Thomas, and the Chinese monk Xuanzang in the seventh century, and the Arab traveller Ibn-Wahab in the ninth century, and later Marco Polo in the thirteenth, and numerous others recalled in this book, Tucker tells these stories well. He is widely respected as a connoisseur of ancient artefacts. He knows, through handling, a Khmer statue, a Chinese celadon and a Bactrian chariot fitting – and much else; he has travelled the length and breadth of the Silk Road, and he is widely read so his book is learned and felicitous.

I wish I'd had this book 33 years ago when I was first in China, and on subsequent trips, when I was trying to understand the scattered remnants and tumbled walls of the ancient city of Turfan in remote Xinjiang, and the caves at Dunhuang and the (then vandalised) Buddhas in the Yungang caves outside Datong. As for the monumental Buddhas hewn from rock at Bamiyan, 'among the greatest artistic creations of the earth', Tucker does those full justice in his text, though they have been destroyed by fanatics. Many of the towns and cities still exist, yet some of what remains of the Silk Road befits the hubris of Ozymandias. I am thinking of Turfan and the Peshawar valley, and the dusty foundations of Merv, in present-day Turkmenistan, an enormous set of interlocked cities, now little more than an elegant crater.

Since the Silk Road was not one road, but many, it represented a series of suggestive directions, taking in – not cities, since cities are a recent phenomenon on earth – but a multitude of bazaars. Many of the bazaars still flourish, the Tolkuchka Bazaar – just outside Ashgabat in Turkmenistan – is a desert encampment retailing camels and carpets and silver, and the Silk Road Bokhara remains a venerable and busy town, and Xian (resurgent Changan) is a metropolis once more. The presence of mosques, synagogues, temples and Christian churches in such places demonstrates the complexity of belief on the road. Jewish travellers from the Levant found their way to Changan and Luoyang, and not only became involved in the production of silk, but their Chinese descendents, the Chinese Jews of Kaifeng, are still living in Henan province. There may be Nestorians in China too. Nestorians found their way to China when they expanded to the East – the Silk Road was thick with schismatics.

Recognising this back-and-forth of believers and thinkers, Tucker makes one of his shrewdest judgements when he describes the arrival of Buddhism in China along the ancient routes: 'one of many instances of the passage of ideas (one of the Silk Road's most important commodities)'. We take for granted objects, sculptures, terracotta, textiles, instruments, weapons and finery, and the excesses of Qin Shi Huangdi in his desire for immortality; but it was the exchange of ideas – faiths, beliefs, and songs and poems too – that gave the Silk Road its vitality.

This book is a good companion in all respects, a history that is readable, a guide for the traveller that is invaluable, a handbook for the seeker of antiquities, an essential vademecum for the puzzled and bewildered tourist; and for the chair-bound person who does not wish to experience firsthand the howling Taklamakan Desert, or the upsets of Turkmenistan or Uzbekistan, or the exotic cuisines en route, it is a wonderful reference book and an enlightening journey in itself.

Note on the Translation of the Poetry and Prose

When poetry and other forms of literature are translated from another language, the quality of translation is almost as important as the original text. The interpretations of Chinese literature by Burton Watson, Arthur Waley and Vikram Seth, quoted in many places in this book, are superb. So, too, are the translations from the Persian by Gertrude Bell, Reuben Levy and A. J. Arberry, and when several versions of the same text are available I have tried to use the one that is the most evocative and best captures the atmosphere of the time or place.

MAP 1
The Silk Road – land and sea routes.

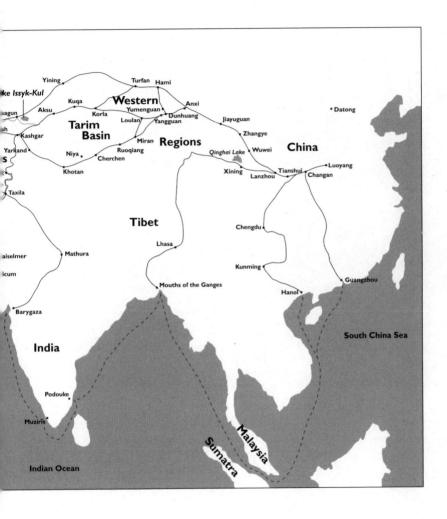

INTRODUCTION

The Early Development of the Silk Road, Principal Routes and Goods Carried

When the towns go down there are stains of
Rust on the stone shores and illegible
Coins and a rhyme remembered of swans, say,
Or birds or leaves or a horse or fabulous
Bull forms or a falling of gold upon Softness.
(Archibald MacLeish (1892–1982), '…& Forty-Second Street')

Baron Ferdinand Von Richtofen first coined the term 'Silk Road', or *Seidenstrasse*, in 1877, but it is a misnomer. It was not really a road at all; it was a vast network of land-based and maritime trade routes and the merchants who used it carried far, far more than just silk. The beginnings of land-based trade between Orient and Occident can probably be pinpointed to around 105 BC, when the Chinese Emperor Wudi (r.140–87 BC) sent a group of Chinese emissaries to the court of Mithradates II (r.123–88 BC), the Parthian ruler of Persia. Wudi's mission appears to have marked the beginnings of trade with Persia. In 53 BC the Persians unfurled dazzling silk banners during their battle with the Romans at Carrhae. The Romans are said to have fled in terror at the sight of the banners and were routed.

By 46 BC, however, Chinese silks had reached Rome. A triumphal procession for Julius Caesar in that year included silk canopies, and it was not long before the commentators of the day were lamenting the Romans' obsession with the new material and the drain it placed upon the economy. So pervasive was the new fashion that in 14 BC Rome's Senate was obliged to issue a ban against men 'disgracing themselves with the effeminate delicacy of silk apparel', but to little effect, it seems. The Roman commentator Seneca, writing in the first century AD, makes no attempt to hide his disapproval of women who wore silk:

> Silk garments provide no protection for the body, or indeed modesty, so that when a woman wears them she can scarcely […] swear that she is not naked.
>
> (Seneca, first century AD, *On Benefits*)

During the first century AD, as trade increased between Rome and the East, many commentators criticised the apparently insatiable appetite among Romans for luxury goods:

> we have come now to see […] journeys made to Seres[1] [China] to obtain cloth, the abysses of the Red Sea explored for pearls, and the depths of the earth scoured for emeralds. They have even taken up the notion of piercing the ears as if it were too small a matter to wear those gems in necklaces and tiaras unless holes were also made in the body into which to insert them […] at the lowest computation, India and Seres and the [Arabian] Peninsula together drain our empire of one hundred million sesterces every year. That is the price that our luxuries and our womankind cost us.
>
> (Pliny the Elder, *Natural History*)

Trade between East and West was to continue, despite interruptions caused by wars, pestilence and politics, until maritime routes pioneered by European explorers in the fifteenth and sixteenth centuries superseded the old highways. At different times and throughout its history, trading centres grew and prospered along the highways of the Silk Road. Great cities like the Abbasid capital of Baghdad, the Sogdian town of Samarkand and the Bactrian metropolis of Merv became dynamic entrepôts where goods were traded in both directions. Merchants did not lead their caravans across the whole route – they would transport their goods between two commercial centres and would then sell them on to other merchants. The caravan cities of the Silk Road benefited both from the trading of these goods and from the taxes and customs duties levied upon merchants. Along with trade goods came new ideas: religions, medical knowledge, scientific and technological innovations all passed in both directions and the Silk Road became a great network of veins and arteries, carrying the life-blood of nations across the known world.

Silk Road commerce was driven by three basic factors: first, the obvious desire for profit; second, a fascination with the exotic; and third, as a means to enhance the political power of a particular nation. All three issues will be discussed at length throughout this book. If anyone doubts that Silk Road commerce was truly global in nature, consider the following three items, each unearthed in distant corners of the earth in extraordinary circumstances. An Indian ivory mirror handle from the first century AD, found in the ruins of Pompeii, an Egyptian Pharaoh mask found in the thirteenth-century grave of a Mongol woman at Genghis Khan's capital of Karakorum in Mongolia, and a seventh- or eighth-century bronze Buddha from Pakistan's Swat valley, found in a Viking grave at Helgö in Sweden, all reveal the extent to which the Silk Road disseminated its products.

As already mentioned, silk was the principal, but by no means the only, commodity. A search through a substantial part of the extant literature on the Silk Road reveals literally dozens of different commodities, and the following chart, which is by no means exhaustive, attempts to summarise the principal ones. There are also references throughout this book to the products of individual Silk Road cities, gleaned mainly from the writings of commentators of the time. Individual commodities are discussed in greater detail elsewhere in the book.

A SUMMARY OF TRADE GOODS FROM EAST AND WEST CARRIED BY LAND AND SEA

Commodities from the East

From India:

Household slaves, pets and arena animals, exotic furs, cashmere wool, raw and finished cotton (cotton plants have been cultivated in India for 4,000 years), spinach (probably mainly from Nepal), sandalwood and other exotic woods, palm-oil, cane-sugar and perfumes (aromatics), gems (rubies, sapphires and emeralds although diamonds, surprisingly, were not prized by the Chinese).

From China:

Silk, skins, iron, mirrors, weapons, porcelain (first manufactured around the eighth century), lacquerware, nephrite jade (from Khotan), rhubarb, tea.

Paper, traditionally thought to have been invented by the court eunuch Cai Lun in AD 105.

Gunpowder, invented in China around the seventh century and first used by them for military purposes around the twelfth century. It reached Europe during the fourteenth century.

Medicines: ephaedra (Chinese: mahuang – used for millennia in China to treat asthma and hay fever. Ephedrine – now synthesised – was originally made from ephaedra), Epsom salts, elixirs for immortality (which often shortened, rather than extended life), ginseng (the best was from Korea), snake bile (collected in southern China and Indochina) and seaweed (a diuretic), among many other examples.

From Various Parts of Asia:

Precious and semi-precious stones: including lapis lazuli (mined in Afghanistan), jadeite (from Burma), rock crystal, carnelians and other quartzes, rubies (from Sri Lanka and Southeast Asia), sapphires (from India, Southeast Asia and Sri Lanka).

Jewellery, ivory, tortoiseshell, rhinoceros horn, seashells and pearls.

Ornamental woods, gum resins and aromatics (camphor from China, Japan, Borneo and Indochina was highly coveted).

Silver and gold (especially from southern China, Tibet and Indochina but also imported from many other parts of the world).

Spices (especially pepper, ginger, cardamom, turmeric, nutmeg and cloves, and, from India, Sri Lanka and Southeast Asia – cinnamon).

Cochineal and indigo used for dyeing fabrics and cosmetics.

Minerals: sulphur (for elixirs, imported from Indonesia); realgar (or arsenic sulphide, found in many parts of the world – although the best comes from Hunan province in China – and used as an elixir, to treat skin diseases and, so it was believed, to convert copper into gold).

Ceramics.

Horses (Central Asian breeds were especially prized in China) and camels.

Flowers, including peonies, roses, camellias and chrysanthemums and tulips (tulips from Central Asia and Turkey first arrived in Europe in the 1550s and were so coveted in seventeenth-century Holland that a single bulb could sell for 5,000 guilders, more than the price of a house!).

Alfalfa for animal feed, millet.

Human beings: acrobats, Central Asian jugglers and musicians, Central Asian grooms, dwarves, household slaves, South Sea Island pearl divers, Southeast Asian dancers, foreign guards.

From Persia and the Countries of the Middle East:
Incense (from southern Arabia), dates, pistachios, peaches, walnuts, Tyrian purple (from the *Murex trunculus* shellfish) and indigo for dyeing; frankincense and myrrh; storax (an aromatic resin), muslin cloth, wines, glassware, olive oil and silver vessels (especially the work of the Sasanian craftsmen of Persia).

Commodities from the West

Merchants on the land-routes and Roman ships, crewed by men from many nations, conveyed:

Wool and linen textiles, carpets, Baltic amber, Mediterranean coral, asbestos, bronze vessels, lamps, glass vessels and glass beads, wine and papyrus, huge quantities of coins and bullion, ambergris (from the sperm whale, used in the manufacture of perfume and collected along the African coast), entertainers, exotic animals and opium (opium poppies probably originated in the eastern Mediterranean and reached China in about the seventh century).

Religions (Spread Along the Trade Routes in all Directions)

Buddhism (arose in India and spread in both directions as far east as Japan and as far west as modern day Turkmenistan).

Islam (founded in the seventh cenury, it spread in all directions and now attracts a worldwide following of more than 1 billion devotees).

Christianity (arose in the eastern Mediterranean and spread throughout the Roman world. Nestorian Christianity spread eastwards after the expulsion of Nestorius, patriarch of Constantinople, during the fifth century. It reached China by 635).

Manichaeism (developed in the Middle East during the third century and reached China by the seventh or eighth century).

Zoroastrianism (the state religion of Persia until the arrival of Islam in the seventh century, it had spread eastwards to China and India by the seventh or eighth century).

Technology and Innovations

Acquired by China from the Lands to the West:
Harnesses, saddles and stirrups (from the steppe nomads), construction methods for bridges and mountain roads, knowledge of medicinal plants and poisons, cultivation of cotton and seafaring techniques.

Acquired by the West from Asia:
  Chinese inventions (summarised in the table below).
  Medical techniques (especially from Arab scholars such as Ibn Sina).
  Science and mathematics – algebra, astronomy and the Arab numerals that
    we use in the West today.
  The use of passports (a Mongol innovation, known as the *paizi* or *gerege*).
  Military techniques and strategies.
  Architectural styles and devices (the Persian invention of the squinch
    allowed the addition of a dome and led to the construction of many of
    the world's great buildings).

The westward flow of Chinese technology occurred throughout the existence of the Silk Road. The renowned scholar Joseph Needham, in his monumental work *Science and Civilisation in China* (1954), summarised the plethora of new inventions that reached Europe between the first and eighteenth centuries, often after a time-lapse of several hundred years. There are many other examples, not listed below, such as the use of paper money, the abacus and the use of coal for fuel. The modern world owes a great debt to ancient China:

CHART SUMMARISING THE TRANSMISSION OF MECHANICAL AND OTHER TECHNIQUES FROM CHINA TO THE WEST

Type of device	Approximate time lag in centuries
Square-pallet chain-pump	15
Edge-runner mill	13
Edge-runner mill with application of water power	9
Metallurgical blowing engines, water power	11
Rotary fan and rotary winnowing machine	14
Piston-bellows	approx. 14
Draw-loom	4
Silk-handling machinery (a form of flyer for laying thread evenly on reels appears around the eleventh century and water power is applied to spinning mills in the fourteenth century)	3–13

Type of device	Approximate time lag in centuries
Wheelbarrow	9–10
Sailing-carriage	11
Wagon-mill	12
Efficient harness for draught animals: Breast-strap (postilion)	8
Collar	6
Crossbow (as an individual arm)	13
Kite	approx. 12
Helicopter top (spun by cord)	14
Zoetrope (moved by ascending hot air current)	approx. 10
Deep drilling	11
Cast iron	10–12
'Cardan supension'	8–9
Segmental arch bridge	7
Iron-chain suspension bridge	10–13
Canal lock-gates	7–17
Nautical construction principles (including watertight compartments, aerodynamically efficient sails and fore-and-aft rigging)	up to 10
Stern-post rudder	approx. 4
Gunpowder	5–6
Gunpowder for military use	4
Magnetic compass (lodestone spoon)	11
Magnetic compass with needle	4
Magnetic compass used for navigation	2
Paper	10
Printing (block)	6
Printing (movable type)	4
Printing (metal movable type)	1
Porcelain	11–13

(Adapted from Joseph Needham, 1954)

The Migration of Peoples Along the Trade Routes

There was considerable traffic in human beings in both directions along the Silk Road and there were also many instances of mass migration of entire communities. We will examine the migration of the Yuezhi, founders of the Kushan Empire, elsewhere in this book, and also look briefly at the Europoid mummies of the Tarim Basin. But perhaps the farthest wanderings of any single people are contained in the migration of the Roma, or Gypsies, who now number between 8 and 12 million souls and reside mainly in eastern Europe. The origin of the Roma is uncertain but there are linguistic similarities between the Romani language and some dialects of India. It appears that the Roma originated in north-western India and departed from their homeland in about the ninth century. They moved slowly westwards through Iran and the Near East and by the fourteenth century were settled in the Balkans. Centuries of persecution and pogroms have caused the Roma to live in close-knit communities, often avoiding contact with non-Gypsies. The notion that contact with non-Gypsies, known as *Gadjo* (feminine: *gadji*) to the Roma, is corrupting, may originate in the group's Hindu origins.

CHAPTER ONE

Precursors of the Silk Road

Alexander the Great

The life and achievements of Alexander the Great (r.336–23 BC) preceded the establishment of the Silk Road by some three centuries but the route that he followed approximates in many places to the highways that merchants of later years would come to use. His empire was vast but its existence was fleeting: within 12 years of embarking upon his conquest of Asia he lay dead in Babylon and his satraps began, almost immediately, to rebel. At the time of his death Alexander's empire encompassed all of the lands between Greece and India, and the many cities that he founded became pockets of Greek culture that continued to exert a profound influence long after his passing. He took with him an army of up to 40,000 men and the soldiers that he left behind to garrison these new cities married local women. Greek ideas began to permeate through the societies of the East: religion, politics, medicine and the arts were all strongly affected by Alexander's legacy, and the foundations for the subsequent development of the Silk Road were firmly laid. After Alexander's time it could never again be said that the Orient and Occident were two separate, unconnected worlds. A fully developed network of trade routes between Europe and Asia does not appear to have been in place until the first century BC but, in the years after Alexander's death, exotic goods are known to have reached the West in significant quantities. Ivory, spices and unusual pets (parrots and peacocks were especially prized) are all recorded among the possessions of the wealthy citizenry of ancient Athens.

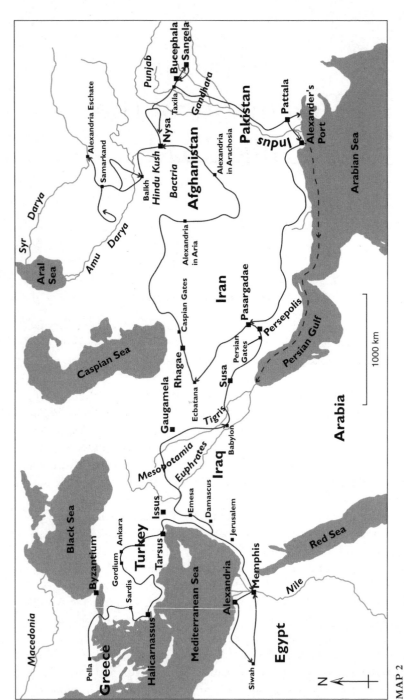

MAP 2
Alexander the Great's journeys and the extent of his empire.

Figure 1
Marble head of Alexander
the Great. Hellenistic
period, first half of the
second century BC. Height
42 cm. From Pergamon
(Bergama), Izmir province,
Turkey.

Chinese Legend

The *Travels of Emperor Mu*, written around the third century BC, describe the exploits of King Mu of the Western Zhou dynasty (1050–771 BC). Emperor Mu is thought to have lived around 1000 BC and the journeys ascribed to him are a mixture of legend and fact: 'Emperor Mu wished to satisfy his ambition by touring around the world and by marking the countries under the sky with the wheels of his chariots and the hoofs of his horses' (from a commentary on *Classic of Spring and Autumn*, quoted in Franck and Brownstone, 1986).

Emperor Mu is said to have departed from China through the Yumenguan (the 'Jade Gate') with an army and travelled in a jade-inlaid gold carriage to the lands of Central Asia. Legend has it that, after crossing the desert of the Taklamakan, he reached first the Pamirs and then journeyed through the Kunlun Mountains on the northern edge of the Tibet-Qinghai plateau, the domain of Xi Wang Mu, the Queen Mother of the West. After presenting her with lavish gifts of jade and silk – the earliest mention of the precious commodity as tribute – he turned homeward, stopping en route to hunt. But Mu's exploits are legend. There are tantalising clues that the authors knew of the people of the western regions and had knowledge of their customs, but the evidence is inconclusive. The only solid evidence for early Chinese contacts with the lands beyond its borders comes from studies of nomads and the processes of trade and tribute along what came to be known as the 'Steppe Route'.

Nomads

Sworn to sweep out the Huns
without regard for my own safety:
Five thousand sable hats and silk coats
Were lost in the border dust.
I grieve for those crumbling bones
scattered along the river bank of Wuding,
They are still in the hearts of lovers
Who dream of them in inner chambers.

> (Chen Tao (ninth century), 'March on Western Lun',
> from Z. C. Tang, 1969. Western Lun, or Lung-Hsi,
> was an outpost in Gansu)

The Steppe Route

It is important to make brief mention here of what some scholars have termed the 'Steppe Route' and its relation to the Silk Road. The Steppe Route is not literally a route, since it does not follow a precise track in the way that the Silk Road does. Instead it covers a region as far west as the steppes of southern Russia and the Danube, through the Kazakh Plain and Mongolia as far as the Great Wall of China. Nomadic equestrian tribes moved across the area in both directions in search of pasture for their cattle, horses and sheep, a practice that has been followed since Neolithic times. Because of their peripatetic lifestyle there are few remains of permanent settlements to be found and this makes identification of a precise route impossible. These nomadic groups (called 'Hu' by the Chinese), conducted trade with neighbouring regions from a very early period, including the purchase of silks, bronze mirrors and weapons from China; furs and gold from Siberia; nephrite jade and wool from east Turkestan, and horses and wool from west Turkestan. The contents of *kurgans* (burial mounds) of the Scythian-Sakae period (sixth to fourth centuries BC), most notably at Pazyryk, show that contacts with the Chinese were taking place from an extremely early date. The Pazyryk mounds lie at a height of 1,600 m above sea level in the eastern part of the Altai, a range that begins 450 km south-east of Novosibirsk and extends southwards through Kazakhstan, China and Mongolia. Among thousands of items unearthed at Pazyryk are Chinese bronze mirrors, woollen textiles that may come from Iraq, and a cream-coloured Chinese silk saddle cover, embroidered with phoenixes and birds.

By the time of the Western Han dynasty in China (206 BC–AD 9), there was a constant demand for Chinese silk, part of an essential barter process through which the Chinese obtained horses. An early description of this trade by a Chinese official reflects a belief that the Han were simultaneously receiving tribute and impoverishing the nomads. They did not regard it as trade.

A piece of Chinese plain silk can be exchanged with the *Hsiung-nu* [Xiongnu] for articles worth several pieces of gold and thereby reduce the resources of our enemy. Mules, donkeys and camels enter the frontier in unbroken lines; horses, dapples and bays and prancing mounts, come into our possession. The furs of sables, marmots, foxes and badgers, coloured rugs and decorated carpets fill the imperial treasury, while jade and auspicious stones, corals and crystals become national treasures.

(Ascribed to the Lord Grand Secretary of the Han Council in 81 BC, and quoted in Franck and Brownstone, 1986)

The Xiongnu peoples, the most powerful and bellicose of all the Hu tribes, first appear in Chinese annals during the late fourth century BC, and come from the region between the Yellow River and the Yingshan Mountains. The term *Xiongnu* is extremely derogatory, meaning something along the lines of 'slave bastard' and reflects the contempt with which the Chinese regarded the nomadic peoples along their northern frontier. Sima Qian's *Shiji* ('Records of the Grand Historian')[1] gives a fascinating account of the Xiongnu. He states that they had no walled cities or fixed dwellings and wandered from place to place in search of water and pasture for their animals. They did not engage in agriculture and had no means of writing. Their strength as warriors derives from the practice of training boys to hunt with bow and arrow from an early age. During times of peace, the Xiongnu were content to herd their flocks but, in times of war, they lived by 'plundering and marauding'. Sima Qian describes them as being without honour: 'Their only concern is self-advantage, and they know nothing of propriety or righteousness.'

In recent years, historians have attempted to augment our knowledge of the Xiongnu, and recent discoveries indicate that they were a more highly developed society than Sima Qian's annals would lead us to believe. By the Warring States period (475–221 BC), the Hu peoples had established a strong, cohesive and prosperous society that posed a major threat to China's borders. The quality of their gold work suggests that they had attained a high level of sophistication.

The Chinese adopted various methods to counter the threat from the Hu. Early Chinese accounts describe how, in 307 BC, King Wuling of Zhao instructed his troops to adopt Hu dress and to change from a strategy of chariot warfare to one of fighting on horseback with bows. This enabled the Zhao to push back the Hu and to solidify their control of northern China by the mid-third century BC. Around 400 BC the Chinese had begun to erect an immense wall to keep out the nomads and the Zhao added sections of their own. The wall was strengthened and extended during the centuries that followed, most notably during the reign of Qin Shi Huangdi (r.221–210 BC). During the Ming dynasty (1368–1644) the masonry and earth structure we know today as the Great Wall was completed.

Other strategies employed by the Chinese to contain the Hu included the payment of tribute and forging conjugal ties. By about 200 BC the Xiongnu were at the zenith of their power under the leadership of the chieftain (or *Shanyu*) Maodun. Maodun conquered the Ordos area to the south of the Yellow River as well as expanding his empire into Central Asia and defeating the Yuezhi, another of the Hu tribes. Attempts by the Chinese general, Liu Bang, the founder of the Han dynasty, to attack the Xiongnu almost ended in disaster when his forces were cut off and surrounded by Maodun's army. A peace agreement was negotiated involving the payment of vast amounts of tribute in the form of silks and foodstuffs, a strategy that the Chinese continued to use for much of the Western Han dynasty (206 BC–AD 9). The Xiongnu Empire was formally recognised by the Han, who declared, according to Sima Qian, 'Let the state holding the bows beyond the Great Wall follow the rules of the *Shanyu* and let the Han govern the state of overcoat and hat, which lies inside the Great Wall.' Inscriptions on pottery architectural tiles unearthed at Baotou, Inner Mongolia, reveal the practice of exchanging marital ties in order to placate the Xiongnu.

Many of the Chinese women who were sent to marry nomads were extremely reluctant to go. A poem from around 107 BC describes the anguish of Liu Xijun (Liu Hsi-chun), daughter of a disgraced prince of the Han ruling dynasty, who was sent to marry an aging nomad chief:

> My family has married me
> in this far corner of the world,
> sent me to a strange land,
> to the king of the Wu-sun.
> A yurt is my chamber,
> felt my walls,
> flesh my only food,
> kumiss to drink.
> My thoughts are all of my homeland,
> my heart aches within.
> Oh to be the yellow crane
> Winging home again!
>   ('Song of Sorrow'. Translated by Burton Watson in B. Watson, 1984)

It is quite clear from the excavation of burial mounds (known as *kurgans*), that the relationship between the Chinese and the Xiongnu was not merely adversarial, however. Excavations of the *kurgans* at the Noin-Ula site north of Ulan Bator in Mongolia, by Russian archeologists during the 1920s, reveal that there was a tremendous amount of interaction between the two groups. Fragments of bronze mirrors and lacquer bowls were discovered, all of Chinese manufacture, as well as a silk textile from Sichuan with tree and bird motifs. One of the lacquer bowls has a long inscription in Chinese which includes the date 2 BC and it seems likely that the site itself is of the same era.

Zhang Qian

Despite their best efforts, Han strategies for pacifying the Xiongnu were ineffective and raiding continued unabated until the reign of Emperor Wudi (140–87 BC). Wudi's attempts to counter the Xiongnu threat were a pivotal event in the history and development of the Silk Road and are described at length by Sima Qian in 'Records of the Grand Historian'. After the death of the king of the Indo-Scythian Yuezhi peoples at the hands of the Xiongnu leader Maodun, they were driven westwards from the Gansu corridor to Bactria in modern Afghanistan, where they eventually established the Kushan Empire. Emperor Wudi decided to send an envoy to the Yuezhi in the hope of persuading them to open a second front against the Xiongnu. He selected a palace courtier called Zhang Qian, together with a Xiongnu slave named Ganfu who was sent as interpreter. The expedition set out in 138 BC with over 100 men. As it passed westwards through Xiongnu territory the party was taken hostage. Zhang was detained for more than ten years, taking a Xiongnu wife who bore him a son, but he eventually escaped and continued his journey to Bactria. He was unable to convince the somewhat indolent Yuezhi king to form an alliance against the Xiongnu and, after a year as their guest, he started for home. On the way back to China, Zhang was again captured by the Xiongnu and spent a further year with them before escaping with his Xiongnu wife and the slave Ganfu. Of the 100 men in his party only Zhang Qian and Ganfu returned safely to China.

Zhang's report to Emperor Wudi is recorded in the annals of Sima Qian. He describes the regions to the west of China, including those of Dayuan (Ferghana, between the Oxus and the Jaxartes rivers in present day Uzbekistan and Kyrgyzstan), Daxia (Bactria) and Kangju (Transoxiana). He also related anecdotal information about more distant lands, describing 'a great shoreless lake' (probably the Caspian Sea), the Persian kingdom of Anxi (Parthia), where 'great birds lay eggs as big as pots' and the 'Western Sea' (possibly the Persian Gulf or the Red Sea). His descriptions of the land of Shendu (India) must have sounded outlandish to the Chinese:

> When I was in Daxia (Bactria) [...] I saw bamboo canes from Qiong and cloth made in the province of Shu [Qiong and Shu are in the area of present day Sichuan, Guizhou and Yunnan provinces in south-western China]. When I asked the people how they had gotten such articles, they replied, 'Our merchants go to buy them in the markets of Shendu.' [...] The region is said to be hot and damp. The inhabitants ride elephants when they go into battle. The kingdom is situated on a great river.

Emperor Wudi immediately recognised an opportunity to increase trade with China's neighbours and to use that trade as an instrument of foreign policy to extend his dominions. Wudi was transfixed by accounts of the horses of Dayuan (Ferghana). Zhang Qian saw animals there that he described as having been foaled from those of heaven, and which sweated blood (probably the result of parasites). Wudi had consulted the oracle, the 'Book of Change' which warned that 'divine horses are due to appear from the northwest', and he believed the Ferghana animals to be the fulfilment of that prediction. Wudi's desire to acquire these horses may have been linked to his search for immortality, and two poems (one quoted here) that survive from the Han dynasty were probably written to express his joy when he acquired some of them:

From Great Unity heaven-sent,
The horse of heaven comes down,
Soaked with crimson sweat,
Froth flowing russet.
His courage is superb,
His spirit marvellous.
He prances through floating clouds,
Darkly racing upwards.
His body free and easy
Leaps across a myriad leagues.
Now who is his equal?
Dragons are his friends.

('The Horse of Heaven', Anonymous,
Han dynasty (206 BC–AD 220). From Birrell, 1988)

The idea of the heavenly horse and its connection with dragons became embedded in the Chinese psyche. The Tang dynasty poet Li Bai (also known as Li Po, 701–62) has immortalised the way in which these horses were revered by the Chinese: 'The Horses of Heaven come out of the dens of the Kushanas [Yuezhi], Backs formed with tiger markings, bones made from dragon wings.'

Heavenly horses are popularly believed to have been Arab stallions,[2] now long disappeared, and were far superior in strength and endurance to the small local breeds used by the Chinese. The Chinese used the wild tarpan of the Asian steppe, identified as *Equus Prjewalski* (Prjewalski's Horse).[3] Ferghana horses, if they could be obtained in sufficient numbers,

Figure 2
Bronze
figure of a
flying horse,
one leg
resting upon
a swallow.
Eastern Han
dynasty,
(AD 25–220).
Height
34.5 cm,
length
45 cm.
Unearthed
at Leitai,
Wuwei,
Gansu, in
1969.

might enable the Chinese to subjugate the Xiongnu, and missions were sent out to secure them, resulting in further contacts with neighbouring states and the establishment of routes which came to be known as the Silk Road. 'Heavenly horses' figure in the art of the period again and again, the most sublime example being the celebrated 'Flying Horse of Gansu', unearthed at Wuwei in 1969 (Figure 2).

Sima Qian relates that Wudi sent Wang Ranyu, Bo Shichang and other envoys to search for a new route to Bactria via India, through the 'barbarian regions' of south-west China. The bellicosity of these tribes is described at length by Sima Qian. One of the groups he describes – the Dian peoples of Yunnan – are referred to as riders of elephants who traded with neighbouring states. Dian bronzes show that they wore the trousers and short tunics of the equestrian nomads of Central Asia.

Attempts to establish a route to Bactria were unsuccessful and the project was abandoned but the Chinese continued to make contact with their neighbours. Zhang Qian's last expedition was to visit the Wusun people, who lived in the Ili River valley south of Lake Balkash in modern day Kazakhstan, to seek allies against the Xiongnu and to secure more 'heavenly horses' in fulfilment of Wudi's augury. Horses from Dayuan (Ferghana) were found to be even more robust than those

supplied by the Wusun, and Chinese trade with both states increased
to the point where the Han began to construct fortifications along the
route to protect travellers. By the time of Zhang Qian's death in 113 BC,
he had become one of the most senior ministers of Wudi's court with
the title of Grand Messenger. Sima Qian describes the return of envoys
that Zhang Qian had dispatched to the kingdoms of Central Asia and
the importance of this process to the development of China's relations
with neighbouring countries. His words are a fitting valediction for a
man who can safely be described as the father of the Silk Road:

> For the first time relations were established between the lands of the
> northwest and the Han. It was Zhang Qian, however, who opened
> the way for this move, and all the envoys who journeyed to the lands
> in later times relied upon his reputation to gain them a hearing.

A charming vignette about Emperor Wudi reveals that his long reign
was not wholly devoted to military adventures. Wudi's mausoleum at
Maoling, 40 km west of Xian, is the largest of all the Western Han
tombs and is said to have taken 53 years to build. The attendant tombs
contain the remains of important officials such as General Huo Qubing
(see below). Nearby is the tomb of his favourite concubine, Lady Li, an
honour denied even to his two wives. She was a sister of the musician Li
Yannian, who presented her to Wudi with a poem:

> There's a beauty in the north
> Who stands alone in the world.
> A smile from her would cause the fall of a city;
> Another smile would ruin a country.
> What do you care about the downfall of a city or a country?
> A beautiful lady would be hard to meet again!
>
> (Quoted in He Zhenghuang, 1990)

A story from the time suggests that their love endured even after their
deaths: whenever the moon rose a thin thread of smoke would rise
from Lady Li's tomb, circle round the mausoleum of Wudi, and then
disappear.

The long series of military campaigns that Wudi had begun in about
129 BC resulted in the gradual subjugation of the Xiongnu. One of
Wudi's most celebrated and successful generals was Huo Qubing (140–
117 BC), an acquaintance of Zhang Qian. Huo's mausoleum is adjacent

to Wudi's and is presided over by spectacular life-size stone sculptures of horses, one of which tramples a Xiongnu warrior.

Huo Qubing was a gifted military strategist who was given command of his first army at only 18 years old. He was victorious in six consecutive campaigns against the Xiongnu and was honoured by Wudi who named him the 'swift Cavalry General'. Sima Qian describes him as 'a man of few words [...] but [...] [that] he possessed great daring and initiative'. He is also described as having declined the emperor's offer of a mansion, remarking that: 'While the Xiongnu have still not been wiped out there is no time to think about houses.' Another episode involving Huo occurred in 121 BC, when he led a force of 10,000 cavalrymen from Longxi in Gansu, about 500 km beyond Mount Yanzhi, to engage the Xiongnu. He killed or captured 18,000 of the Huns but, more significantly perhaps, is described by Sima Qian as having succeeded in defeating the Xiutu king – whose kingdom lay in the western part of Xiongnu territory – and 'seizing the golden man which he used in worshipping Heaven'. There has been considerable speculation among scholars that this incident marked China's first contact with Buddhism.

When Huo died in 117 BC at the age of only 24, Wudi ordered that soldiers from the defeated Xiongnu tribes line the road to his mausoleum. His grave mound was constructed in the shape of the Qilian Mountains of Gansu, where many of his greatest victories had occurred.

The gradual reduction in the threat from the Xiongnu facilitated greater contacts with the lands to the west. It was not all plain sailing, however. By about 111 BC it seems that Emperor Wudi's desire for horses had exceeded the appetite of his neighbours for the goods he was offering in exchange. Returning emissaries had informed him that the horses of Ershi (Sutrishna), capital of the Dayuan region between Khujand (Khodjent) and Samarkand, were the most magnificent of all the Ferghana steeds. He sent a gift of 1,000 gold coins and a golden horse, and a request for some of the Ershi mounts. But Dayuan, by this time, 'was overflowing with Han goods' and the king felt sufficiently removed from Chinese influence to refuse to supply them. The incensed Han envoy smashed the golden horse and departed for Dayuan's eastern border. He and his party were overtaken, however, by agents of the king from the town of Yucheng and massacred.

Emperor Wudi was enraged by the murder of his envoys and dispatched Li Guangli, a second brother of his favourite concubine Lady Li, to exact revenge. In 104 BC, Li Guangli set off at the head of a force of 6,000 cavalry and 20,000–30,000 conscripts. As the army travelled west, the terrified occupants of the towns along the route barricaded themselves in and refused to supply provisions. By the time Li Guangli reached Yucheng he had lost all but a few thousand of his men and even they were exhausted. General Li attacked Yucheng but was beaten back and lost yet more men. He withdrew to Dunhuang, sending a message to Wudi to request permission to disband the army until reinforcements became available. Permission was refused and the troops were instructed to remain outside the Jade Gate (Yumenguan), China's western frontier. After some delay, a vast army of 60,000 men, 100,000 oxen and more than 30,000 horses was assembled and marched to Ershi with General Li in command. The town's water supply was diverted by the Chinese and after a siege of 40 days it was on the verge of falling. Its occupants sought terms with the Chinese, who killed the king and acquired 20 or 30 of their best horses as well as over 3,000 ordinary stallions and mares. Li Guangli's two campaigns had lasted four years and he acquired only a small number of 'heavenly horses'. But as he marched triumphantly back towards China the rulers of the small states he encountered on the way, having heard of the defeat of the Dayuan kingdom, swore loyalty to the Han and sent tribute to the court at Changan (modern Xian). This process enabled China to impose suzerainty on the entire Tarim basin, thereafter known as Xinjiang ('New Dominion'). At about the same time, commanderies were established at Zhangye, Jiuquan, Dunhuang and Wuwei, and a line of defensive fortifications built to protect the new routes to the West. This process of consolidation was completed by the formidable General Ban Chao (AD 31–103), who progressively subdued all of the kingdoms of the Tarim basin and opened up the routes to the West (see page 50).

A postscript to the story of China's perennial foe, the Xiongnu, was that their fortunes continued to decline long after the death of General Huo Qubing. In about 57 BC, riven by internal disputes, the Xiongnu Empire split into northern and southern factions. Following the death of the northern Xiongnu ruler in 36 BC, and a treaty agreed with the southern leader, Huhanye, a long period of relative calm was achieved. Huhanye was presented with a Chinese concubine for a wife and was also paid generous annual tribute: the ensuing peace lasted well into the first century AD. By the end of that century the Xiongnu were thoroughly defeated and the remnants of their empire fled west into Central Asia or were transformed into fragmented, heavily sinocised communities in Gansu and Shaanxi. There they engaged in raising cattle and horses and were also recruited as mercenaries to fight for whichever Chinese ruler happened to hold power. The Xianbei (Toba) tribes were similarly occupied in parts of Hebei and Liaoning and both groups were subjected to discrimination and oppression by the Chinese. At the beginning of the fourth century the nomads rose against their rulers and proclaimed independent kingdoms in northern China: the Xiongnu proclaimed independence in 304, first calling their new state the Han and later the Zhou (names taken from great Chinese dynasties). With their equestrian and archery skills the Xiongnu proved unstoppable and, by 316, they had captured both Luoyang and Changan (Xian). There followed a period of civil war lasting nearly 150 years, in which various nomadic groups fought each other to create as many as 16 different states, each as ephemeral as its predecessor. An enormous southward exodus of Chinese occurred and the country was effectively divided in two: the north was controlled by the nomads and the south by the Han. At the end of the fourth century the Toba (Xianbei) emerged as the most powerful force in north China and, in 386, established the Northern Wei dynasty (386–534) with their capital at Datong (see page 29).

The Xiongnu were never again regarded as a serious and unified threat, although another branch of the tribe – how distant a branch is hotly disputed – appears, also during the fourth century, on the southern plains of eastern Europe. Contemporary accounts of the Huns leave little doubt that Europeans feared them as much as the Chinese feared the Xiongnu:

> Lo, suddenly messengers ran to and fro and the whole East trembled, for swarms of Huns had broken forth from the far distant Maeotis between the icy Tanais and the monstrous peoples of the Massagetae, where the Gates of Alexander pen in the wild nations behind the rocks of the Caucasus. They filled the whole earth with slaughter and panic alike as they flitted hither and thither on their swift horses [...] May Jesus avert such beasts from the Roman world in the future!
>
> (St Jerome. Quoted in Sinor, 1990)

After the defeat of the Alani and the Goths, an immense confederation of Huns was created under the command of Attila, 'the scourge of God'. By 452 Attila had conquered Gaul and northern Italy but died unexpectedly of excessive feasting in 453. At his funeral, the Inner Asian traditions of the Huns were not forgotten: they slashed at their faces as a sign of mourning and raced horses around the coffin. After Attila's death the Hun tribes disintegrated and its members were eventually dispersed and absorbed into local populations.

CHAPTER TWO
The Introduction of Buddhism to China

One night in a dream emperor Mingdi saw a deity flying in front of his palace which had a golden body and emanated sunlight from the neck. The next day he asked his ministers to explain the identity of this deity. One of them, Fu Yi, replied that he had heard of a sage in India called 'the Buddha', who had attained salvation, who was able to fly and whose body was of a golden hue.

> (From the *Sutra in Forty-two sections*, probably late Han dynasty (first–third century AD). Quoted in Paludan, 1998)

A branch of the great Silk Road ran over the Karakorum Range to the Gandhara kingdom of the Kushans and on to India. Along this long and treacherous highway came what Rudyard Kipling calls a 'river of life',[1] conveying exotic goods and new ideas about philosophy, literature, science, art and architecture into the Middle Kingdom. The arrival of the Buddhist faith in China along the ancient routes is one of many instances of the passage of ideas (one of the Silk Road's most important commodities). China's first Buddhists were those of the Mahayana school (the 'Greater Vehicle'), which teaches that all beings can achieve enlightenment and enter nirvana; less emphasis is placed on the renunciation of worldly pleasures and salvation can occur instantaneously. The rival Hinayana school (the 'Lesser Vehicle') is based on the original teachings of the Buddha himself and teaches that man can achieve enlightenment and escape worldly misery only by a long series of births and rebirths and by leading a life of monastic self-denial.

During its early existence, Chinese Buddhism allied itself with the Daoists. Daoism is believed to have been developed by Laozi during the sixth century BC and is concerned with an individual's relationship to nature and the spirit world. Until the third century AD, Buddhism was little more than a minor sect, regarded by most Chinese as a variety of Daoism. Its early followers were foreigners: merchants from Central Asia and India, hostages of the Chinese and envoys from neighbouring states.

The dream of the Han dynasty emperor, Mingdi (r.AD 57–75) was a pivotal event in the history of the Silk Road. Mingdi is said to have sent envoys to India to discover more about the teachings of the Buddha. They returned with a group of Indian monks, a number of sacred texts (sutras) and several statues carried, according to legend, on the back of a white horse. These objects were placed in the appositely named White Horse Temple at Luoyang – founded by a Parthian missionary named An Shigao in 148 (some sources say AD 67), and regarded as the earliest Buddhist establishment in China.

After the downfall of the Han dynasty in 220 Buddhism spread more rapidly through China. An important figure in the early dissemination of Buddhism was the monk Dao An (*c.*312–85). He worked first in Xianyang and then at the capital, Changan (Xian). Dao An attempted to understand Buddhist ideas on their own terms rather than simply equating them to Chinese beliefs, and produced an immense catalogue of all Buddhist texts known to exist at that time.

It was not until the Northern Wei dynasty (386–534) that Buddhism was adopted as the state religion, however, and even then it was mainly for reasons of political expediency. The Wei were nomadic peoples of the Toba tribe and preferred the imported ideas of a foreign 'barbarian' god to the Chinese philosophies of Confucianism and Daosim – which they neither trusted nor fully understood. They may also have felt that a populace devoted to the ideals of peace and humility would be easier to govern. One of the Toba rulers is recorded as saying: 'we were born out of the marches [...] Buddha being a barbarian god is the one we should worship'. The Northern Wei also encouraged the acquisition and translation of Buddhist texts from India. They brought the celebrated monk Kumarajiva (343–413) to the capital at Datong in Shanxi province. Kumarajiva – son of an Indian father and a princess from Kuqa – translated some 300 Mahayana Buddhist texts from Sanskrit

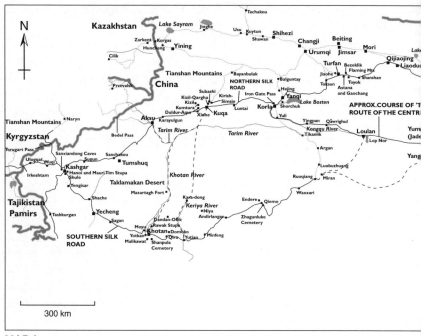

MAP 3
The Silk Road through China.

into Chinese and expounded the doctrines of the new faith. Many of the monks who made the hazardous journey to India are unknown to history but two – Fa Xian (337–422) and Xuanzang (600–64) – have left records of their travels.

Fa Xian and Xuanzang

The first of the many Chinese pilgrims to journey to India and return safely to China was Fa Xian (337–422). In 399 he embarked on a 15-year journey, travelling outward through Khotan and across the Himalayas to India. He travelled to at least 30 kingdoms – studying Buddhism under the great Indian teachers of the day at Benares, at the Gandhara capital of Taxila, and in Ceylon. He remained in Ceylon for two years before attempting a return to China by sea. During the journey he was shipwrecked on the island of Java and was forced to continue his journey aboard a different vessel. When he returned to China in 414 he devoted himself to translating into Chinese the Buddhist sutras

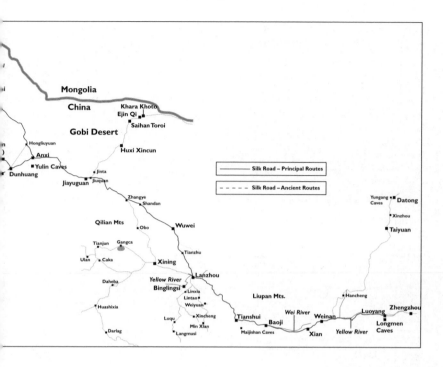

that he had acquired during his journey. The record of his travels, *A Record of Buddhistic Kingdoms* (Fa Xian, 1886) is an invaluable source of information about the geography and customs of some of the ancient kingdoms of the Silk Road and is referred to on many occasions in this book. His contribution to the growth of Buddhism in China can also not be overstated.

The celebrated Chinese monk Xuanzang, perhaps the most accomplished of all of the Silk Road's many travellers, set out in 629 from the Tang dynasty capital of Xian. His departure was contrary to the precise instructions of Emperor Taizong (r.626–49), and his intention, like that of Fa Xian before him, was to obtain Buddhist sutras from India. A number of modern historians have retraced his journey, involving more than 15,000 km and 16 years of the most arduous travel imaginable. His journey took him along the Northern Silk Road to Turfan and Kuqa; then across the Tianshan Mountains to Tashkent, Samarkand and Bactria; over the Hindu Kush to the Gandhara kingdom; on a vast circuit of India, and finally back to China through the Pamirs and along the Southern Silk Road.

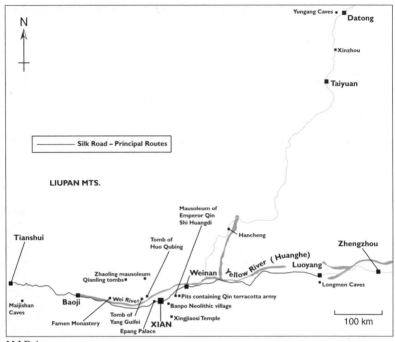

MAP 4
Datong, Luoyang and Xian, with surrounding sites.

On his return to China, the clandestine nature of his departure was forgotten and both the emperor and the population of Changan fêted him. The Great Goose Pagoda in Xian was built to house the 657 Mahayana and Hinayana texts and relics that he brought back, and he continued to work for the remainder of his life – translating some 1,300 volumes of sutras into Chinese. Seven Buddha images that he carried with him were among the relics and may have provided the inspiration for the Chinese Buddhist sculpture of the age. The record of his journey, *Buddhist Records of the Western World* (*Si-yu-ki*) (Xuanzang, 1884) is, like Fa Xian's volume, an immensely important source of information about the countries of the Silk Road.

The Northern Wei as Patrons of Buddhism

Under Northern Wei patronage many of the greatest Buddhist monuments were constructed – at Yungang and Longmen for example – where immense sculptures of the Buddha and his followers both glorified the new religion and legitimised the rule of the new dynasty.

Yungang Caves

The Yungang ('Cloud Ridge') caves are about 16 km from the first Northern Wei capital of Datong, Shanxi province. They were, for the most part, built between 460 and 494, when the Wei capital moved to Luoyang. There are 53 caves, extending about 1 km along the Wuzhoushan cliffs and containing more than 50,000 Buddhist images. These images represent the middle period of Northern Wei art, when influences from the art of Gandhara and Chinese Central Asia were particularly strong. We know from the accounts of travellers that the immense rock-cut Buddhas of Bamiyan in Afghanistan had an enormous impact on the people who encountered them for the first time. It is therefore easy to understand why they came to serve as models for the early cave-temples constructed in China. These influences are most evident at Yungang in the earlier caves. Five immense Buddhas – including one at Cave 20 which is about 14 m in height – recall not only the great Buddhas of Bamiyan but also sculpture from the classical world (Figure 3).

The later caves at Yungang, built just before the removal of the capital to Luoyang, are a riot of detail and fuse elements from the Hellenistic world (such as acanthus leaves and arabesques), with Persian lions, Gandhara draperies, Indian gods (including Siva and Vishnu) and Chinese dragons to create a more indigenous style. At Cave 6 we encounter the fully developed Yungang style at its most magnificent. The walls are arranged in a series of horizontal tiers with seated or standing images of the Buddha, surrounded by heavenly beings, musicians and flying *apsaras* (celestial beings). The lower sections contain reliefs depicting episodes from the Buddha's prior lives (known as *jatakas*).

After the relocation of the Wei capital in 494, a number of smaller caves were executed. Figures from this period are more slender and sit in a more relaxed posture reminiscent of Persian sculpture of the Sasanian period. A crowned *bodhisattva* in the Metropolitan museum, New York, recalls the Gandhara murals of Bamiyan and later at Fondukistan, themselves the recipients of motifs from Iran – but the style is essentially Chinese. According to Laurence Sickman (Sickman and Soper, 1988), the singular facial expressions of Northern Wei sculpture are characterised by a 'lingering archaic half-smile'.

During the coming pages we will examine the major sites along the Silk Road as we head west towards the Gandhara region. This was the route along which Buddhism came to China, and the artistic styles that we encounter at these places reveal the manner in which Chinese art

Figure 3
Rock-cut
image of
a seated
Buddha.
Northern
Wei
dynasty,
erected
c.460–5.
Height:
14 m.
Location:
Cave 20,
Yungang,
Shanxi.

This colossal image sits with his hands held in the pose of meditation, known as dhyanamudra. *His thin clinging robe with its sharp creases, the raised cranial protuberance* (usnisha) *and the overall naturalism of the sculpture recall images from Gandhara. The face has a rather child-like quality, a characteristic trait of Northern Wei sculpture. The ceiling and the front wall of this cave have collapsed, exposing the figures to the outside air.*

came to develop its own, unique identity. In 486, the Northern Wei emperor declared that Chinese dress would be worn at court and this had a profound effect on artistic styles. More slender forms with sweeping robes and a greater sense of movement and spirituality replace the heavy stiffness of the Yungang images. Robes that cascade downward to cover the throne characterise seated figures of the period, and standing images are graceful and delicate. When the Northern Wei moved their capital to Luoyang, Henan province, in 494, they occupied a city already tied inextricably to the history of the Silk Road from its days as the capital of the Eastern Han dynasty. At the Longmen caves, near Luoyang, we encounter the apogee of the more refined and delicate Wei style.

Longmen Caves

The Longmen ('Dragon Gate') caves are situated about 13 km south of Luoyang and were constructed by the Northern Wei between 493 and about 535, and by other dynasties at various periods thereafter until around 900. There are more than 2,300 caves and niches at Longmen, containing some 100,000 images of the Buddha and his attendants.

The Wei sculptures of the early sixth century and the Tang dynasty creations of the late seventh century represent the main periods of creativity. During this 200-year period, 12 principal caves and many smaller ones were constructed. The carvings from the Binyang cave were begun in 505 and include an immense central figure (in Cave 140) of Amitabha Buddha flanked by his two disciples: Ananda and Kasyapa. Their appearance owes much to the art of Gupta India, probably because of the infusion of ideas from monks journeying to and from the sub-continent.

The second high point at Longmen, the latter part of the seventh century, is revealed at Longmen's largest structure – the Fengxian temple. The gigantic sculptures at Fengxian were commissioned by the Tang emperor, Gaozong (r.649–83), in about 672, and completed around 675. The work was financed by Gaozong's ambitious consort, Wu Zetian, who declared herself ruler of China in 690 and dominated the country for the next 15 years. An immense statue of Vairocana, the most important of the five cosmic Buddhas, is believed to resemble Wu Zetian herself (Figure 4).

A *bodhisattva* and two guardian figures to the right of the Vairocana Buddha are stupendous manifestations of Tang dynasty art. They illustrate the transition from the linear, heavily robed images of the

Figure 4
Vairocana Buddha with a *bodhisattva* and a disciple. Tang dynasty, *c*.672–5. Height (Buddha, including pedestal): 17.14 m. Fengxian temple, Longmen, Henan province.

Northern Wei to the dynamic, fleshy sculptures of the Tang – further evidence of the influence of Gupta India. The left hand figure is a *bodhisattva*, the middle one a *lokapala* (a 'heavenly king' who protects one of the four corners of space – in this case Vaisravana, Guardian of the North) and the right hand figure is a *dvarapala*, heroic guardian of the Buddhist faith. The *lokapala* holds a model stupa (a Buddhist reliquary) in his right hand, his left placed upon his waist in a gesture of triumph and his right foot on the head of a dwarf – representing the powers of evil and ignorance.

CHAPTER THREE
The Old Capital of Luoyang

Luoyang in Henan province has been a capital of China at various times since the Western Zhou dynasty (1050–771 BC), when it was known as Chengzhou. During the Western Han dynasty (206 BC–AD 9) a new city was established on the Zhou site but with the capital situated at Changan. The Nangong (South Palace) and the Beigong (North Palace) were the most important of the city's buildings during the Western Han dynasty. China's capital was moved to Luoyang in AD 25 by the first Eastern Han emperor, Guang Wudi (r.AD 25–7). The reason for the move was that Changan had been destroyed during the bitter two-year civil war that followed the death of the usurper Wang Mang (r.AD 9–23). Guang Wudi embarked on an ambitious project to construct a new city wall of about 13 km in length. Records from the time reveal that the wall contained 12 city gates, the most important being the Pinchchengmen gate which faced south and provided access to the South Palace. The North Palace was enlarged by Guang Wudi's successor Mingdi (r.AD 57–75), whose dream may have led to the introduction of Buddhism to China. Its extent was such that it could accommodate 10,000 people and, it is claimed, could be seen from a distance of 18 km.

The city's commercial activities were centred upon three markets: the Gold Market (Jinshi) within the city walls and the South Market and Horse Market (Nanshi and Mashi), situated outside the city walls. Within these three markets were said to be 120 different bazaars, each peddling a different type of merchandise, as well as innumerable shops and godowns. There were three Zoroastrian temples in the city, serving the growing number of Persians who had come to reside and conduct business there. A poem, written during the Han dynasty, provides a glimpse of the splendours of Luoyang:

> In Lo Town how fine everything is!
> The 'Caps and Belts' go seeking each other out.
> The great boulevards are intersected by lanes,
> Wherein are the town houses of Royal Dukes.
> The two palaces stare at each other from afar,
> The twin gates rise a hundred feet.
>
> > (Translated by Arthur Waley. Quoted in Loewe, 1973.
> > 'Caps and Belts' are high-ranking officials)

Luoyang prospered until the reign of the last Han emperor, Xiandi (r.189–220). Peasant uprisings in China increased, in protest against the tax burden on smallholders, and there was a simultaneous growth in the power of the great landowning families that led to an undermining of government authority. In 190, the rebel Tung Cho, of the 'Yellow Turban' sect, forced the emperor to abandon Luoyang and seek refuge in Changan. The city was then destroyed in a fire which lasted for more than three days and which reduced palaces, temples and the renowned imperial library to ashes. The poet Ts'ao Chih (Cao Zhi) saw the stricken city about 20 years later and has left an account of what remained:

> How desolate is Loyang,
> Its palaces burned down,
> The walls fallen in ruins,
> As brambles climb to the sky…
> There are no paths to walk,
> Unworked fields have run to waste…
> Lonely is the countryside,
> A thousand *li* without one smoking hearth.
>
> > (Written in about AD 211 by the poet Ts'ao Chih
> > (Cao Zhi, 192–232). Quoted in Jenner, 1981)

The Han dynasty finally ended in 220 and China slid relentlessly into an abyss. A period of almost 400 years of disunity and suffering followed.

Luoyang was rebuilt as the capital under the succeeding Wei dynasty of the Three Kingdoms period (220–65) on the site of the Han capital, but was destroyed yet again in 311 at the hands of the now heavily sinicised Xiongnu nomads of north China. The period from 304–439, known as the Sixteen Kingdoms, consisted of a succession of northern tribal chieftains fighting for dominance. It was not until the late fourth century that the Toba Wei (or Xianbei) managed to unify northern China and establish the Northern Wei dynasty.

When the Northern Wei established their capital at Luoyang in 494, the city finally regained its former glory. The old custom of having two palaces – northern and southern – was abolished and a vast new structure was built on the site of the old Eastern Han North Palace. The building was so large that it occupied about one-tenth of the entire city. In the northern part of the metropolis were imperial buildings and parks and, in the southern section, were government offices, temples and the homes of the nobility. The Northern Wei began a concerted programme to adopt Chinese customs and dress, progressively relinquishing their nomadic origins. Many of the influential Toba families resisted this process of sinification and attempted to preserve their nomadic way of life, leading to tensions at court. Luoyang's new lease of life under the Northern Wei was extremely brief – the city's great buildings were not completed until 502, in 523 the Wei's northern armies began to rebel, and in 529 they attacked the city. By 534 the city had been abandoned once again but, during a brief 20-year hiatus between 502–23, Luoyang flourished as a Silk Road entrepôt and many of its inhabitants became immeasurably rich. Prince Shen of Ho-chien was the richest of them all, it seems. Yang Hsuan-chih's *Record of the Monasteries of Luoyang*, written in 547–50, is the main source of information about this period (see Jenner, 1981). Yang describes how Prince Shen owned 300 dancing girls, a dozen or so Persian horses and a concubine who played the flute so beautifully that she was able to quell rebellions. Prince Shen once laid on a banquet at which guests were served delicacies in vessels of gold, silver, crystal, agate and red jade: 'all exquisitely made in ways not known in the central lands as they all came from the West'. His warehouses, Yang tells us, were 'full of brocade, felt goods, pearls, ice gauze, and mist silk; the quantities of embroidery, coloured silk, and all kinds of silk textile, patterned or plain, as well as money were incalculable'.

The expatriate population of Luoyang lived in the southern suburbs, across the Lo River, and there were said to be 10,000 families of foreigners in the city at the beginning of the sixth century:

From the Ts'ung-ling [Pamir] mountains westwards to *Da Qin* [Rome] 100 countries and 1,000 cities all gladly attached themselves to us; foreign traders and merchants came hurrying in through the passes every day. This could indeed be called exhausting all the regions of heaven and earth.

(From *Record of the Monasteries of Luoyang*, by Yang Hsuan-chih, written in 547–50. Quoted in Jenner, 1981)

Foreign merchants congregated at the 'Four Directions Market' – popularly known as the 'Eternal Bridge Market' – south of the Lo River; but the main market was located in the western part of the city. The western suburb was home to Luoyang's nobility and to the town's merchants, and for this reason the Great Luoyang Market developed here. Yang Hsuan-chih has left a rare portrait of an individual merchant, the commodities trader Liu Bao who was the richest commoner in Luoyang:

he traded wherever boat or cart could go or foot could tread. Thus the goods from the whole area within the seas were assembled in his establishments. His property was comparable to a copper-bearing mountain, his wealth to a cave of gold. The scale on which his house was built exceeded the proper limits, and its pavilions and towers soared up through the clouds. His carriages, horses, clothes, and ornaments were like those of a prince.

(Ibid.)

The area west of the Great Market was occupied by brewers, men whose grog was so potent that those who consumed it were said to remain inebriated for a month. The best known of Luoyang's brewers was Liu Pai-to. His wine was exported far and wide and once led to the capture of a gang of brigands, rendered powerless to resist the forces of law and order after imbibing quantities of it. The wags of the day composed a ditty to commemorate the event:

No need to fear the sword or bow
But Pai-to's hooch will lay you low.

(Ibid.)

In the winter of 534 the entire population of Luoyang – as many as 2 million people – was ordered to move to the new capital of Yeh. In 535 the Northern Wei disintegrated into two rival states – the Eastern and

Western Wei – and the two factions fought over the discarded bones of the city. By 538 the palaces and monasteries of Luoyang lay in ruins and only about 15,000 of the city's original population remained. The schism did not prevent the continuing decline of nomadic practices among the Wei, and the Toba were eventually absorbed into the general Chinese population, finally disappearing as a race.

It is not surprising that trade along the Silk Road tended to decline during periods of civil war and political division. It did not cease, however, and China remained cosmopolitan and culturally vibrant.

By 589, Yang Jian – a man of mixed Chinese and nomad blood who became the first emperor of the Sui dynasty – had forcibly reunified all of China. Ruling as Emperor Wendi (r.581–604), he disarmed the private armies of the preceding Period of Disunity, undertook vast public works at his capital of Changan, repaired the Great Wall and became a fervent sponsor of the Buddhist faith. The Sui dynastic annals record that during Wendi's reign there were 230,000 monks, 3,792 temples and shrines, and 106,580 new images erected. A determined campaign to redistribute land to the peasants increased the flow of revenue and ushered in a period of great economic prosperity in China. Wendi died in 604, probably murdered by his son Yangdi (r.604–17). Yangdi embarked on an extravagant scheme to rebuild Luoyang as China's second city. With a display of the profligacy that would eventually lead to his downfall, some 2 million labourers were employed to construct a vast pleasure park of some 155 km^2. When Yangdi visited the park during the winter months, silk flowers and leaves were attached to the bare branches. His tours, one to the area south of the Yangtze and another to the Western Regions, were acts of magnificent lunacy still marvelled at by the Chinese. During the first, he ordered the construction of canals to link the Yellow River, the Huai and the Yangtze, a vast network approximately 2,000 km long. This network eventually became known as the Grand Canal and extended from Hangzhou in the south-east to Luoyang in the west. A branch also led northwards, almost as far as Beijing. Yangdi sailed southwards from Luoyang to Jiangdu (modern day Yangzhou) in a four-storey dragon boat accompanied by an entourage of 100,000–200,000 people. Several thousand more vessels followed in his wake, propelled by 80,000 boatmen pulling on ropes of green silk, and the inhabitants living along the canal for a distance of about 250 km were instructed to make piles of expensive delicacies for the party to consume. The historian Witold Rodzinski described them as 'a swarm of imperial locusts'.

During Yangdi's second tour, in 609, he travelled to Longxi in Gansu, west to Qinghai and north as far as Zhangye prefecture in the Hexi Corridor. Yangdi's journey followed the precise route of the Silk Road and, at the time of his visit, Zhangye had already become an important entrepôt for merchants from the Western Lands. At Zhangye, Yangdi held an audience for the kings and emissaries of the Western Regions, intended as display of imperial Chinese power. Many of the rulers accompanied him back to Luoyang where a vast reception was arranged outside Duanmen Gate. Performers from all over the Western Regions entertained the visitors, and the city's merchants were ordered to provide them with as much free food and wine as they could consume.

The excesses of Yangdi's rule weakened China's economy. The situation was made worse by three disastrous attempts to subjugate the Koguryo kingdom of Korea in which as many as 300,000 Chinese soldiers lost their lives. Major flooding of the Yellow River, famine, and uprisings among the peasants, soon followed, and the northern general Li Yuan who, like the Sui emperor Wendi, was of mixed Chinese and nomadic origins, seized the opportunity to bid for power. He captured Changan in 617, followed a year later by Luoyang. Yangdi sought refuge in Yangzhou – where he was eventually strangled with a silken cord – and Li Yuan proclaimed himself first emperor of the Tang dynasty. With its capital at Changan, China entered its golden age and the Silk Road achieved its apogee.

CHAPTER FOUR
The Old Capital of Changan (Xian)

A Brief History of the City

Xian[1] is situated in the southern part of Shaanxi province and its temperate climate, abundance of rainfall and soft loess soil have attracted settlements since the Paleolithic Age. A fossilised skull unearthed in Dali county to the north-east of Xian has been dated to about 200,000 years ago. Neolithic sites have been discovered all around Xian, most notably at Banpo in the city's eastern suburbs. Banpo – described by archeologists as a Yangshao culture site – was occupied from about 4500 to about 3750 BC. Banpo's culture was highly sophisticated, producing pottery of red clay decorated in black paint with designs of fish, animals, human faces and geometric patterns. The inhabitants produced stone tools for farming, fishing and hunting, and built grass-roofed roundhouses for their families. Their burial practices, in which husbands and wives were interred separately, indicates that a highly developed society already existed in China even at this early date, and the mysterious symbols and signs engraved on their pottery suggests that they possessed a primitive form of writing.

The Xian area has been a pivot of Chinese civilisation for much of the past 3,500 years, beginning with the Zhou State during the second millennium BC. The homeland of the Zhou peoples was along the Jinghe River valley in the western part of central Shaanxi province. They lived under constant threat of attack from northern nomads known as the Xunyun (later known as the Xiongnu). They were also

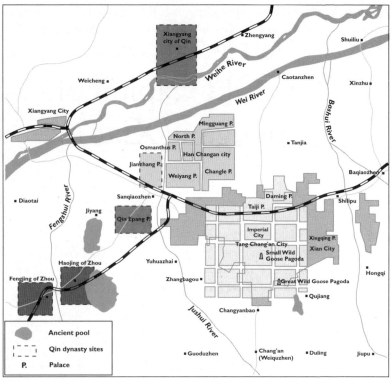

MAP 5
Sites around Xian that have served as dynastic capitals in Chinese history.
(Adapted from Ma *et al.*, 1992)

threatened by the Shang peoples to the east and by other nomadic groups. The Zhou eventually migrated to a more secure area just west of Xian, settling at Zhouyuan between Qishan and Fufeng counties. The city was protected by Mount Qi to the north and the Wei River to the south, and remained as the Zhou capital until the final defeat of the Shang in about 1050 BC. A new capital – divided between the twin cities of Feng and Hao to the south-west of modern Xian – was then established by King Wen and King Wu of the Zhou, and remained there for the next 300 years – while Zhouyuan remained a fortress town and a centre for the performance of dynastic rites. Evidence of the latter function is provided by the large numbers of bronze vessels and inscribed oracle bones discovered there.

Excavations near the village of Zhangjiapo, on the west bank of the Feng River, have revealed what is believed to be the site of the two later capitals of Feng and Hao. These were large well-planned cities with palaces and workshops, underground pipes for water supply and sewage, and an agrarian economy supplemented by hunting, fishing and animal husbandry. Slavery was widespread, with some unfortunate slaves being compelled to enter the afterlife with their masters – the grave of one Zhou nobleman, excavated at Zhangjiapo, contained two carriages, six horses and a driver!

The Western Zhou fell in about 770 BC after attacks from the north by the Quanrong nomads of north-west China. The capital was destroyed and the Zhou abandoned the Xian area and moved their capital to Luoyang.

The Qin People and the Formation of a Unified China

The Qin people originated from the west, in the Tianshui area of Gansu province. During the Eastern Zhou period, between 770–221 BC, they gradually migrated eastwards, moving their capitals as they went. Xianyang (sometimes spelt Xiangyang), 15 km north-west of modern Xian, was selected as the Qin capital in about 350 BC, probably on the council of the influential chief minister of Qin, Shang Yang (d.338 BC). From their base at Xianyang the Qin systematically defeated the six other rivals of the Warring States period. By 221 BC they had unified the country and established the Qin dynasty, with its capital at Xianyang. Xianyang was relatively small but was part of a network of palace sites in the area. The early annals record that, by the reign of King Zhuang Xiang (r.c.250–247 BC), the network of buildings and roads extended for about 25 km across the city. Each time a rival state was defeated, it is reported that a new palace was built in the style of that territory. More than 120,000 of the country's most powerful families were forcibly relocated to Xianyang and it became an extremely cosmopolitan city. With the establishment of Xianyang as the dynastic capital in 221 BC, a programme of expansion was undertaken which involved the movement of the city's centre to the south of the Wei River. The Epang Palace, the construction of which started in about 212 BC with a building force of 720,000, was colossal. The dais could accommodate 10,000 people and the entire palace complex – with lesser buildings, parks and gardens – covered an area some 150 km in circumference. Before the front hall of Epang stood 12 colossal statues, each weighing about 120 tons and made from the confiscated and melted-down weapons of the Qin's former enemies. The Epang Palace was destroyed by fire in 206 BC but now rises again in the western suburbs of Xian, recently rebuilt by the Chinese government.

The rule of the Yellow emperor, Qin Shi Huangdi (r.221–210 BC), was autocratic and relatively short but he consolidated Qin control of the country by the introduction of far-reaching reforms that still affect life in China today. Standardisation of Chinese scripts, units of measure, dress, calendars, coinage and even the axle-lengths of carts was carried out. The road network was extended by about 7,500 km to the furthest reaches of the Qin Empire, existing sections of rammed earth wall along China's frontier were bolstered and new sections built. The wall was eventually unified as China's first Great Wall, extending some 5,000 km from the Chihli Gulf to the borders of Tibet. A series of forts and watchtowers along the route countered the threat from northern nomads (see boxed text on pages 44–6). An army of 300,000 men, led by the Qin general, Meng Tian, entered the land of the Xiongnu nomads in Gansu province and secured the area for large numbers of Han Chinese who were forcibly resettled there. By means of large-scale deportations to the remote reaches of the empire, the Qin were able to extend their territory. Even China's name comes from the Chinese pronunciation of 'Qin'. Qin Shi Huangdi's achievements were many but they were made at great cost to his people. One of his contemporaries, before fleeing the imperial court, described him as follows:

> The King of Qin is like a bird of prey [...] There is no beneficence in him, and he has the heart of a tiger or a wolf. When he is in diffi-culties, he finds it easy to devour human beings [...] If he realises his ambitions concerning the empire, all men will be his slaves.
>
> (Wei Liao, adviser to Qin Shi Huangdi. Quoted in Sima Qian's *Shiji* ('Records of the Grand Historian'))

Qin Shi Huangdi and Immortality

Here at the quiet limit of the world,
A white-haired shadow roaming like a dream
The ever-silent spaces of the East.

(Alfred, Lord Tennyson (1809–1892), 'Tithonus')

Qin Shi Huangdi's love of ceremony and extravagant display is apparent in the vast scale of each of his undertakings. Nowhere is this more apparent than at the site of his own mausoleum, begun soon after he became ruler of Qin in 246 BC. The tomb is one of the largest construction projects ever undertaken by humankind and was the result of Qin Shi Huangdi's desire for immortality. In Sima Qian's *Records of the Grand Historian* – written about 100 years later – he describes how Qin Shi Huangdi sends the envoy Xu Fu and 3,000 young men and virgins to the Isles of the Immortals, at Penglai in the Eastern Sea. Three spirit mountains, reputed to exist in the Gulf of Bohai (or Chihli), were populated by immortals who possessed the elixir of eternal life. Daoist alchemists are recorded as having prescribed various immortality potions, some containing lethal poisons.

As king of Qin and then as emperor of China, Qin Shi Huangdi ruled for a total of 37 years. The construction of his mausoleum took 36 of those years and the entire mausoleum area covers around 56 km². The actual tomb consists of a tumulus some 50 m high and 1.5 km in circumference. The tomb has never been excavated because of the scale of archeological work that would be required, but descriptions of the construction and contents by the Han dynasty historian Sima Qian give some idea of what is in store for the world when the tomb is finally opened:

> Shortly after he ascended the throne, the First Emperor ordered the Lishan Hills to be prepared for the building of his tomb. When the country was unified, he sent over 700,000 convicts there to build his tomb. Three waterways were dredged and joined together. Coffins were reinforced with copper, and the whole tomb was filled with costly and exotic things. Craftsmen were ordered to make crossbows, which were positioned in such a manner as to shoot down any would-be grave robber. Channels and pools of mercury were installed to represent rivers and seas. The vault and floor of the main coffin chamber were designed to resemble the sky and earth. Candles were made of animal fat, which supposedly could burn forever.
>
> (Sima Qian, *Shiji* ('*Records of the Grand Historian*')
> Translated by Burton Watson, 1993)

The pits to the east *have* been excavated, however, revealing one of the great archeological finds of the twentieth century. Since 1974, when the first discoveries were made by farmers digging a well, an army of 8,000 life-size terracotta soldiers and horses has been unearthed from three immense rectangular pits (Figure 5). These figures are arranged in offensive battle formation, facing east and standing to attention, awaiting orders from the emperor to attack. Infantrymen, archers and crossbowmen, charioteers and cavalry make up the emperor's army for

Figure 5
A group of terracotta warriors. Qin dynasty (221–207 BC). Pit 1 at the tomb complex of the Emperor Qin Shi Huangdi. Xian, Shaanxi province.

the afterlife. Figures were made in moulds, using precise mass production techniques, with individual details added afterwards. This technique was used to produce tomb figures during later dynasties. Their weapons are bronze, many as sharp as the day they were first made, and treated with a thin layer of chromium to prevent corrosion.

THE GREAT WALL OF CHINA

A man'd be better off to die in battle
than eat his heart out building the Long Wall!
The Long Wall – how it winds and winds,
winds and winds three thousand *li*;
Here on the border, so many strong boys;
In the houses back home, so many widows and wives...

(Chen Lin (d.217), 'I Watered My Horse at the
Long Wall Caves'. Translated in Burton Watson, 1984)[2]

In 214 BC, Qin Shi Huangdi's gifted general, Meng Tian, led a force of 300,000 men (mostly forced labourers and convicts) to defeat the Xiongnu nomads along the northern frontier. Meng Tian proceeded to join up already extant sections of the wall and built a series of forts and watchtowers. The Qin wall was 10,000 *li* (about 4,500 km) in length but the cost of its construction in human life was appalling. Sima Qian describes the sufferings of Meng Tian's army, many of whom were interred within the structure as they died:

Figure 6 The Great Wall. This section dates to the Ming dynasty (1368–1644).

The dead reached incalculable numbers, the corpses lay strewn for a thousand *li*, and streams of blood soaked the plains. The strength of the common people was exhausted and five families out of every ten longed for revolt.

(From Sima Qian, *Shiji* ('Records of the Grand Historian'). Translated by Burton Watson, in Sima Qian, 1993)

The wall's defensive value was incalculable but it also held symbolic significance for the Chinese. It was a dividing line between the agrarian societies of the south and the nomads of the north. From the Qin dynasty onwards, the Great Wall was assiduously maintained as a barrier between civilised China and the barbarian regions beyond. An important point to note about the Qin dynasty wall is that large sections of it were much further north than the present day wall, completed during the Ming dynasty. The Ming dynasty wall extends from Hebei province in the north-east through Shanxi, Shaanxi and Ningxia provinces to Gansu province in the west. Locally obtainable building methods and materials were used so that different sections of the wall are constructed in different ways. Tamped earth, stone, wood and tiles were used in sections of wall built before the Ming dynasty; and rubble faced with stone and paved along the top with bricks, during the Ming. The height of the wall varies, depending on the terrain, but averages about 8 m with a base width of 6.6 m and a top width of about 5.8 m – wide enough for five horses or ten soldiers to travel abreast along

> its ramparts. The length of the wall was punctuated by more than 2,500 watchtowers with gates set at intervals to permit access to the trade routes and oases of the Silk Road. Contrary to conventional wisdom, the wall is *not* visible from the moon.

Qin Shi Huangdi died in 210 BC, probably as a result of ingesting the very immortality potions that were supposed to prolong his life. He was interred in his mausoleum with many of the workers who built it, all of his childless concubines, and his eternal terracotta army. He was briefly succeeded by his son Er Shi (r.210–207 BC), a madman and a puppet of the eunuch Zhao Gao. Er Shi lived a life of idleness as the peasants finally rebelled against the tyranny of the Qin regime and the empire dissolved around him. After Er Shi's death by suicide in 207 BC, the insurgent leader Xiang Yu destroyed Xianyang and slaughtered the entire imperial family. The Epang Palace is said to have burned for three months. There followed a period of five years of war between the states of Chu (led by Xiang Yu) and of Han (led by the former peasant Liu Bang), and large areas of China were destroyed. Liu Bang was eventually victorious and, in 206 BC, established the Han dynasty – a state of affairs that lasted, with only a brief interruption, for the next 400 years.

Xian During the Han Dynasty – China's First 'Golden Age'

The capital of the Western Han (206 BC–AD 9) is located about 10 km north-west of modern Xian and 2 km south of the Wei River. The Qin capital of Xianyang is just to the north of the river. The plan of the city follows an approximate square and is oriented according to the four directions. Its grid pattern still survives today and can be seen clearly in satellite photographs. The city walls were constructed of rammed yellow earth up to 18 m in height and were about 30 km in length, encompassing an urban area of about 36 km². During its heyday, in the reign of Wudi (r.140–87 BC), it was the largest city on earth with a population of over 500,000. The city walls contained a total of 12 gates – three on each axis – and eight major avenues ran through the city in straight lines from east to west or north to south. The centre lane of each avenue was reserved for the emperor, as was the middle arch of each gate. Two immense palaces were built in opposite corners of the city – Weiyang in the south-west and Changle in the south-east, each 5 or 6 km² in area. The Jianzhang Palace was built later, in about 104

BC, just west of the city and within the Shanglin Gardens. The Changle Palace was used for administering state affairs during the early part of the Western Han dynasty and later served as a residence for the dowager empress, while the Weiyang Palace was the centre of power throughout the Western Han and was also used for great ceremonial occasions. The Shanglin Gardens were built by Wudi at the same time as the Jianzhang Palace and contained 3,000 varieties of flowers and fruit trees; rare animals such as birds from West Asia, Indian rhinoceroses and some of the 'heavenly horses' of Central Asia.

Michael Loewe paints a vivid picture of the affluent lifestyles of the citizens of Changan during its glory days. His account (Loewe, 1973) is based on a Han document of 81 BC that fulminates against the profligate behaviour of the rich and the well-to-do, in contrast with the wretched conditions endured by the poor. The rich lived in multi-storeyed houses constructed with richly carved crossbeams – their floors covered with embroidered cushions, wool rugs or rush matting, and even the middle classes could afford felts or wild boar hides. The beds of Changan were of fine timber and hung with delicate embroideries and there was so much silk around that even ordinary citizens were said to wear garments fit for queens. The rich wore squirrel and fox furs and wild duck feathers, and the less wealthy wore wool and ferret skins. Their footwear was equally lavish – the rich with shoes of inlaid-leather or silk-lined slippers. At weddings the rich flaunted red badger furs and tinkling jades and the well-to-do wore long skirts and jewels. Game was taken out of season, young fish were caught without regard for preserving stocks and it was common to see banquets at which dish after dish was served.

The rich paraded up and down Changan's streets in gold or silver carriages – their horses decked out in breastplates and jewellery, and wearing gilt or painted bits, and gold or inlaid-bridles. The middle classes had lacquered equipment, sometimes hung with tassels, for their horses. For entertainment the rich would often keep their own orchestras and choirs and liked to watch tiger-fights and performances by foreign girls. The merely 'well-off' would arrange flute or lute concerts. The extravagance of the age extended to religious practice and the burial of the dead while, the observer notes, the rural poor were treated worse than the animals of the urban rich.

Commerce was conducted at nine markets – referred to collectively as the East and West Markets – and situated in the north-west part of the city on either side of one of the main avenues. Watchtowers were built within each market to maintain law and order and to supervise commerce. During the early part of the dynasty, the markets of Changan were centres for trading in the agricultural produce of the outlying regions. Peasants brought produce to the city and bartered it for farm implements, livestock and household goods. The markets were also used for the practice of divination and for the public execution of criminals and traitors.

The nature of commerce in Changan altered during the reign of Wudi (r.140–87 BC). Under his rule China expanded its frontiers as far as Korea, Vietnam and Central Asia, secured the rebellious areas in the south and south-west of the country, and contained the threat from Xiongnu nomads. After Zhang Qian's journeys from Changan to the Western Regions in 138 and 116 BC, exotic goods began to appear in Changan. Zhang Qian himself is known to have brought back alfalfa (lucerne), grapes and a small number of horses. Trade with the countries to the west began as a process of barter – exchanging silk and weapons for grapes, walnuts, alfalfa, pomegranates and, above all, for horses. Chinese silks, mirrors, lacquer and weapons from the Han dynasty have been found at archeological sites all over the Western Regions, in Afghanistan, and in the graves of nomads in Mongolia (see the section on Noin-Ula on page 15). Wudi's need for horses was acute: during his campaign against the Xiongnu in 119 BC he is said to have lost more than 100,000 of them.

Commerce and Conquest

In 115 BC or 105 BC, Wudi sent the first Chinese embassy to Anxi (Persia) – to the court of the Parthian king, Mithradates II. The Han historian Sima Qian records that the emissaries were greeted at the Persian border by a force of 20,000 horsemen and escorted to Mithradate's court. They were presented with ostrich eggs and conjurers from Alexandria as gifts for Wudi, and were accompanied back to China by a Persian ambassador. The Chinese were already aware of lands to the west of Persia and believed that they might be the place where the sun sets, the domain of Xi Wang Mu (the Queen Mother of the West) – a figure in Chinese mythology who was thought to possess the elixir of immortality. Wudi's mission appears to have been the starting point for trade with Persia and culminated in the unfurling of dazzling silk banners at the battle of Carrhae in 53 BC. Marcus Licinius Crassus, governor of the Roman province of Syria, led an army of infantry against the Parthians near Carrhae. The battle was a disaster for the Romans. They were outmanoeuvred and fled in panic when the Parthians unfurled huge silk banners – the first Roman contact with the new material. Within seven years silk had reached Rome – in 46 BC the silk canopies displayed during a triumphal procession of Julius Caesar are given mention.

In 104 BC, 102 BC and again in 42 BC, Chinese armies conducted campaigns across the Pamirs as far west as Sogdiana and Ferghana in Central Asia – opening up the Silk Road even further. During the 42 BC campaign they laid seige to a walled settlement in Sogdiana, probably by the Talas River, an event described in the *Han Shu* ('History of the Former Han'). The defenders were Xiongnu but the settlement was said to have been protected by a wooden palisade, a structure favoured by the Romans and previously unknown in the East. The Han annals also relate that the defenders adopted a 'fish-scale' formation, perhaps a reference to the Roman *tetsudo* strategy in which legionnaires stood with overlapping shields like the scales of a fish. The sinologist Homer Dubs (1957) postulated that the Xiongnu defenders were assisted by Roman soldiers – probably captives taken at the Battle of Carrhae and sent east as slaves. The Chinese were victorious and captured 145 of the soldiers. Dubs speculated that they were Romans (although the annals are vague), and that they were taken back to China and permitted to settle in one of the frontier towns of the Gansu Corridor. Was this China's first contact with Europeans? The evidence is inconclusive but the story is fascinating, nonetheless.

The growth of commerce with the lands to the west was accompanied by the arrival of small numbers of foreigners at Changan and the beginnings of foreign influence on the art of the period. Many of the early foreigners were entertainers, sent as tribute from far-off lands. As China expanded its borders into Central Asia merchants and envoys began to arrive in China to swear allegiance to the Han court and to bring exotic goods as tribute. Chinese merchants joined many of the expeditions to the Western Lands and a process of trade and cultural interchange gradually developed. There is abundant evidence of the technical innovations that the Han dynasty acquired from neighbouring countries. These innovations were critical in the development of Chinese civilisation and were absorbed via early trade and military contacts on the Silk Road. Jacques Gernet (1982) lists a number of them, including harnesses, saddles and stirrups (from the steppe nomads), construction methods for bridges and mountain roads, knowledge of medicinal plants and poisons, the cultivation of cotton and seafaring.

The processes of trade and tribute were often difficult to distinguish. Merchants frequently masqueraded as emissaries to the Han court in order to ensure a favourable reception for their goods. During the reign of Chengdi (r.33–7 BC), it was said that of all the delegations who had come to pay tribute to the Han, not one of them contained a member of a royal family or even a nobleman. During another celebrated mission in 166, a merchant passed himself off as an envoy of the Roman emperor Marcus Aurelius and arrived at the Indochinese port of Tonkin to offer elephant tusks, rhinoceros horn and tortoiseshell. The commentator's dismissive description of his merchandise indicates that trade was so highly developed by this point that such hitherto priceless items were no longer regarded as valuable:

> In the beginning of the Yuan-jia period of the emperor Huan the king of Da-Qin, Antun sent envoys who offered ivory, rhinoceros horns, and tortoise shells from the boundary of Annam; this was the first time they communicated with us [...] Their tribute contained no precious stones whatever, which makes us suspect that the messengers kept them back.
>
> (From the *Hou Han Shou* ('History of the Later Han').
> Quoted in Vollmer *et al.*, 1983)

From AD 73 onwards General Ban Chao (AD 31–103), brother of the great Han historian Ban Ku, began the process of restoring Han rule in Central Asia. By AD 91 the various states of the Tarim Basin had submitted to Han rule – a process achieved by Ban Chao at minimal expense and using local troops. This enabled China to resume its control of the Silk Road. The same year, he was appointed 'Protector General of the Western Regions' and, in AD 97, led an expedition across Central Asia as far as the Caspian Sea – the most distant point yet reached by a Chinese. Also in AD 97, Ban Chao dispatched an emissary called Gan Ying to Da Qin (Rome). He is believed to have reached the Persian Gulf and, upon arriving, enquired of the Parthians how to proceed further. He was informed that the crossing could take as long as three years and that many who attempted it were afflicted by violent pangs of homesickness that often led to the sufferer's death. Gan Ying was deterred from continuing his journey, thereby preserving the lucrative role of the Parthians as middlemen in the silk trade between China and Rome. Both countries remained remarkably ignorant of each other – the Romans refer repeatedly to China as the 'land of Seres', a country where silk was produced by combing it from trees – and the Chinese were equally ill-informed about the Romans; they believed that the people of Rome were physically similar to the Chinese (they even called the country 'Great Qin' after China), and that they also practised sericulture. The *Hou Han Shou* relates that, 'The people of this land are all inhabitants of great height, with regular features; they are similar to the inhabitants of the Middle Kingdom, and that is why the country is called Da Qin.' The first century AD was a period of thriving trade between China and the West when, as the *Hou Han Shou* relates, 'peasant colonies were founded in the fertile lands; inns and posts for changing horses were established along the main routes; messengers and couriers travelled in every season of the year; and the Merchant Strangers knocked daily on our gates to have them opened'.

The Western Han dynasty was an epoch of great affluence and cultural vitality. A number of scholars have remarked that many Western Han works of art are a blend of the mythology and superstitions of the south of China and the rather hard-edged realism of the north. The best of Western Han art is to be found in tombs. The art of the Western Han has a slightly naïve quality, with the theme of entertainment occurring again and again; in addition to storytellers, musicians and acrobats, figures of dancing women – unearthed in large numbers from Han tombs – are a favourite.

The art of the Han dynasty does not readily reveal direct influences from the West – despite the fact that trade and contacts with other countries were flourishing. Motifs from steppe art, such as confronting animals or openwork narratives and landscapes, are to be found on Chinese bronze belt plaques and harness fittings. These were probably absorbed via their trade with the Xiongnu, and from commercial and military contacts (both land and sea) with the lands to the south of China that occurred at least as early as the Western Han dynasty. After the fall of the Qin dynasty in 207 BC, one of the regime's surviving generals – Zhao Tuo – fled south and declared an independent kingdom. The kingdom of Nanyue, comprising modern Guangdong, Guanxi and northern Vietnam, lasted until 111 BC when it was defeated by the armies of the Han emperor, Wudi. The second king of Nanyue – Zhao Mo – died in about 122 BC and the site of what is thought to be his grave was excavated in 1983. He wears the same style of jade suit as Prince Liu Sheng, interred 3,500 km away in Mancheng, Hebei province, metropolitan China; and contacts with the southern regions are also revealed by the presence of perfumes and ivory. A silver box and a jade *rhyton* (drinking horn) found in the tomb reflect contacts with western and Central Asia. After 111 BC, when the region was absorbed into the Chinese Empire, the new Han rulers of the south introduced Chinese culture and craftsmanship – but indigenous styles were not entirely displaced.

Western themes are harder to identify in the early art of metropolitan China. It seems that a sense of cultural superiority among the Han meant that their creations were their own, or were so heavily sinicised that their origins are rendered unrecognisable. Three rare exceptions are the winged horse – a popular motif in the art of Han China and also passed to its neighbours (see Figure 2); an extraordinary and possibly unique example of a *putto* hunting fish with a trident among vine scrolls; and the motif of the 'goat-man'. The naked, cherub-like *putto* appears on a lacquer plate unearthed at the tomb of General Zhu Ran (d.249) in Ma'anshan, Anhui province. The plate dates to the Eastern Han dynasty (AD 25–220) and contains an inscription that suggests it was manufactured in Chengdu, Sichuan province. This motif occurs many times in Roman mosaics, and on silver vessels, and the fact that it has travelled so far and in a virtually unchanged form is little short of amazing.[3]

Jenny So and Emma Bunker (1995) suggest that such motifs reached China through the intermediary of nomadic art. New metallurgical techniques such as granulation, loop-in-loop chains and an early form of cloisonné were acquired from the West via Chinese contact with the nomads during the Eastern Zhou dynasty and perfected during the Qin and Han dynasties. Bunker describes these new metalsmithing techniques at length in relation to Chinese personal ornament (White and Bunker, 1994).[4]

Artistic styles such as the carving of narrative scenes on stone and the production of stone sculpture in the round have no precedent in previous dynasties. Their origins may be traced to the sculpture and carved reliefs of the Greco-Roman world and of Assyria – by a process of gradual dissemination along the Silk Road. This is also the case with the more naturalistic style of Han art. During the feudal societies of previous dynasties art was produced almost exclusively for ritual use, but during the affluent years of the Han dynasty it was created to beautify the home, and the new qualities of dynamism, naturalism and humour must be due – at least in part – to ideas imported from the classical world.

The financial strain of supporting Wudi's military adventures undermined the economy and after his death in 87 BC the Western Han dynasty was progressively weakened by a succession of ineffectual rulers and by a growing rivalry among the families of imperial consorts. In AD 9 a nephew of the dowager empress named Wang Mang declared himself emperor of the short-lived Xin dynasty. Wang Mang's attempts at land reform and curbing the excesses of the rich left him isolated – in AD 23 rebellion broke out and Changan was attacked. Wang Mang took refuge in a tower but was sought out and beheaded – seated in full imperial regalia upon his throne.

After Wang Mang's death the Han nobility regained the throne, establishing the Eastern Han dynasty (AD 25–220). The capital was moved from Changan to Luoyang, although Changan continued to be an important commercial and political centre. During the chaos of the Period of Disunity (221–589) the fortunes of the city rose and fell with every change of ruler. It was the capital of, among others: the Western Wei, the Northern Zhou and the early Sui kingdoms. The city was attacked yet again in 316 during the Western Jin dynasty when, it was said, 'there were not more than one hundred families. Weeds and thorns grew thickly as if in a forest'.

Changan's fortunes did not fully revive until 581 when Emperor Wendi (r.581–604) founded the Sui dynasty. Wendi established the Sui capital on a new site, 2–3 km to the south-east of the Han city of Changan. The old city was abandoned and turned into an imperial garden and the name Daxing ('Great Resurrection') was given to the new city of Changan. It is on this site that Changan has remained until today.

One of the most tragic of the players on Changan's stage during the Sui dynasty was Princess Li Jingxun, who died on 30 June 608 at the age of only eight. Princess Li came from a family that was noble and yet was beset by calamity. Her grandfather died in battle against the nomadic tribes of the north, and her father, Li Min, was an official in the government of the Sui dynasty (581–618). Soon after her own early death, Princess Li's father was executed on the orders of the Sui emperor, and her mother, too, was poisoned a few months later. At the time of Princess Li's death her family were still affluent and powerful and, perhaps because of regret at her premature death, her funeral was particularly lavish. She was buried just outside one of Xian's gates with an inscription on the sarcophagus that states: 'Open this and you will drop dead.' The curse appears to have been effective since, when the tomb was excavated in 1957, the contents were found to be intact (Figure 7).

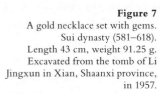

Figure 7
A gold necklace set with gems.
Sui dynasty (581–618).
Length 43 cm, weight 91.25 g.
Excavated from the tomb of Li
Jingxun in Xian, Shaanxi province,
in 1957.

This exquisite necklace consists of 28 gold beads each set with ten pearls. In the middle of the clasp is a dark blue pearl incised with a deer. The square ornaments at either end are set with lapis lazuli – a stone found solely in Afghanistan. The two large stones at the bottom are a chicken-blood stone (a type of pyrophyllite), and a large pale blue cabochon, variously described as a sapphire or a lapis bead. The workmanship and design of this necklace recall Persian art; it has also been suggested that such necklaces were the inspiration for the adornments worn in the monumental Chinese stone sculptures of Avalokitesvara.

Xian During China's Second 'Golden Age': The Great Tang Dynasty

A hundred thousand *li*[5] of journey, how many dangers?
Desert dragons, when you wag your tongue, will hear and be humbled.
The day you reach India's five lands, your hair will be white –
The moon sets on Ch'ang-an and its midnight bells.

(Li Tung, ninth century, 'For the Monk San-tsang on
His Return to the Western Regions'. Translated by Burton Watson
in B. Watson, 1984)

By the time of the Tang dynasty (618–907) Buddhism was firmly established in China and in Changan alone there were 81 monasteries and temples and 28 convents – more than any other city in China. Emperor Taizong (r.626–49) built the city's most famous landmark, the Dayan ('Great Goose') Pagoda for the monk Xuanzang – to house the scriptures and relics that he had brought from India (Figure 8).

Taizong's successor, Gaozong (r.649–83), erected the adjacent Daciensi ('Temple of Great Mercy') in memory of his late mother Empress Wende in 648, while he was still crown prince. The Daciensi, more than 24 hectares in extent, has no fewer than 11 courtyards, 1,800 rooms and accommodation for 300 monks. Other examples of imperially sponsored Buddhist temples in Changan are the Dajianfusi ('Temple of Great Fortune') – comprising the 15-storey 'Little Goose' pagoda and covering an area of 10 hectares – and the Zhangjing Temple; built outside the East Gate by Emperor Daizong and containing 48 courtyards and over 4,000 cubicles for monks.

The Tang emperors were enthusiastic patrons of Buddhism and members of various sects became involved in court intrigue to advance their own particular cause. A number of monks achieved great wealth and fame at the Tang court and monasteries acquired vast landholdings. Tang dynasty records show that a monk was entitled to 5 acres of land and a nun to about 3, while individual monasteries were allowed an additional holding. This meant that a monastery of 100 monks would be entitled to as many as 600 acres of land – all tax-exempt. By the time of Daizong (r.762–79), monasteries had acquired most of the cultivable land in the Changan area and people were actually becoming monks to avoid paying tax. This trend generated bitter resentment among the landlord classes and threatened China's economy. The Buddhist Church was an economic power in Tang dynasty China. Gernet describes the contents of a set of monastic accounts from Dunhuang, listing the monastery's various sources of revenue:

income from lands
interest on loans (virtually all monasteries derived income from usury)
levies on gardens
rent from oil presses (oil was used for lamps and for cooking)
rent from mills (for grinding millet and wheat flour)
miscellaneous gifts (made on the occasion of festivals)
fees received for the recitation of sutras, 'spring and autumn Buddha
    food', and alms given during vegetarian feasts.

> (Extracted from Pelliot ms P4081 from Dunhuang.
> Quoted in Gernet, 1995)

Figure 8
The Dayan
('Great Goose')
Pagoda, Xian,
Shaanxi
province.
Tang dynasty,
completed 652.
Height 64.5 m.

Monks performed services such as the recitation of sutras for the dead, divination, healing and the practice of magic. Charlatanism was rife and many monks paid little more than lip service to Buddhist principles. In 842 an imperial decree issued by the Daoist emperor, Wuzong (r.840–6), resulted in the layicising of more than 3,000 of the most profligate of these 'monk-sorcerers':

> All monks and nuns in the empire who practice alchemy, sorcery, or incantations; draft evaders; those who bear the marks of flagellation, tattoos or forced labour [as a result of previous offences]; who indulge in debauchery, maintain wives, and disregard the Buddhist

precepts; all these shall be defrocked. All money, provisions, grains, lands, estates, and gardens owned by these monks and nuns shall be confiscated by the government.

(Quoted in Gernet, 1995)

A campaign of persecution of Buddhist orders and other foreign religions continued until 845 and culminated in the destruction of temples and monasteries. Buddhist images were melted down and vast areas of land were expropriated by the state. These events by no means eradicated Buddhism in China, but the religion never regained the political and economic dominance that it had hitherto enjoyed. The Nestorian, Manichaean and Zoroastrian religions fared far worse – they all but disappeared from metropolitan China and were only preserved at all by the presence of adherents among border peoples such as the Uighurs and Mongols.

The xenophobia of the ninth century marked the beginning of the end for the Tang dynasty. Intrigue at court and the behaviour of increasingly exploitative landlords led to a worsening economic situation and outbreaks of famine during the second half of the century. Widespread peasant uprisings followed – the largest led by the rebel leader Huang Zhao. Huang's army attacked Guangzhou (Canton) in 879 and massacred 120,000 of the town's 200,000 Arab, Indian, Persian and Southeast Asian residents. In 880 he rode into Changan in a golden carriage, at the head of an army dressed in brocade, and proceeded to tear apart the city. By the time he had finished 'grass grew on the streets and hares and foxes ran everywhere'. One of the manuscripts discovered at Dunhuang contains a searing description of the aftermath of Huang Zhao's attack on Changan. The remnants of the great Tang dynasty lingered for another 27 years, with power in the hands of warlords.

★ ★ ★

Changan looks like a chessboard – Won and lost for a hundred
     years, sad beyond all telling.
          (Li Bai (also called Li Po, 701–62), 'Autumn Mediation')[6]

Foreigners in Xian

At its height, during the seventh and eighth centuries and until the An Lushan Rebellion of 755, Changan was the largest city on earth – almost

2 million people lived within its walls and suburbs. Foreigners came to the capital from all over Asia: from the north came Koreans and the emissaries of various Turkic tribes such as Uighurs and Tokharians; from the west came Persians, Sogdians and Khorezmians as well as Arabs, Jews, Indians and Armenoids (from west of the Caspian); from the lands to the south came Javanese, Malays, Singhalese and Chams; and from further afield came small numbers of African slaves. The Chinese attitude to foreigners was contradictory. On the one hand they dismissed all foreigners as barbarians (or *hu*), ridiculing and caricaturing them at every opportunity. Tomb figures of foreigners were invariably modelled with humorously exaggerated features (see the section on the Tang terracotta figurines on page 71), and written documents from the time almost always refer to them in a disparaging way. Foreigners were confined to segregated sections of Changan and were generally forbidden to intermarry with the Chinese – although this did not apply to 'strategic' marriages with the rulers of friendly states.

The Tang government strictly regulated the activities of merchants. Control was exercised over both the sale and distribution of goods from abroad – particularly when they were exotic items of interest to the court. Such items were often regarded as tribute from a submissive nation, and a merchant was expected to present a portion of his wares to the court or to hand them all in to a government warehouse at the point of entry. Even those goods that could be sold without restriction were confined to specified outlets – such as Changan's Western Market, where merchants were carefully supervised by government officials. The laws regulating imports to China were ever-changing and often subject to the whim of a particular customs official. The sinologist Edward Schafer, in his book *The Golden Peaches of Samarkand* (1963), refers to the Arab trader Abu Zaid Al-Hasan's complaint that he was obliged to hand over a third of his goods to the imperial warehouse upon arrival in the country.

Similar obstacles were placed in the way of merchants as they sought goods for the return journey to their home countries. The more desirable and profitable the goods, the more tightly they were controlled. Schafer describes an edict of 714 that forbade 'the export or the sale to foreigners of tapestries, damasks, gauzes, crepes, embroideries, and other fancy silks, or of yaktails, pearls, gold or iron'. If a foreigner died in China without a wife or heir his property was confiscated by the state, and even in cases where he was able to avoid this rule by taking a Chinese spouse, he could not take her back to his homeland.

Foreign emissaries to the Tang court were treated more courteously but were also subjected to numerous restrictions. Countries which conducted regular diplomatic relations with the Tang were issued a number of bronze tokens in the shape of fish. The envoy carried one half and the court retained the other. Upon arrival at Changan the emissary would be received by the *Hung-lu* office and questioned in great detail about the customs and geography of his homeland. Based on this information, Schafer tells us, the office would create a map of the envoy's country.

The emissary would wait until the day appointed for his audience with the emperor and would prostrate himself before the throne. Extravagant gifts were *de rigueur* and these were handed over to the Officer of Protocol. The envoy seldom received a word from the emperor but was often bestowed with grand titles. Schafer tells us of a visit to the court of Xuanzong (r.712–56) by an envoy from the King of Srivijaya in Sumatra. After presenting his gifts to the emperor the envoy was presented, in the name of his king, with a purple caftan and a gold belt. The title of 'Great Army Leader of the Militant Guards of the Left' was conferred upon the king, through his envoy – and the latter was then ushered out of the imperial presence. A mural in the tomb of Prince Zhanghuai – second son of Emperor Gaozong and Empress Wu Zetian – gives us an idea of the various protocols required of an embassy to the Tang court.

On the other hand, despite their apparent enmity towards foreigners and the restrictions they placed upon their activities, the Tang Chinese enthusiastically embraced foreign fashions in music, dress, diet and the arts. There were intermittent persecutions of foreign religions but, particularly during the early part of the Tang dynasty, there was a surprising degree of tolerance. Zoroastrianism reached China from Persia at about the time of the Northern Wei dynasty (386–534) and was flourishing by the time of the Tang dynasty. There were a number of Zoroastrian temples in Changan and another in Luoyang – the religion's spread propagated by refugees from the Sasanian Empire of Persia after the regime had, by 651, been completely overthrown by the Arabs. A tombstone unearthed in Xian in 1955 was found inscribed in Chinese and in the Pahlavi script of Persia, and it records the story of the tomb occupants – a man called Su Liang and his wife. They were both Persian Zoroastrians, descended from the rulers of the Sasanian Empire, but who had fled to China when that dynasty collapsed.

Manichaeism came to China from Central Asia during the Tang dynasty. It was endorsed by an imperial edict during the reign of Empress Wu Zetian (690–705), but despite an order in 732 forbidding its practice by Han Chinese the religion endured among the Uighur communities of Gansu and Xinjiang. In 786 the Manichaeans were permitted to construct the Dayunguangming Temple in Changan. Mani (216 or 217–76), the religion's founder, was born in southern Babylonia. He was probably a Parthian – the dynasty overthrown by the Sasanian king, Ardashir I, in 224. His father had gone to live in the city of Ctesiphon on the Tigris (south of Baghdad), where he is said to have heard voices ordering him to abstain from meat, sexual activity and the drinking of wine. He joined a group that adhered to these strictures. Mani subsequently journeyed to India where he founded his first Manichaean community, apparently influenced heavily by Buddhist ideas. Upon his return to Ctesiphon he was permitted to practise his faith but was eventually brought to trial for apostasy at the behest of orthodox Zoroastrian priests at the court of Bahram I. He was sentenced to crucifixion and put to death at Belapat in Susiana in 276. Manichaeism continued to take root, however, and soon spread across the Roman Empire to North Africa. One of its most vociferous opponents was the colourfully named St Augustine of Hippo (354–430). St Augustine was the son of a pagan who converted to Christianity and eventually became bishop of Hippo in North Africa (now Annaba in Algeria). He wrote a series of polemics fulminating against Manichaeism and it was this opposition – coupled with condemnation of it by the Roman Empire – that brought about the decline of Manichaeism in the West. Many of Mani's followers had fled eastwards, however. They settled in Central Asia and eventually reached China – where Manichaean communities were set up during the seventh and eighth centuries. Manichaeism is based on two principles: Light (the Spirit) and Darkness (the Flesh). These two principles of darkness and light, representing good and evil, struggle to gain control of the universe. It is man's duty to separate the two forces and render the latter harmless. He must avoid all activities that are detrimental to the light and attempt to free it from the darkness with which it is merged. If the principles are correctly adhered to separation of the two forces will occur immediately after death.

The Nestorians, too, flourished in Changan. The religion's founder, Nestorius, former Roman Catholic Patriarch of Constantinople, was expelled from the Church in 432 as a result of a schism with the Pope over the nature of the divinity of Christ and the role of the Virgin Mary. Nestorianism spread eastwards along the Silk Road to Central Asia, reaching China in 635. A Nestorian priest from Persia known as Adam (Aluoben to the Chinese) brought scriptures to Changan and was permitted to construct the Yiningfang Temple in the city. By the time of Emperor Xuanzong's reign (712–56) there were Nestorian temples in Changan, Luoyang and in other cities, and Yiningfang Temple was renamed Da Qin ('Rome'). A stele, discovered near Xian in 1625 and now housed in the city's Forest of Stelae Museum, commemorates Aluoben's arrival and the introduction of Nestorianism to China. Emperor Taizong (r.626–49) embraced the new religion with open arms. This 2.36 m tall stele is dated 781 and inscribed in Syriac and Chinese with the following words:

> At the time when Taizong, the brilliant emperor, was gloriously and splendidly beginning his prosperous reign, governing the people with far-sighted wisdom, there was in the land of Da Qin [Rome] a man of high virtue named Aluoben who, upon the augury of blue clouds, brought hither the true writings. After studying the harmony of the winds, he hastened to confront the dangers and difficulties and arrived in Changan in the ninth year of the Chen-kuan period [AD 635]. The emperor sent his minister, the duke Fang Hsüan-ling, with an escort, to receive the visitor in the western suburb of the city and conduct him to the palace. When the books had been transferred to the library and the doctrine examined in his private apartments, the emperor perceived its quality and truth and ordered that it should be preached and spread among the people.

At the bottom of this stele is a list, in Syriac, of 70 Nestorian priests.

Islam made modest inroads into China after the collapse of the Sasanian era, introduced mostly by merchants and former soldiers of the Arab armies. Even after the defeat of a Tang army at the Talas River in 751, Islam remained a religion of foreigners and of a number of the Turkic border tribes. There is some debate over whether the Grand Mosque on Changan's Huajue Lane was established during the Tang dynasty – it has been rebuilt many times and is more often ascribed to the Song dynasty (after 960). Mosques were undoubtedly in existence in Tang China, nevertheless – the Huaisheng Mosque in Canton was established as early as 627 by a relative of the Prophet Mohammed – one of the first Muslim missionaries to the Middle Kingdom.

Finally, there were a number of Jewish traders living in both Changan and Luoyang and they too were permitted to practise their religion. Jewish merchants were the most resourceful and adaptable of people and were active the length and breadth of the Silk Road. Jews were especially active in the production, dyeing and trading of silk textiles. Their descendants can be found among the several hundred Chinese Jews still living in Kaifeng, Henan province. The reign of Emperor Wuzong (840–6) – an ardent Daoist – witnessed the major persecution of foreign religions and the climate of religious toleration that had characterised the early Tang was but a distant memory.

During the tolerant atmosphere of the early Tang period many Chinese developed friendships with foreigners living in China. Abe no Nakamaro, friend of the poet Li Bai, was one such person (see the section on Japanese visitors below). Some foreigners attained high positions in government and acquired great power and fortune. The most infamous of these was the part-Sogdian general, An Lushan – a favourite of Emperor Xuanzong – who attempted to usurp the throne in 755. But many other foreigners gave years of faithful service to the Tang.

Japanese Visitors to China

Throughout the Tang dynasty Japanese envoys visited Changan, making the perilous crossing of the East China Sea. Many, such as Monk Min, lived in the Chinese capital to study Buddhist doctrine. Others, like the scholar Takamuko no Kuromaro, who stayed for 34 years, learned about processes of government. He took his ideas back to Japan where he became involved in the Taika reform movement.[7]

Abe no Nakamaro (701–70) was a close friend of the well-known Tang poets Li Bai and Wang Wei. He lived in Changan for 54 years and was given an official appointment by the Tang court. During the reign of the Tang emperor, Suzong (756–62), Abe decided to return home to visit his aging parents. The ship carrying him almost capsized, drifting as far as the south China coast before he was rescued. Believing him lost, Li Bai wrote the poem 'Mourning Chao', one of the greatest masterpieces of Tang literature:

Chao left our imperial city for his Japanese homeland
a lone flake of sail. Now he wanders islands of immortals.
Foundering in emerald seas, a bright moon never to return

Leaves white, grief-tinged clouds crowding our southlands.

('Mourning Chao' by Li Bai (also called Li Po), 701–62.

In Hinton, 1996)

The ultimate expression of the close cultural links between China and Japan during the Tang dynasty can be found in the Japanese cities of Kyoto and Nara – both modelled on Changan – and in the contents of the Shosoin repository.

The scholar Kibino Makibi (693 or 695–775) remained in Changan for 18 years, using the basic structural parts and radicals of Chinese writing to create Japanese Katakana script. His fellow countryman Kukai (Kobo Daishi) studied Esoteric Buddhism at Changan's Qinglong Temple and returned to Japan to found the Shingon sect. Kukai also invented Hiragana script – a simplification of the phonetic Kanji script that revolutionised the writing of literature during Japan's Heian period (794–1185). It enabled women – who were considered incapable of learning to write complex Chinese characters and were hence not given an education – to express themselves in writing. As a result, it was women who wrote many of the first published works in Japan – the most celebrated being *Genji Monogatari* ('The Tale of Genji') by Murasaki Shikibu.

Persians, Sogdians and Other Foreigners

Where shall we say adieu?
Why not the Ching-I Gate of Changan
Where the Persian waitresses beckon with white hands,
Enticing customers to drink their fill of fine wine?

(Li Bai (also called Li Po), 701–62.

Quoted in Hayashi, 1975)

The splendours of Tang dynasty Changan captivated the Arab traveller Ibn-Wahab, who visited in about 815:

The town was very great, and its population extremely numerous. It was divided into two vast halves separated by a long, broad track. The emperor, his ministers, his guard, the supreme judge, the eunuchs, and all those who belonged to the imperial household lived in the eastern part of the city. The ordinary population could not communicate with them and were not admitted to the places there, watered by many canals whose banks were planted with trees and decorated with sumptuous residences. The western part of the town was inhabited by the ordinary people and the merchants. They had great squares there and markets for the necessities of life. At day-break, officers of the royal household would be seen there, together with purveyors and the servants of the courtiers. They came to this part of town to visit the markets and the merchants' dwellings in order to buy all they wanted, and they did not return until the fol-lowing morning.

(Recorded in about 915 by Abu Zaid Al-Hasan.
Quoted in Drège and Bührer, 1989)

Persians and Sogdians were by far the most active among the merchants. Many Persians were quick to acquire wealth and soon controlled the medicine, spice and jewellery bazaars. The commercial activity of Changan was centred on the East and West markets, each containing innumerable bazaars for many tradesmen including gold and silversmiths, tailors, tanners, herbalists, metalworkers, saddlers and purveyors of food and drink. There were also establishments offering various services: pawnshops, moneylenders, printers and brothels – to name but four – and the Western Market, with over 3,000 shops lining its narrow lanes, was the more bustling of the two.

Perhaps the most distinguished among the many thousands of foreigners who made China their permanent home was Peroz (or Firûz), son of Yazdegerd III (r.632–51), the last of the Sasanian rulers of Persia. Peroz and his son Nyas sought refuge in Changan in about 670 and were appointed 'Generals of the Left and Right' in the Tang army. Peroz was also appointed as ambassador, representing the large Persian community in Changan. One of the 61 statues of ambassadors that stand before the tomb of Gaozong and Wu Zetian is believed to be of Peroz.

Musicians, singers and dancers came to Changan to entertain the Tang court and many of them achieved great fame and wealth. Cao Bao, from Kebud in modern Uzbekistan, became a celebrated *pipa* (lute) player – a tradition continued by his son and grandson. During the reign of Xianzong (805–20) a renowned singer from Maimargh (a state in Central Asia) performed at court and, during Xuanzong's reign (712–56), dancing girls from Chach (near modern Tashkent) would dance provocatively until, at the climax, they would pull down their blouses to reveal naked shoulders:

Purple net shirts are set in motion – the Chach dancers come!
Girdles droop from gilded thighs, flowered waists are heavy,
Hats revolve with golden bells, snowy faces turn.
I watch – too soon the tune is done, they will not be detained;
Whirling in clouds, escorted by rain, they are off to the Terrace of
  the Sun.

(Bai Juyi, 772–846. 'The Geisha of Chach'.
Quoted in Schafer, 1963)

The most cherished of all the dancers from the Western Lands were
the 'Sogdian twirling girls' – the best coming from Samarkand. These
girls – presented as tribute by rulers of Central Asian states – were all the
rage at the beginning of the eighth century. Dressed in crimson robes
and green damask pantaloons, they balanced and twirled on the tops of
balls that rolled about the stage. Xuanzong was inordinately fond of this
dance and his inamorata, Yang Guifei, is said to have mastered it.

Musicians and dancers also came from southern and eastern Asia.
In 802 the Pyu kingdom of Burma sent a 35-man orchestra which
played compositions based on the Buddhist scriptures, accompanied
by conches and bronze drums. In 777, 11 Japanese dancing girls were
sent to the Tang court, and musicians from the kingdom of Funan (in
what is now Vietnam) came to live in the Tang capital. Not all of the
musicians sent to Tang were allowed to remain, however. Schafer tells
the story of the two girls sent to the Tang court by its ally, the Silla
kingdom of Korea. They appear to have been chosen as much for their
looks as for their musical ability. Emperor Taizong (626–49) decided
that they were to be pitied as an exotic parrot would be, and promptly
sent them back.

Of all the musical styles to enter China during the Tang dynasty, it was
the instruments and compositions from the kingdom of Kucha (Kuqa)
that had the most influence. Kuqa musicians introduced the four-stringed
pipa, a small lacquered drum, and the flute. The Gigaku performances of
Japan appear to have their origins among the musicians of Kuqa (see the
sections on Kuqa and the Shosoin on pages 142 and 82 respectively).
The indefatigable monk Xuanzang visited Kuqa during the seventh
century and stated that, 'the musicians of this land outshine those of other
kingdoms by their talent on the flute and the guitar'.

The Sogdians – of eastern Iranian descent and speaking an
Indo-European dialect – were consummate merchants whose language
became the *lingua franca* of the Silk Road. A Chinese commentary of the

time, *Memoir on the Barbarians of the West*, refers admiringly to the traders from Sogdia:

> They are clever traders. When a boy reaches the age of five years, he is sent to study books. When he begins to understand them, he is sent to study trade. To make profits is regarded by most of the inhabitants as an excellent thing.
>
> (Wei Jie, *Memoir on the Barbarians of the West*. Quoted in Drège and Bührer, 1989)

Caravans from the Sogdian cities of Samarkand, Varakhsha (near Bukhara) and Penjikent (near the Tajik–Uzbek border) brought gemstones, perfumes, silver, wool and cotton textiles, and horses across the Gobi via Dunhuang to China. In return the Sogdians purchased raw silk – both as yarn and as woven pieces – and resold it to the Persians, the Byzantines (until the end of the sixth century), the Indians and the nomads of the steppe. A bundle of letters sent between Sogdian merchants – discovered in a watchtower at the western extremity of the Great Wall by the British-Hungarian archaeologist and explorer Sir Marc Aurel Stein (1862–1943) in 1907 – are dated to around 313 and indicate that trade between Sogdiana and China was conducted from an early date. The letters refer to the political instability of the Silk Road at the time, and one describes the destruction of the northern capital, Luoyang, by the Xiongnu: 'And, Sir, the last Emperor – so they say – fled from Saragh [Luoyang] because of the famine, and his palace and walled city were set on fire [...] So Saragh is no more, Ngap [the city of Yeh, to the north] no more!' (quoted in Paludan, 1998). Inscriptions in Sogdian language found at Shatial, in Pakistan's upper Indus valley, demonstrate the extent to which they travelled in search of trade. (For more on the Sogdians, see the box below and the sections on Shatial and Chilas on page 198.)

THE SOGDIANS

Perhaps the greatest of the many Silk Road traders were a people of Persian stock known collectively as the Sogdians. Little is known about them – they could never have been said to constitute a nation or empire, rather they were more of a loosely affiliated group of city-states. What is not in doubt, however, is that they possessed great commercial prowess – evidence of the activities of Sogdian merchants has been found at many locations and over a wide area of the Silk Road. They seemed to have travelled anywhere and everywhere in search of profit, and traces of them are found in the documents and murals of Xinjiang, in the petroglyphs at Chilas in northern Pakistan, and in the poems and stories of Tang dynasty Xian. By the second century AD they were playing a key role in Silk Road trade in both directions – the Chinese bought jade, precious stones, exotic animals and slaves from Sogdian merchants, while the countries to the west purchased the silks, mirrors and weapons that they acquired in China. There were colonies of Sogdian merchants in many Chinese towns and they carried their religion and customs with them as they travelled. The Sogdian language became the Silk Road's *lingua franca* and, from the second century until they were invested by the Arabs during the eighth century, Sogdian cities were centres of cultural excellence. Every work of art that the Sogdians produced – their paintings, their metalwork, their textiles, their sculpture and even their grave artefacts – are flamboyant expressions of wealth and power, acquired from Silk Road trade.

Figure 9
Mural depicting visiting ambassadors at the royal court at Samarkand. Sogdian, seventh century. From the south wall of Room 1, Afrasiab, Samarkand, Uzbekistan.
This and the other murals at Afrasiab adorned the walls of the ruler's palace and the houses of his nobles. They were installed at the museum in the exact arrangement in which they were discovered. In this celebrated and richly painted mural, members of the Chaghanian mission are seen visiting the court of the Sogdian ruler Vargoman. An inscription on the painting refers to the visit of ambassadors from Chaghanian (the area around the Surkhan Darya valley near modern Denau) and Chach (modern Tashkent). Leading the procession is a princess seated beneath a canopy upon a white elephant – the accompanying inscription suggesting that she is destined to marry the Sogdian ruler. Her entourage, on camelback and on horseback, brings gifts for the ruler including a flock of sacred swans. The Chaghanian ambassador himself, lavishly dressed, holds aloft his official mace as he approaches on horseback.

Excavation of the Sogdian burial grounds at Orlat, situated on dry sections of the Saghanaq riverbed to the north-west of Samarkand, have revealed much about their burial practices and their fondness for hunting and jousting. The Sogdian dead were either exposed on towers – their flesh stripped by vultures or dogs before the bones were placed in ossuary caskets – or they were interred in pits or catacombs. At Orlat they were interred and, despite the fact that many graves were looted in antiquity, many artefacts remain. Weapons, ceramics and bone belt buckles were found in a total of ten burial mounds and some, like a jade scabbard slide from China, were of foreign manufacture. The bone belt plaques are all superbly worked with themes that are strangely reminiscent of the European knights of medieval times.

By the early eighth century the Sogdians were finished as an economic and political force in Central Asia. They and Divastich, the last ruler of Penjikent, fled the city with the Arabs in pursuit. They sought refuge at Mount Mugh in modern Tajikistan but were eventually overrun and slaughtered in 722. This was not the end of the Sogdians, however. During the 1930s, Soviet researchers discovered that the inhabitants of several villages in the remote Yagnob valley of northern Tajikistan still spoke the ancient language of the Sogdians. More than 1,000 years after they disappeared from the Central Asian stage, these precious few descendants of the men who helped to sustain the Silk Road during its most vibrant years are still to be found in the mountains of Tajikistan. The modern descendants of the Sogdians, it is said, are the Tajiks, but – as with so much of Central Asian history – the subject is a matter of fierce debate.

Tokharians

Over the past 35 years a number of mummified corpses have been discovered in the Taklamakan Desert of Xinjiang. Their physiognomy appears to be Caucasian or 'Western' and several are decorated with tattoos that resemble the animal style of early nomadic peoples. Furthermore, the textiles worn by other Caucasoid mummies – found near Hami on the Northern Silk Road – resemble the 'tartans' worn by both modern-day Scots and by the ancient Celts before them. This twill, woven in light brown with light blue and white stripes, resembles some of the cloth fragments discovered in the salt mines of Hallstatt in Austria. The latter were the remains of cloth discarded by ancient Celtic miners and date from about 1300 to about 400 BC. Their approximate dates of manufacture, and the colours and designs used, correspond closely to the twills found at Hami.

All of these factors have given rise to the theory that the mummies are the remains of a lost tribe of European nomads who may have migrated eastwards in very early times and settled in the oasis cities of Chinese Central Asia. A detail of a cave painting found at Bezeklik shows Tokharian worshippers making donations to the *bodhisattva* (see Figure 10). Their reddish hair and pale eyes are similar to the mummies discovered around Urumqi, despite the fact that a gap of as much as 2,000 years separates them. There is also speculation that the Tokharians were a tribe of the Yuezhi confederation – founders of the Kushan Empire – who were driven out of the Tarim basin in about 165 BC by the Xiongnu (see the section on the Kushans on page 206). The main evidence for this is that they both spoke dialects of the same Tokharian language found in the Tang dynasty manuscripts of the Tarim basin – especially those discovered around Kuqa. The Yuezhi left no written texts but etymological links have been established with a number of words that were adopted by the Chinese from the tribe's language long before they were expelled during the second century BC. These include the word 'Qilian', the mountains referred to by the Han historian Sima Qian as the domain of the Yuezhi. The name Qilian apparently derives from the Tokharian word *klyom*, meaning 'heavenly' – the Chinese now call this range (on the northern side of the Tarim basin), the Tianshan or 'Heavenly Mountains', while today's Qilian Mountains are to the south. There is an intriguing quote in Pliny's *Natural History*, written around AD 70–80 and containing the Roman view of the world at the time. He refers to the people of China as 'Seres', the name given to the country by the Greeks, but the physiognomy he attributes to them is strange indeed:

> The Seres are of more than average height; they have red hair, blue eyes and harsh voices, and they have no language in which to communicate their thoughts. The merchandise [of the Cingalese] was deposited on the bank on the Seres' side of the river, and they would carry it away and leave the price if they agreed to it.

Admittedly, the information was obtained second-hand from a Sri Lankan ('Cingalese') ambassador to Rome but the possibility that this is an early reference to the Tokharians is a fascinating one.

If the mummies of the Taklamakan were Tokharians, what remains to be answered is where people with such self-evidently Caucasoid features came from. The question is still hotly debated by scholars but

Figure 10
Detail of a
mural depicting
Tokharian donors
offering bags of
money.
Uighur period,
ninth century.
From Cave
20, Bezeklik,
Xinjiang
province.

what is undeniable is that many of the residents of modern day Xinjiang possess distinctly 'European' features.

The Tokharian traders of the Tang dynasty were to be found at Kizil, Kuqa and Karashahr on the northern section of the Silk Route; and in Kashgar, Yarkand and Khotan on the southern section. They were city dwellers and were therefore important traders with the Chinese, and their influences on Chinese culture were extensive. Music and dance from Kuqa were admired and imitated by the Tang Chinese, and the Tokharian ladies – renowned for their beauty – introduced new fashions, hairstyles and make-up to the Middle Kingdom (see the section on Kuqa on page 142).

Not all Chinese approved of the infusion of foreign customs. The conservative poet Yuan Zhen (779–831), who eventually served as prime minister, was extremely vocal on the subject at the end of the eighth century:

Ever since the Western horsemen began raising smut and dust,
Fur and fleece, rank and rancid, have filled Hsien and Lo.
Women make themselves Western matrons by the study of Western
    makeup;
Entertainers present Western tunes, in their devotion to Western music.
                     (Yuan Zhen, 779–831. Quoted in Schafer, 1963.
                     'Hsien' is Changan and 'Lo' is Luoyang)

Yuan Zhen paints a rich and colourful picture of a typical foreign trader of Tang China, depicting him as a man who would travel to the ends of the world, who would exploit nature, and buy or sell anything to turn a profit:

In search of pearls, he harnesses the glaucous sea –
He gathers his pearls, and ascends to Ching and Heng.
In the north, he buys the Tangut horses,
In the west, he catches Tibetan parrots.
Fire-washed linen from the Continent of Flames,
Perfectly woven tapestries from the Land of Shu;
Slave girls of Yüeh, sleek of buttery flesh;
Houseboys of Hsi, bright of brow and eye.
                     (Yuan Zhen, 779–831. Quoted in Schafer, 1963.
          'Fire-washed linen' is asbestos, imported from the Roman Empire
        and the 'Continent of Flames' is the mythical name for the lands to
    the south of China. 'Shu' is Sichuan and 'Hsi' was the name given to a
                          tribe from Manchuria)

Tang Terracotta Figurines

During the Shang dynasty (*c*.1500–1050 BC) and most of the Zhou period (1050–221 BC), members of Chinese nobility were interred with their servants, charioteers and horses in order that they could be served in the afterlife. By the time of the Emperor Qin Shi Huangdi (r.221–210 BC), real horses were still buried with the emperor but his retinue was represented by vast number of figures in terracotta (see the section on Qin Shi Huangdi on page 42).

By the early part of the Tang dynasty the practice of burying *mingqi* ('objects or articles of the spirit') was widespread. Foreigners were a great source of fascination to the Tang Chinese and are frequently depicted on tomb figures. Among these *voix du silence,* representations of Arab and Semite merchants from the lands to the west are common, as are pearl divers from the islands of Southeast Asia, Central Asian grooms and acrobats, and occasional figures of curly-haired Africans. These figures provide a wealth of information about the society and attitudes of Tang China. They are modelled in a naturalistic and often humorous way and are a reflection of the manner in which the Chinese regarded foreign visitors to the country. By the early part of the eighth century they were being made in vast numbers and tombs of the nobility could contain hundreds of terracotta figures. Prince Li Xian (d.706), for example, son of Emperor Gaozong, was interred with no fewer than 777 terracotta figures. Emperor Ruizong (r.684–90 and 710–12) decried the growing use of *mingqi* as a means to show off the wealth and social status of the deceased and his or her family, rather than as a genuine expression of grief. Grave goods were carried in processions up to 10 km long and officials competed with each other to see who could produce the most ostentatious display. The problem became so acute that in 742 sumptuary laws were enacted to specify the size and quantity of figures permissible for different official ranks – officials above the third rank could have 90 figures, those above the fifth were allowed 60 and those above the ninth, 40.

During the early part of the dynasty they were generally unglazed, modelled in a somewhat stiff manner, and generic in style. From the end of the seventh to the middle of the eighth century, pottery figures were modelled in a dynamic and particularised fashion and were expertly glazed. Tri-coloured (or *sancai*) glaze was made by blending copper, iron or cobalt with colourless lead silicate to produce cream, amber, green and (less frequently) blue. As well as figures of humans, camels, horses, ferocious *lokapalas* (guardians) and creatures from mythology were produced. The best figures from this period are technical *tours de force* (Figure 11).

Terracotta figures also include depictions of the peoples of Kunlun (or Kurung), a general term used by the Tang to describe the kingdoms of the South China Sea said to have dark skin and curly hair. In fact, the Chinese appear to have been singularly ill-informed about the lands to the south of the Kunlun mountain range on the Tibetan plateau – the source of the name. Some Tang records contemptuously describe all of

Figure 11
Tri-colour (*sancai*) glazed figure of a camel carrying a party of musicians. Tang dynasty, *c.*745. Height (camel) 48.5 cm; height (figures) 11–16.1 cm. Unearthed in 1959 from a tomb at Zhongbao Village, Xian.

This image is a paragon of Chinese ceramic art. The musicians are a mixture of Chinese and Central Asian individuals who play string, wind and percussion instruments including reed pipes, a flute and a type of lute. The central figure dances, or perhaps sings, to the music as their mount stretches his neck and bellows.

the peoples of the lands to the south as Kunlun peoples, even applying the term to Persians and Indians. The term is most often used, however, to denote the people from the Southeast Asian archipelago – a source of slaves for the Chinese. The Chinese seem to have admired not only their skill in taming wild animals – such as elephants and rhinoceroses – but also their ability to stay under water for long periods of time. They were sought after and trained as pearl divers.

A small number of Africans reached Changan, probably as slaves aboard Arab ships. Official records from the Tang dynasty indicate that the first African country known to the Chinese was Shunai, located in the southern part of modern day Somalia. The kingdom is recorded as having sent an ambassador to Tang China in 629. The Chinese sometimes refer to Africans as *Zangi*, apparently after the island of Zanzibar, and also grouped them under the somewhat confusing heading of *Kunlun*. This means that they can be only tentatively identified among the terracotta tomb figures of the Tang.

Terracotta figures of Chinese subjects are a barometer of fashions current among the Tang nobility. The pulchritudinous Yang Guifei – celebrated concubine of the Tang emperor, Xuanzong (r.712–756) – was regarded as the ideal of feminine beauty by the ladies of Tang. Her Rubenesque proportions and towering 'cloud-tresses' were widely imitated and are represented in many of the tomb figures of the mid-eighth century. The celebrated Tang dynasty poet Bai Juyi (772–846) captures the moment when Xuanzong is first smitten as he sights Lady Yang emerging from her bath:

> Her hair like a cloud,
> Her face like a flower,
> A gold hair-pin adorning her tresses.
> Behind the warm lotus-flower curtain,
> They took their pleasure in the spring night.
>
> (Bai Juyi, 772–846. 'Song of Eternal Sorrow')

Each year the emperor would take her to the hot springs built specially outside Changan so he could watch her bathe. When Xuanzong played board games and was losing, Lady Yang would set loose her Samarkand lapdog or her pet parakeet to upend the pieces and preserve the emperor's dignity. So besotted was Xuanzong that he neglected his official duties and almost brought the dynasty to an end. An Lushan – an illiterate former slave of Turkish and Sogdian descent – succeeded in gaining the emperor's favour through a combination of intrigue and cunning. In 755 he attempted to seize the throne, marching from Beijing with an army of 150,000. After taking Luoyang he declared himself emperor and Xuanzong fled towards Sichuan. En route, Xuanzong's troops mutinied and he was allowed to escape, but only after agreeing that Yang Guifei be strangled. The rebellion was not quelled until 763, the conflict prolonged by the involvement of Tibetans. Imperial power was eventually restored with the assistance of a large force of Uighurs and an army led by the gifted general, Guo Ziyi (697–781). In return for providing assistance the Uighurs demanded the right to sack the city of Luoyang and this they did at the end of 757, and again in 762. A secondary consequence of the An Lushan Rebellion was that a marked reduction in the production of ceramic figurines occurred – perhaps because of the destruction of the kilns. Figurines continued to be produced throughout the late Tang era but in smaller numbers and without the exuberant vitality of the middle period.

Tomb Sculpture and Paintings

Two other aspects of Tang funeral practice provide information about the affluent and cosmopolitan nature of the society of the time: above-ground stone sculpture, and tomb paintings. Stone sculpture placed above tombs dates back to 117 BC and the mausoleum of General Huo Qubing. From the first century AD onwards, the Chinese adopted the practice of erecting 'spirit roads' – an avenue of statues and engraved stele lining the approaches to the tomb of an important figure. Statues of men and animals – often mythical beasts – served as a guard of honour for the deceased in the afterlife and a reminder of his or her status. The spirit roads erected at Tang dynasty tombs reflect an empire at the height of its power. The earliest Tang tombs, such as that of Emperor Taizong (r.626–49), were erected during a period in which China became the dominant power in Asia; the Ordos region, Inner Mongolia and the Tarim basin were brought firmly under Chinese control and Taizong's defeat of the eastern Turks in 630 resulted in some 10,000 Turkish families moving to the capital. Contacts with Tibet were enhanced by the marriage, in 641, of the Tang princess Wencheng to King Songtsän Gampo – the country's ruler. Campaigns were also launched against Korea although it was not until 668 – long after Taizong's death – that the entire country was finally subjugated as a result of an alliance with Silla, one of its states. Taizong's mausoleum at Zhaoling, north-west of Xian, was built into the side of a mountain and required 13 years to complete. Some 14 statues of foreign rulers once stood at the northern gate, while the east and west galleries contained stone reliefs of his six favourite horses – each of which played a role in one of his military campaigns. The carvings are based on drawings by the court painter, Yan Liben.

Taizong's eldest son and heir, the hapless Li Cheng Qian, was a Turkophile of absurd proportions. He preferred to speak Turkish rather than Chinese and set up a complete Turkish encampment in the palace grounds where he sat, dressed as a khan, eating mutton cooked over a camp-fire. He was eventually caught plotting and removed from the line of succession.

At the Qianling Mausoleum, north-west of Changan, is the joint burial place of Emperor Gaozong (r.649–83) and his implacable consort Wu Zetian (r.690–705) – the only woman ever to become emperor of China. The inner wall contains an area of 240 hectares (about 600 acres) and all over the site are reminders of a country enjoying its glory days. A stele at Qianling, erected on Wu Zetian's orders and in memory of her achievements, is without an inscription – the idea is that her accomplishments were so great that that they could not be expressed by mere words. Statues of winged horses at Qianling recall Assyrian reliefs, and a large stone ostrich on Gaozong's tomb is a reminder of the Tang fascination with distant lands. A group of 61 stone figures of foreigners stand within the inner enclosure at Qianling, representing the foreign rulers and envoys who were resident in Changan or who came to attend the funeral of Emperor Gaozong. Of the 61 original statues, one has disappeared and the remainder have been damaged at some time in the distant past – perhaps during a period of xenophobia in China. On the back of each statue is an inscription giving the subject's name, title and country of origin. These inscriptions are now illegible but were, according to records from the time, still visible during the Song dynasty (960–1279). Two Persians were identified, including a certain King Balāsh – thought to be King Peroz of Persia – the last ruler of the Sasanian dynasty who sought refuge in Changan from the Arab invasion of his country (see the section on Persians in Changan on page 63). They now stand in silent serried ranks, paying homage to the late emperor.

Qianling has a large number of ancillary tombs containing royal relatives – 17 in the south-east area alone. A number have been excavated in recent years and the murals that line their passageways are a captivating record of court life during the Tang dynasty. Princess Yongtai (684–701), a granddaughter of Gaozong and Wu Zetian, died at the age of 17 – almost certainly at the hands of the latter. An exquisite mural – depicting two groups of palace maids who appear to be walking in a slow, silent candle-lit procession towards her bedchamber – was found on the eastern wall of the front chamber of Yongtai's tomb.

Figure 12
Mural depicting a group of foreign envoys to the Tang court. Tang dynasty, 706. Height 184.5 cm, width 252.5 cm.

Discovered in 1971 at the tomb of Prince Zhanghuai (Li Xian), Qianling, near Xian, Shaanxi province. In this mural, the three Chinese officials on the left greet the three foreign ambassadors on the right as they wait to see the emperor. The envoys have been tentatively identified from their dress and appearance as representing (left to right): the eastern Roman Empire, Japan or Korea, and one from the north-east Chinese minority peoples.

The murals adorning the walls of Crown Prince Zhanghuai's tomb are quite different. Zhanghuai, born Li Xian, was the second son of Gaozong and Wu Zetian. He was deposed by Empress Wu in 680, banished to Sichuan province, and eventually forced to commit suicide in 684. He was not formally buried until after Empress Wu's death and the restoration of Emperor Zhongzong to the throne in 705. The murals of Crown Prince Zhanghuai's tomb are more exuberant than those of Yongtai and are a splendid record of aristocratic pursuits during the Tang dynasty. More than 50 paintings were found in the passageways of the tomb and it is quite clear from their content that Prince Zhanghuai was inordinately fond of hunting and polo. In the hunting scenes, well-dressed Tang nobles hunt with falcons, trained cheetahs and small dogs. Cheetahs and dogs were used for a brief period at the beginning of the eighth century and there are records of both types of animal being imported as tribute – particularly from Samarkand. Another of the murals from Prince Zhanghuai's tomb depicts a group of foreign emissaries at a time when numerous countries maintained diplomatic relations with the Tang court (Figure 12).

The many images of beautiful women form the last category of murals found in Zhanghuai's tomb. Artists began to depict individual aspects of character and physiognomy, and an air of confidence – apparent at the beginning of the eighth century – is reflected in the humour contained in many of the paintings. In one, a rather lecherous man with a bulbous nose leers suggestively at a court beauty holding a rooster. In another, a well-built older lady is accompanied by a female attendant, dressed in the clothing of a Central Asian man, and by a female dwarf – all indicative of the new fondness for exotica.

Other Works of Art from Tang Dynasty Xian

The Daming Palace (the 'Palace of Great Brightness') in the north-east section of Changan was the largest of the three palaces built for the Tang rulers – the two others being the Taiji and Xingqing palaces. Built in 662 on the orders of Emperor Gaozong, Daming was situated on high ground and faced south. The remains of the front hall at Daming – the Hanyuan Hall – were excavated between 1956–60 and the dimensions of the building were discovered to be about 67 × 29 m with a floor space of almost 2,000 m². It sat above a vast open area of about 600 × 750 m. The relics found in the remains of the Daming Palace include large numbers of tiles and bricks with geometric designs, some inscribed with the phrase, 'Made by an Official Artisan' to show that they had been inspected and approved by the Ministry of Public Works. A sensuous and graceful marble statue of a *bodhisattva* found in the ruins of Daming is inspired by the Gupta sculpture of India. The manner of depicting the *bodhisattva* revealed in this sculpture became the norm in Chinese art for centuries afterwards. Typically, one hip is thrust out to the side, the arm on the same side is bent at the elbow and held in a raised position, and the arm on the opposite side hangs pendent. The robes cling to emphasise the contours of the body and the figure is then adorned with a layer of jewellery. The Daming *bodhisattva* is the most supreme example of it type and has been described – with a concession to gender – as the 'Venus of the East'.

During the An Lushan Rebellion of 755, two large terracotta urns were buried for safekeeping in the village of Hejia on the southern outskirts of Changan – on land that had been the residence of Li Shouli, son of Prince Zhanghuai. The pots were discovered in 1970 and were found to contain more than 1,000 objects of incalculable value. The treasures include precious medicines and coins from Japan, Sasanian

Persia, the eastern Roman Empire (Byzantium), and a large number from China itself. Some 270 gold and silver objects were discovered, some in Chinese style and others showing clear foreign influence.

A gilt silver octagonal cup, excavated with a second cup at Hejia, has facets decorated with four musicians and four dancers – all foreign in appearance – and a handle with two addorsed heads of Central Asian men. The shape of the cup is Near Eastern in origin and may have been made by one of the many Persian or Sogdian silversmiths living in Changan at the time. The popularity of foreign entertainers was at its height during the period before the An Lushan Rebellion and an elaborate musical arrangement called the *Shibu Yue* ('Ten-Part composition') was performed at important banquets and celebrations. Each part was composed in the musical style of a certain country or nationality, and the figures on this cup appear to be conducting a performance of this arrangement (see also the section on foreigners in Xian on page 57).

Another of the relics from Hejia village, a gilt-silver wine flask with the design of a dancing horse, is a reminder of the intense Chinese affection for horses. It follows that of the leather bottles used by the northern nomads. The Tang annals relate that Emperor Xuanzong (r.712–56) owned 400 horses that were trained to dance. Arthur Waley's account of the sad fate of the horses is the most colourful. Each year, on the emperor's birthday, a group of them would perform a complex dressage to a suite called the 'Tune of the Tilted Cup'. The horses would be ridden up a steep slope to perform on top of a tall platform, or would dance while held aloft on benches. They would conclude their performance by kneeling before the sovereign with wine cups held in their mouths, as if offering a toast. During the An Lushan Rebellion the horses were dispersed and eventually fell into the hands of a warlord who knew nothing of their imperial pedigree. One day, during a banquet, marching music was played in the camp and the horses began to dance. The grooms believed them to be possessed and, at the instigation of the warlord, they began to beat them with brooms. The horses thought they were being beaten for not keeping proper time to the music and the more they were beaten the harder they danced. Eventually the horses fell dead on the stable floor (abridged from Waley, 1952).

Famensi

The last of the Tang dynasty sites in the Xian area that we will examine in this book is the Famen monastery in Fufeng county, 120 km west of

Xian. Originally founded during the Eastern Han dynasty (AD 25–220) as the Asoka Temple, it was renamed the Famensi during the Tang dynasty. From the Northern Wei (386–534) onwards it was a place of pilgrimage and was said to contain relics of Buddha Sakyamuni himself. The monastery was clearly the recipient of a large amount of largesse, particularly during the Tang dynasty period. There is literary evidence that the relics housed in it were carried, on a number of occasions, as part of a lavish procession between Famensi and the Tang capital – a distance of over 120 km. In 819 the relics were paraded before a rapturous crowd and put on display in the imperial palace. Confucianist poet and essayist Han Yu (768–824), a fierce opponent of Buddhism, submitted a blunt memorial to the court in which he criticised the emperor himself for encouraging the practice of a foreign religion:

> You are […] putting on for the citizens of the capital this extra-ordinary spectacle which is nothing more than a sort of theatrical amusement […] Now that the Buddha has long been dead, is it fitting that his decayed and rotten bones, his ill-omened and filthy remains, should be allowed to enter in the precincts of the palace? […] Without reason you have taken up unclean things and examined them in person.
>
> (Han Yu, in 819, *Lun fogu biao*, 'Memorial Discussing the Buddha's Bones'. Quoted in Lee, 1998)

Han Yu's punishment for this outburst was exile to Guangdong, but the seeds were sown for Emperor Wuzong's campaign of persecution – launched against the Buddhists from 842–5. About 4,500 temples and monasteries were closed or destroyed and 250,000 monks and nuns were layicised. The treasures of Famensi survived, however. In 1981, part of the pagoda collapsed during a storm and during a reconstruction project in 1987 a set of three underground chambers was discovered in the foundations. The chambers were excavated and produced four relics, purportedly finger bones of the Buddha, buried in about 874. Only one appears to be of bone, the other three are circular crystal tubes – an acceptable substitute at a time when genuine relics were in both great demand and short supply. One of the relics was intended to be displayed on a tray held by a gilt-silver *bodhisattva* made especially for Emperor Yizong (r.859–73). Wrapped around the *bodhisattva* are more than 200 saltwater pearls – Silk Road imports from the Persian Gulf. A large number of other treasures were also deposited in the foundations – apparently as a commemorative donation for the relics – including 121 gold and silver articles, 16 porcelain vessels, stone and lacquer objects, 400 pieces of jewellery, imported glass, and over 7,000 pieces of silk textiles. The porcelains included a number of *mise* ('secret colour') Yue-ware vessels, hitherto thought not to have been produced until the Song dynasty. There is room to examine only three of the artefacts from the Famensi here, but each has a strong connection with the Silk Road. A complete set of tea drinking paraphernalia was discovered in the foundations – all in silver and gilded-silver. Techniques for working with precious metals were perfected during the Tang dynasty as a result of contacts with the craftsmen of Central Asia and Persia – many of whom were resident in Changan. Although tea drinking had been known in China since ancient times, by the time of the Tang dynasty it had become an elaborate ritual and was inextricably linked to the practice of Chan (or Zen) Buddhism. Practitioners of this form of Buddhism were expected to meditate for long periods, eschewing both sleep and food. But they were permitted to drink tea – the stimulating effects of which kept them awake. The practice eventually spread to the population in general and the intricate form of the Famensi tea implements indicates that, by the late Tang dynasty, it had become an art form. A Tang dynasty text, *The Classic of Tea* by Lu Yu, is the first treatise ever written on the subject of drinking tea. The presence of salt receptacles at Famensi is a reflection of the fondness among the Tang for taking tea with salt and spice.

Another Famensi article, a blue glass dish, may be foreign in origin. The dish is decorated with incised and gilded plantain leaves and has an Islamic flavour that suggests it was imported – perhaps from Nishapur in Persia or Samarra in Iraq, where similar vessels have been found. The Shosoin repository in Nara, Japan, has a number of Persian glass vessels – but such items, because of their fragility, are rare. Another of the artefacts found at the Famen Pagoda reveals a different type of contact with neighbouring countries. A gilded-silver censer (or incense burner) was discovered together with a small figure of the Hindu god Ganesha: the elephant-headed son of Siva. Only a handful of figures of Ganesha have been identified in Chinese art.

One of the greatest collections of Tang art to survive to modern times is not in China but in Japan – at the Shosoin repository in Nara (see box below). Aside from the Shosoin, Tang silk fabrics were also found in large numbers at the Astana cemetery in Turfan, Xinjiang province, and are discussed in detail in that section.

THE SHOSOIN

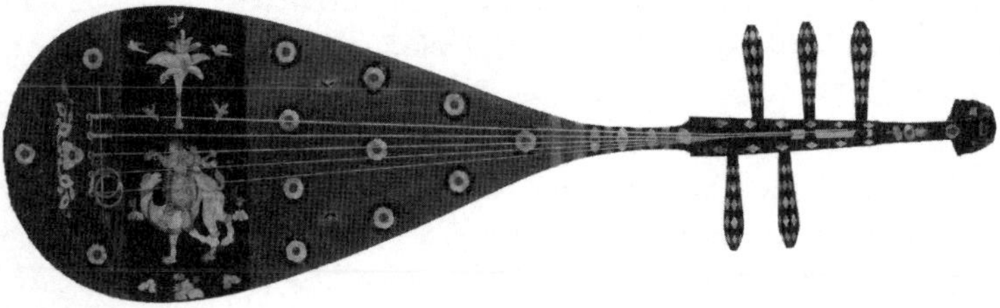

Figure 13
Plectrum guard, part of an Indian five-stringed lute (*biwa*). Eighth century. Length
(plectrum guard only) 30.9 cm; Length (instrument) 108.1 cm.
*This plectrum guard, part of a complete sandalwood and chestnut lute, is inlaid with a mother-of-
pearl depiction of a musician on camel-back. The figure depicted may be Persian.*

The Nara period (710–784) in Japan – also referred to as the Tempyo
period – is contemporary with the early Tang dynasty of China and indeed
was strongly influenced by it. One of the most devoutly Buddhist emperors
of the Nara period was Shomu (r.724–49), who established monasteries in
each province of Japan and made Buddhism the de facto state religion. His
greatest achievement was the establishment, in 743, of the Todaiji temple in
Nara, and the construction of its massive 16 m bronze image of Vairocana
(the cosmic Buddha) – known as the Great Buddha ('Daibutsu'). The temple
was dedicated in 752, and its Great Buddha Hall ('Daibutsuden'), measuring 88 x 51 m, is the largest wooden building in the world. Shomu abdi-
cated in 749, leaving the throne to his daughter Empress Koken, and died in
May 756. At the end of 49 days of official mourning, his widow, Empress
Dowager Komyo (d.760), dedicated his possessions to the Todaiji temple.
Throughout their marriage the emperor and empress remained inseparable.
Komyo's dedication, written in her own neat calligraphy, contains a petition
to the Great Buddha and concludes with the following remark:

> The list given above contains treasures that have been handled by
> the late emperor and articles that served him in the palace. These
> objects remind me of the bygone days, and the sight of them causes
> me bitter grief.
>
> (Empress Komyo (d.760), 22 July 756. From the
> *Kokka Chimpo-cho* ('Catalogue of Rare National Treasures').
> Quoted in Hayashi, 1975)

Until 1953, when they were moved to a modern concrete structure, Emperor
Shomu's possessions were stored in the Todaiji's storehouse – known as the

Shosoin. The original wooden structure, 33 m in length and 14 m high, is raised above the ground by means of 40 pillars. A style of construction known as *azekura-zukuri* – a method that permits the circulation of air on dry days when the logs contract slightly, but seals the interior on damp days – was used to minimise the effects of damp. As a result, the Shosoin's contents have remained in an almost perfect state of preservation for 13 centuries and together they represent the largest and most important single group of Silk Road artefacts in the world. Chinese envoys to the Tempyo court, Japanese emissaries to the Tang capital, and pilgrims – all of them journeying to China in search of Buddhist learning – are believed to have been the source of the Shosoin's treasures, although there are locally produced items as well.

Japanese author Ryoichi Hayashi (Hayashi, 1975) has grouped the Shosoin inventory into 12 categories: manuscripts and documents, writing materials, household furnishings, personal attire, table utensils, musical instruments and accessories, games and games pieces, weaponry and armour, medicines and aromatics, 'regalia for annual observances', Buddhist regalia, and craftsmen's tools. Among the 2,794 complete items and the many thousands of fragments are: Chinese mirrors, paintings and ceramics; glass and silver vessels from Persia; rugs and silk textiles with Chinese, Persian, nomadic and classical motifs; musical instruments that include the world's only surviving example of an ancient Indian lute (Figure 13), and approximately 170 *Gigaku* dance-masks. Two surprising features of the treasures housed in the Shosoin repository are the relatively small number of ceramics (the 50-odd items are mostly functional), and the almost complete absence of gold or silver jewellery. Excavations of Tang sites in China have yielded large numbers of exquisite items of jewellery – the dearth of similar examples among the contents of the Shosoin is a mystery.

Many of the Shosoin's treasures exist nowhere else on earth and provide a priceless glimpse of the culture and tastes of the time – little wonder, then, that Hayashi has called the repository 'the final destination of the Silk Road'.

The Great Poets – the Intellectual Climate of the Tang Dynasty

The writing of poetry flourished during the Tang dynasty. One of the main reasons for this was that the civil service examinations, begun by the Sui rulers to select officials from among the scholar class, were expanded by the Tang to include the writing of poetry. Tang emperors actively encouraged the writing of poems – at imperial banquets the emperor would frequently compose a poem and his ministers would then write replies. Cultural influences from countries to the west of

China also flowed into the capital, encouraging creativity. Furthermore, the prosperity of the time meant that scholars could travel widely and absorb new ideas. During the reign of Xuanzong (712–56) poets held important posts in the government.

Li Bai (also known as Li Po, 701–62) became a friend of Xuanzong and briefly held a position in the Imperial Academy before becoming disillusioned. He was caught up in the An Lushan Rebellion of 755 and joined the staff of Prince Yung who made an unsuccessful bid for the throne. Li Bai was exiled to the south-west of China but, before reaching it, was pardoned and spent the remainder of his life wandering the country. He loved to frequent the wine shops of Changan and, imbibing freely, would write flamboyant verse about the beauty of the women of the city. When he ran out of money he would exchange the gold tortoise that he carried as proof of his official rank, for wine. Li Bai's other favourite themes were friendship, the life of ordinary people, his own hopes and desires, and the splendours of the natural world. He wrote almost 900 poems and many of them, like those of his contemporaries, were set to music. His verse, romantic in the extreme, often possesses a dream-like quality that reflects his boundless imagination:

> I left the rosy clouds of Baidi in the morning.
> Covered a thousand *li* to Jiangling in a day;
> While the apes on both banks were still calling.
> My boat had sailed ten thousand hills away.
>
> ('Leaving Baidi for Jiangling' by Li Bai[8])

Li Bai's close friend, Du Fu (712–70) lived in Changan for ten years before he was finally appointed to a minor government post. His disillusionment and the poverty he endured are reflected in the subject matter of his poems. Like Li Bai, he was caught up in the An Lushan Rebellion and was actually taken prisoner. Many of his greatest poems were written during this period:

> Having a son's a curse today.
> Far better to have daughters, get them married –
> A son will lie lost in the grass, unburied.
> Why, Sir, on distant Qinghai shore[9]
> The bleached ungathered bones lie year on year.
> New ghosts complain, and those who died before

Weep in the wet grey sky and haunt the ear.

(Du Fu, 'Ballad of the Army Carts'.
Translated by Vikram Seth, 1992)

Du Fu lived the last decade of his life in exile in Sichuan province where he wrote about half of the 1,400 poems that survive.

Another of the great Tang poets, Wang Wei (701–62) was almost an exact contemporary of Li Bai, although there is no certainty that they ever met. Wang was the child prodigy of a prestigious family. He experienced mixed fortunes as a government official, passing the official examinations and being appointed assistant secretary for music before falling out of favour and spending the remainder of his life in minor posts and enjoying a life of quiet contemplation. During the An Lushan Rebellion he sided, albeit reluctantly, with the rebels, and was narrowly spared execution when imperial power was restored. Wang Wei's multiple talents included calligraphy and painting, and his poems are more reflective than those of Li Bai and Du Fu. His themes are the natural world, solitude and his own faith in Buddhism:

We send you home to a grave on Stone Tower Mountain;
through the green green of pine and cypress, mourners' carriages
   return.
Among white clouds we've laid your bones – it is ended forever;
Only the mindless waters remain, flowing down to the world of men.

(Wang Wei, 701–762, 'Weeping for Ying Yao'.
Translated by Burton Watson, 1984. Ying Yao was a close
friend of fellow poet Wang Wei)

The troubled and short-lived genius of the later Tang dynasty poet, Li He (or Li Ho, 790–816), produced about 240 poems during his brief life. Thwarted in his attempt to pass the civil service examinations and condemned to life as a low-ranking bureaucrat, he wrote poetry of startling intensity:

A Tartar horn tugs at the north wind,
Thistle Gate shines whiter than the stream.
The sky swallows the road to Kokonor.
On the Great Wall, a thousand miles of moonlight.

(Li He (or Li Ho), 790–816, 'On the Frontier')

Bai Juyi (772–846) is probably the greatest poet of the later Tang period. He wrote almost 3,000 poems – the most famous of which is 'Song of Eternal Sorrow' – which chronicles the misfortunes of Emperor Xuanzong and Lady Yang Guifei (see page 74).

In terms of its sheer volume, the quality of its imagery, and the diversity of its subject matter, Tang poetry has never been equalled in the history of Chinese literature. During the Qing dynasty (1644–1911) an anthology of Tang poetry was compiled, comprising almost 50,000 poems by 2,200 different poets – more than the entire repertoire of the previous 2,000 years of Chinese history.

CHAPTER FIVE

The Silk Road Between Xian and Dunhuang: The Route West from Xian

Xian is regarded as the eastern terminus of the Silk Road, although branches continue on to Korea and Japan. For the sake of brevity, we will treat Xian as the starting point for the journey west. Farewell parties were held in the inns along the banks of the Wei River in Xian; willow twigs were broken off, made into a circle and given to the traveller as prayer for his or her safe return:

> The travellers' willow tokens are fresh and green
> And I offer you a toast
> For you are departing towards the setting sun
> And soon you will be a part of the past.[1]
>
> (Wang Wei, 701–62)

Merchants would leave Xian by the Ximen, or West Gate, and usually travelled in groups in order to reduce the risk of attack. Horses, mules and the two-humped Bactrian camel – already familiar to the Chinese for 1,000 years – were used. But by the end of the eighth century even a decrepit Ferghana horse cost 40 bolts of silk – a huge amount that only the wealthy and officials of high rank could afford. Ordinary travellers used the tough ponies of the steppe – the tarpan (*equus przewalski*) – or the humble donkey.

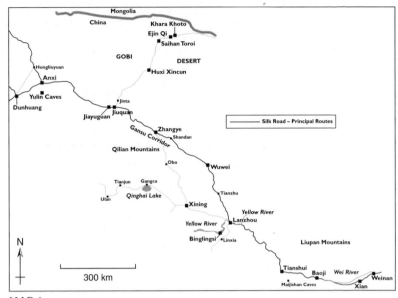

MAP 6
The Silk Road between Xian and Dunhuang.

CAMELS

The camel is an unusual domestic animal. He carries a saddle of flesh on his back. He runs rapidly over shifting sands. He shows his worth in dangerous places. He has a secret knowledge of springs. His knowledge is truly subtle!

(Third century, Guo Pu, *Tuotuo Zan* ('In Praise of the Camel').
Quoted in J.-P. Drège and E. M. Bührer, 1989)

Exhort all men to make the pilgrimage. They will come to you on foot and on the backs of swift camels from every distant quarter.

(From the Qu'ran, XXII: 27.
Translated by N. J. Dawood, in *The Koran*, 1999)

Bronze belt buckles and lamps from China's Warring States period (475–221 BC) contain depictions of two-humped Bactrian camels and their riders – suggesting that they had already been in use for some time. At this early date the Chinese appear to have acquired them from the nomadic tribes of the northern frontier – the Xiongnu in particular – evidenced by their frequent appearance on Ordos region belt buckles. By the time of the Han dynasty, camels were bred in large numbers by the Chinese government and there were large herds in Shaanxi and Gansu provinces. Schafer notes that in 754 the Tang government herds in Gansu alone numbered 279,900 cattle, sheep and camels. The animals were kept by wealthy Chinese as mounts, and by merchants as beasts of burden. The fastest camels were reserved for the 'Bright Camel Envoys' and used to convey messages during times of military emergency. The 'Bright Camel Envoys' were strictly for use in times of national crisis and the Chinese were scandalised when, in 751, the emperor's ill-starred consort Yang Guifei used them to convey a gift of rare Borneo camphor to the Turkic-Sogdian general, An Lushan. Based on the records available to us, and on depictions of camels and their riders in Chinese art, it seems likely that herdsmen and grooms were almost always foreigners – Mongolians, Central Asians and Tibetans. As pack animals, Bactrian camels are without equal: they can survive in high temperatures for seven or eight days without water, and for several weeks in cool weather. They store about 35 kg of fat in their humps and can draw on it when food is scarce – shedding as much as 20–25 per cent of their body weight without ill effect. They can also carry a load of about 150 kg up to 40 km per day, with the broad pads on their feet ensuring sure-footedness. Camels also have remarkable nostrils that they can close during sandstorms. Camel hair can be made into cloth, and additionally their flesh can be eaten – especially the hump, which the Chinese regarded as a delicacy:

> Red camel-humps are brought them from jade broilers,
> and sweet fish is offered them on crystal trays...
> (Du Fu, 712–770, 'A Song of Fair Women')

Scholars have recently examined the loads carried by pottery camels in the tombs of the Northern Wei through to the Tang dynasties (fourth–tenth centuries) – to obtain an idea of what a typical merchant's cargo might consist of. Elfriede Knauer's research in her book, *The Camel's Load in Life and Death*, reveals that the same type of pack saddle has been used since the Han dynasty or even earlier – consisting of two bamboo poles tied lengthways around the humps and interconnected with ropes. Any type of load can then be securely attached to the resulting framework. An improvement on this is a packboard contraption in which lengths of thick reed or bamboo are aligned in parallel and connected by two lateral poles. These packboards may also have served as the collapsible lattice walls of the cameleer's yurt (nomadic tent). Typical loads, based on what can be ascertained from examining tomb figures, might have included skeins and folded lengths of silk fabric, food for the journey (dead rabbits or birds), a pilgrim flask or phoenix-head ewer for water, and sometimes a pet monkey or dog perched on top of the saddle. Fanciful loads such as a musician, or even a complete orchestra (as depicted in Figure 11), are unlikely to have had any basis in real life but they do reflect Chinese curiosity about people living to the west.

The Road West

Near the old caravan route on the Shaanxi-Gansu border are the Lung (Liupan) Mountains. Schafer relates that these mountains were once the source of indigenous green parrots – now hunted to extinction. During the ninth century the men of Lung were obliged to risk their lives to catch parrots to satisfy the insatiable demand for the rare birds at the imperial court in Changan. The highest mountain in the Liupan range – Kongdongshan (2,123 m) – has been sacred to Daoists for centuries.

The Maijishan Caves

Up in the blue sky, in the steep rock cliff, the stone is carved to represent Buddha figures. A thousand niches, although fashioned by human effort, are mistakenly thought to be divine workmanship.

(Written by an early visitor to Maijishan in 949.

Quoted in Swann, 1963)

With their animals laden with silk and other goods, merchants would proceed along the Wei River valley. The first important site, as travellers headed west, are the Maijishan caves in Gansu province – 50 km southeast of Tianshui and about 300 km from Xian. Maijishan ('Wheat Stack Mountain') is so named because of its resemblance to a pile of wheat. Some 194 caves have been carved from its precipitous granite walls, containing among them about 7,000 statues in clay and stone and a large number of murals, the latter in poor condition because of the humidity of the region. The site was active as a Buddhist centre from the fifth century to the Song dynasty (960–1279), with restoration work and some additions made as late as the Qing dynasty (1644–1911). Of the 194 caves, 74 were carved during the Northern Wei period (386–534) and 39 during the Northern Zhou period (557–81). Along with Dunhuang, Longmen and Yungang – all examined elsewhere in this book – Maijishan is one of China's four most important Buddhist cave

Figure 14
The
Maijishan
Grottoes,
Gansu
province.

sights. Because of their location on the main trade route to the West, the sculpture and paintings of Maijishan represent a unique synthesis of artistic styles but the influences of Gandhara and Persia are less apparent. Instead, a number of the sculptures show styles from Southeast Asia and India, perhaps coming up through Sichuan from around the sixth century onwards. The majority of the sculptures at Maijishan are modelled in clay and are warmer and less impassive than the stone statues of Longmen and Yungang.

In an open niche in Cave 9 sits a jewelled figure of Maitreya, the Buddha of the Future, flanked by two attendant *bodhisattvas* and dating to around the sixth century. The influences are those of the Mon (Dvaravati) Buddhas of Thailand, and perhaps of Champa in modern Vietnam. Cave 4 is the largest and is known as the Hall of Scattering Flowers (San Hua Lou). There were originally eight stone pillars supporting the roof of Cave 4, recalling Indian rock-cut temples like Ajanta, but this section has now fallen away. On the wall above Cave 4 are paintings of *apsaras* (celestial beings) that recall those of Dunhuang.

The existence of Maijishan and other Buddhist shrines reflects the fears of travellers along the Silk Road. They were places where the traveller could offer a prayer for perils that were to be faced and to give thanks for dangers that had been safely overcome.

Lanzhou and the Yellow River

After Maijishan, the Silk Road continues west and passes through Lanzhou, the modern provincial capital of Gansu. Lanzhou was an important commercial centre on the Silk Road and sits on the threshold of the Hexi, or Gansu, corridor. The government camel- and horse-breeding stations situated in the Hexi corridor meant that, by the time of the Tang dynasty, Lanzhou was a vital waystation for the movement of animals that were being escorted to Changan. Lanzhou's position on the banks of the Yellow River (Huang He) also meant that it was a trans-shipment point for goods that were to be sent along the river. Many of these goods were transported on goatskin rafts, some of which are still occasionally to be seen. The river itself is 5,464 km long – second only to the Yangtze – and extends from its source in the Bayankala Mountains on the Qinghai-Tibet plateau to the Gulf of Bohai. The Yellow River is the most heavily silt-laden river in the world and takes its name from the yellow ochre colour of its water. The yellow alluvial soils of central China, known as 'loess', are the source of the silt – blown in over a period of millennia from the Gobi Desert and now found in layers up to 300 m thick. The Yellow River has carried the loess across about 300,000 km^2 of the central plain of northern China, creating an immense fertile area from which Chinese civilisation emerged in remotest antiquity. Silting of the river has caused it to breach its banks and change course on innumerable occasions, often with devastating loss of life, and has caused the river to acquire the sobriquet 'China's Sorrow'.

The Silk Road heads north-west from Lanzhou along the Gansu (Hexi) corridor, the route hemmed in by the Gobi Desert to the north and the Qilian Mountains to the south. The corridor is 1,200 km long and between 15–200 km wide and links China with Xinjiang and Central Asia. Emperor Wudi (r.140–87 BC) set up the first of the government horse-breeding stations in the Hexi corridor. According to one contemporary record, alfalfa was planted for pasturage and 36 ranches were established for 300,000 horses – all supervised by a Xiongnu expert named Jinribei. Horses from the Wusun tribe were bred initially but were eventually supplanted by the superior breeds of the Ferghana valley. The Xiongnu believed that the Qilian Mountains to the south of the corridor were sacred and that animals feeding on the vast stretch of pastureland there would thrive and multiply. They also cherished nearby Mount Yanzhi – the occupation of which would, they believed, increase the beauty of their women. Horses are still bred on the pastures of Mount Yanzhi, about 130 km south-east of Zhangye.

Binglingsi

There is some disagreement among historians about the point where the Silk Road crossed the Yellow River. There definitely appears to have been a ferry crossing at the Binglingsi ('Ten Thousand Buddha') caves, located about 100 km south-west of Lanzhou in Yongjing county, Gansu. The river was quite narrow as it passed through Yongjing county – one place is known to the local people as 'Fox Jump' – and there are stories of a ferry and a bridge that once spanned the mouth of the gorge near Binglingsi. The bridge was said to have been built by a Xianbei tribesman named Qifu around 400. Known as the 'number 1 bridge under heaven', it is now deeply submerged beneath the reservoir created when the Liujiaxia hydro-electric dam was built. The ferry is believed to have crossed to a jetty, situated at the foot of the caves, and the Silk Road continued from the opposite side north-westwards towards Zhangye.

When the dam was built the level of the river rose about 20 m and submerged the majority of the lower caves. Many of the sculptures were removed and distributed among the higher ones.

The caves were constructed between the fifth and eighteenth century, with the principal 27 m tall Buddha dating to the Tang dynasty (618–907). The Northern Liang (421–39), like the Toba Wei, were a non-Chinese people and were fervent sponsors of Buddhism. They controlled an independent state with its capital at Liangzhou (modern Wuwei), which dominated a large part of Gansu province. During the early days of the Liang state, cave complexes were constructed at the Jinta Temple and at Mount Madi in Minle county, to the south of Liangzhou. The Binglingsi caves were begun around 420 when the Liang Empire expanded. The Liang also built some of the Mogao caves at Dunhuang at around the same time. Binglingsi comprises some 193 caves and niches (including those now submerged), extending some 200 m along the western side of the river. Many early travellers remarked upon the strange rock formations along this stretch of the

Yellow River – one seventh-century monk marvelling at 'the magic powers of nature' and comparing their shapes to Buddhist stupas and pagodas.

The sculptures in the early caves, with their clinging robes, evoke the styles of Gandhara and Chinese Central Asia far more than the caves at Maijishan. Among the early grottoes is Cave 169, known as the 'Southern Bridge to Heaven Cave', and built over 60 m above the original level of the river (before the dam was built). During excavation of the cave in 1963 an inscription was found dating it to 420. Cave 169 contains Binglingsi's finest art, and sculptures of the type represented within it typically have large heads and hands with drapery-folds created by making deep grooves in the clay. There is a beautiful large painting in Cave 169 of a seated Buddha accompanied by *bodhisattvas* and flying *apsaras* with the name of each deity inscribed to the side. Like the sculptures in the cave, the paintings recall their counterparts in the Gandhara kingdom.

About ten of the caves date to the Northern Wei dynasty (386–534). The thick, enveloping robes and elongated bodies of the Wei sculptures are characteristic of the sixth century. The most notable is Cave 80, dedicated in 520 by its benefactor – a man named Cao Ziyuan, who left a powerful entreaty written on the cliff-face outside: 'may his father and mother and his dependants [...] be reborn in the Paradise of the West; and may all creatures of every description receive the same blessings' (quoted in Akiyama and Matsubara, 1969). There are around 100 Tang dynasty caves at Binglingsi, and sculpture from this period is therefore the most plentiful.

Wuwei

With wine of grapes the cups of jade would glow at night
We long to drink but the *pipa* summons us
If we lie drunk on the battlefield, don't mock us friend;
How many soldiers ever come home?

(Wang Han, *c*.687–735, 'Song of Liangzhou')

In the town of Jiuquan, locally mined black, white and green jade is still used to make cups that are said to glow when filled with wine and placed in the moonlight. The strumming of *pipa* (lutes) was used, like a modern bugle, to rally troops for battle.

After crossing the Yellow River the road heads north-westwards along the Gansu (Hexi) corridor towards Wuwei (formerly Liangzhou). The Gansu corridor was the site of numerous battles with the Xiongnu and, during the first century BC, four commanderies were established at Wuwei, Zhangye, Jiuquan and Dunhuang – all linked by a line of defensive watchtowers and armouries. During the Han dynasty the Great Wall extended as far as the Lop Nor region of Xinjiang, protecting trade along the Silk Road. Wuwei was an important garrison town guarding a section of the wall and it became the main commercial centre for the region.

An important tomb of the Western Han dynasty was excavated at Leitai, north of the centre of Wuwei, in 1969. Dated to 186–219, the tomb contained bronze models of soldiers, chariots and horses – most notably the celebrated 'flying horse of Gansu' (see Figure 2).

During the Period of Disunity – between the collapse of the Han in 220 and the establishment of the Sui dynasty in 581 – Wuwei was the capital of a number of minor states, including the Former Liang and the Southern Liang. Wuwei was then occupied by the Northern Wei dynasty in 420 and thereafter was an important Buddhist centre. The celebrated monk Kumarajiva (343–413) was a prisoner in Wuwei for over 17 years and his achievements were commemorated during the Tang dynasty by the construction of a memorial pagoda that still survives today.

During the Tang period Wuwei continued to be an important Buddhist centre. It was visited by the monk Xuanzang on his way to India and he admired the local wines. Xuanzang crossed the border in secret after Emperor Taizong issued an edict forbidding anyone to leave the country without permission. Wuwei was also a checkpoint for travellers entering and leaving China. It had a population of about 100,000 – many of them merchants from Tibet, India and Central Asia.

In 1036 Wuwei fell to the Xixia (Western Xia or Tanguts), a federation of Tibetan peoples. It continued to be an important trading centre on the Silk Road until the thirteenth century when the Tangut Empire was attacked and its people annihilated by the Mongols. Wuwei remained under the control of the Mongol Yuan dynasty (1279–1368) until Chinese sovereignty was finally restored by the country's Ming rulers during the fourteenth century.

Near the centre of Wuwei is the Bell Tower (Dayun Si), built during the Ming dynasty (1368–1644) but containing a massive Tang dynasty bronze. The sides of the bell are decorated with designs of flying *apsaras*, dragons and tortoises – reminiscent of the murals of the Dunhuang Grottoes. At the beginning of the nineteenth century an inscribed tablet was discovered within the temple precincts where the Bell Tower stands. The tablet, inscribed in both Xixia (Tangut) and Chinese script, has provided the means to understand a language that had defied scholars for centuries.

From Wuwei the Silk Road leads in a north-westerly direction across a desolate landscape. To the north is the Badain Jaran Desert of Inner Mongolia and, to the south, the Qilian Mountains. At the approximate halfway point, near the town of Yongchang, are substantial sections of the old Han dynasty wall.

Zhangye

Approximately 300 km north-west of Wuwei the Silk Road passes through Zhangye – formerly known as Ganzhou – another of the four Han dynasty commanderies. The fortified walls of Zhangye were still intact as recently as the 1900s but have since been demolished. Zhangye was an important trading centre from an early date and local officials regulated the passage of silk.

The excesses of the Sui emperor, Yangdi, have already been described (see Chapter 3 on Luoyang). However, in preparation for his inspection tour of the Western Regions in 609, he made an important contribution to the development of the Silk Road. Yang Di's trusted official Pei Ju (d.627) was appointed minister of trade with responsibility for commerce with the states to the west. Pei Ju's report, *Xiyu Tuzi* ('The Illustrated Account of the Western Regions') has been lost but sections have been preserved in the *Sui Shu* ('History of the Sui dynasty'). Pei Ju delineates the geography, customs and habits of 44 of the states of the Western Lands. Pei organised Yangdi's audience at Zhangye in 609, described by some historians as the first international trade fair on the Silk Road. Emissaries from 27 western states and the entire population of the towns of Wuwei and Zhangye lined the roadside to greet the emperor, all dressed in their Sunday best. The Sui annals relate: 'Horsemen and carts jammed the road while musical performances, singing, dancing and incense-burning created a scene of bustle and excitement.'

There is a large reclining Buddha in Zhangye, at 34.5 m long the largest in China, at the 'Monastery of the Great Buddha' (Dafosi). It was built in 1098 by the Xixia (Tanguts), who had invaded the area in around 1038 and established an independent state.

A famous vistor to Zhangye was Marco Polo, whose great journey between 1271–95 took him through the town. He remained for a year – awaiting permission from Kubilai Khan to continue on to the Mongols' capital – and described the city and its temples in great detail, clearly impressed by what he saw:

> The idolaters have many religious houses, or monasteries and abbeys, built after the manner of the country, and in these a multitude of idols, some of which are of wood, some of stone, and some of clay, are covered with gilding. They are carved in masterly style.
>
> (From *The Travels of Marco Polo the Venetian*.
> Translated by William Marsden, in Polo, 1948)

Marco Polo also describes a journey north of the main Silk Road, from Zhangye to the Tangut city of Edzina or Khara Khoto:

> Leaving this city of Kampion [Zhangye] and travelling for twelve days in a northerly direction, you come to a city named Edzina, at the commencement of the sandy desert, and within the province of Tangut. The inhabitants are idolaters. They have camels, and much cattle of various sorts [...] The fruits of the soil and the flesh of the cattle supply the wants of the people, and they do not concern themselves with trade. Travellers passing through this city lay in a store of provisions for forty days, because [...] that space of time is employed in traversing a desert, where there is not any appearance of dwelling, nor are there any inhabitants.
>
> (Ibid.)

The Xia (Tanguts)

In the centuries before the Mongol conquest of the region, the Xia state or Xixia (Western Xia) controlled large areas of western Inner Mongolia, Ningxia, Gansu and Qinghai. The old Turkic name for the Xia was Tangut and they were descendants of the Qiang tribal group who occupied Qinghai province and Tibet from around the third millennium BC. The descendants of the Qiang are believed by many scholars to be the peoples of modern day Tibet and Burma. The Xia also claimed kinship with the Toba (or Xianbei), the founders of China's

Northern Wei dynasty (see the sections on Northern Wei in Chapters 2 and 3).

The Xia were loyal subjects of the Chinese until the mid-ninth century when internal divisions led to the collapse of the Tibetan Empire and popular dissent weakened the Tang government. After the Tang dynasty collapsed in 907 the Tangut emerged as an independent state. The Tangut Empire (1032–1227) maintained its independence by means of a continuous cycle of alliance and conflict with the Song Chinese and the Liao Khitans. In 1031 a man named Yuan-hao became ruler and achieved recognition of the state by both the Song and the Khitans – expanding Tangut territory to include the whole of western Gansu, including Dunhuang. It was only when, in 1038, he declared himself emperor of the 'Great Xia kingdom' that the Chinese declared him a rebel. A bloody four-year war ensued between the Song and the Tangut at the end of which Yuan-hao agreed to refrain from calling himself emperor in his relations with China, in exchange for a generous annual tribute of 255,000 items of silk, silver, tea and cloth.

From the tenth to the thirteenth centuries, the Xia state controlled and levied taxes upon travellers along the caravan routes within the great curve of the Yellow River, a large part of modern Gansu province. From 1020 onwards their capital was Xingzhou (modern Yinchuan) in today's Ningxia-hui autonomous region. Their economy was based on agriculture and animal husbandry: they grew millet, wheat, rice, hemp and cotton, and raised horses, camels, cattle, sheep and goats. They were renowned for their fine horses, for the salt they refined from lakes in the Ordos region, and for their rhubarb. They also produced their own coinage and excellent iron-work, gold, silver and ceramics. Their creations were heavily influenced by Chinese designs and craftsmen were recruited by the Xia rulers to produce them. The Tangut called themselves 'the White High Great State of Xia', perhaps an allusion to their origins among the snow-capped mountains of Tibet. The population was multi-ethnic, with equal rights afforded to Tangut, Chinese, Tibetan and Uighur alike. The Tangut were originally worshippers of a spirit called Tengri but, by the ninth or tenth century, had become Buddhist – although their shamanistic beliefs also survived. Tangut Buddhism was heavily influenced by both Chinese and Tibetan teachings and documents relating to both schools have been unearthed at Khara Khoto. Daoism and Confucianism were also well regarded.

Khara Khoto

The city of Khara Khoto (the 'Black Town', Heicheng or Edzina) was situated on the edge of the Gobi Desert at the northern border of the Xia state in north-western Inner Mongolia, and was one of the state's principal cities. It was first explored by the Russian P. K. Kozlov in 1908–9 and was subsequently visited by both Sir Marc Aurel Stein and Sven Hedin. Sculptures and paintings found at Khara Khoto represent the earliest expression of Sino-Tibetan art, the style and iconography of which reflect the influence of Tantric Buddhism – noted for its extensive pantheon of deities and lengthy rituals that require a large number of images and paintings. The works of art from Khara Khoto's heyday date mainly from the twelfth to the fourteenth centuries – the city's existence continuing long after it was overrun by Genghis Khan's soldiers in 1227. Among the sculptures found at the site is a beautiful double-headed figure of Buddha, the finest among the large number of Khara Khoto artefacts in the State Hermitage Museum in St Petersburg. The image recalls the story of two poor men who each dreamed of owning an image of the Buddha. They could afford only one, and the Buddha – moved by their piety – caused the image to be divided into two. The method of manufacture of this image (clay, modelled around an armature of reed and straw) is used throughout Central Asia.

Among the paintings acquired by Kozlov at Khara Khoto, and also to be seen in the Hermitage Museum, are silk scroll depictions of Amitabha, Buddha of the Western Paradise. The cult of Amithabha was immensely popular among the Xia. They believed that rebirth in the Pure Land of Amitabha was attainable with prayer and simple faith. Amitabha is frequently shown accompanied and assisted by Avalokitesvara (Guanyin, in Chinese), the *bodhisattva* of compassion. He is often shown towering above diminutive figures in the foreground, donors dressed in the robes of the Tangut nobility.

An interesting aside to the paintings unearthed at Khara Khoto is the discovery that a number of the paintings from the site – all produced between the twelfth and fourteenth centuries – are on a plaid (tartan) background. The suggestion has been made that the Tokharians – probably a tribe of the Yuezhi confederation who were driven out of the Tarim basin in about 165 BC – are descendants of a lost tribe of Celtic peoples. The theory is that they may have migrated eastwards during ancient times and settled in the oasis cities of Chinese Central Asia (for more on this subject, see the section on Tokharians on page 68). Plaid is not found in Tibet, or in China proper – only in the western areas of Gansu, Xinjiang and the Ningxia-hui autonomous region. If the resemblance of the plaid of the Khara Khoto paintings to Celtic tartans is not merely the result of chance, these patterns may represent the remains of a Celtic tradition in Asia.

Khara Khoto fell to Genghis Khan in 1227 after its water supply was diverted. A number of legends that surround the city assert that the treasury, comprising some 80 carts of gold, was lowered into a well to keep it from falling into Mongol hands and, to this day, it has never been found. Shards of blue and white porcelain have been unearthed at Khara Khoto, all dating to the Yuan dynasty of the Mongols (1279–1368). This indicates that the town was still an important trading centre during the period of Mongol domination.

The large number of Yuan dynasty blue and white shards found at sites located far inland is at odds with the conventionally held view that Chinese porcelain reached the West exclusively via the sea routes. It may well be that porcelain was carried on camel-back along the entire length of the Silk Road. Recent work by Professor Li Zhiyan of Beijing's National Museum of Chinese History, and by John Carswell, provides a clue about how this might have been accomplished without the fragile shipment being broken en route. According to Professor Li, the porcelain would have been packed into containers with a mixture of sand, soil, soya bean and wheat – all soaked in water. The concoction then dried to form a solid mass. When the merchant reached his destination, water would have been added and the porcelain retrieved intact.

The Mongols put a large part of the Tangut population to death, but the city of Khara Khoto appears to have lingered on until about 1372, when it was taken by the Ming Chinese general, Feng Sheng. After its capture by the Chinese the city seems to have fallen into decline, perhaps because of the encroaching desert and the development of sea routes in preference to land-based trade. The Chinese renamed the bulk of the territory that constituted the Tangut kingdom Ningxia ('Pacified Xia'). It is now known as the Ningxia-hui autonomous region of China.

Jiuquan

The province of Gansu takes its name from the first characters of the old names for Zhangye and Jiuquan, *Gan*zhou and *Su*zhou. Jiuquan (meaning 'wine spring') sits at the western end of the Hexi corridor and had been a garrison town since 121 BC, together with Wuwei, Zhangye and Dunhuang. It takes its name from a legend surrounding the great Han general, Huo Qubing (see the section on the Xiongnu in Chapter 1). Huo was presented with a gift of fine wine by the emperor but elected to share it with his troops by pouring it into a pool.

Foreign merchants lived in the Dongguan section of the city, and a wooden drum tower, erected during the fourth century and rebuilt many times since, points the way to the Western Lands. Inscriptions over the four gates on each side of the tower declare: 'North is the Gobi Desert, South are the Qilian Mountains, East is the Huashan [a mountain east of Xian] and West is Yiwu [Hami in Xinjiang].'

The city was a capital of the Western Liang state (400–21) of the Sixteen Kingdoms period (304–439) and was occupied during the eighth and ninth centuries by Tibetans – but its role has always been that of a frontier town, the first on the Chinese side of the Great Wall. The Mongols ravaged the area during the thirteenth century, but as late as the seventeenth century Jiuquan was still an important place of congregation for foreign merchants. The Portuguese Jesuit Benedict de Goes died of disease in Jiuquan in 1606, after three years of travelling the Silk Road.

His diary describes a thriving city that was still home to large numbers of foreigners:

> Suzhou City is the place where Western merchants converge [...] The city is divided into two sections. Chinese residents live in one section, and in the other are Muslims who hail from the Western Regions. They were traders and most of them married local women and had children. Burdened with family, they settled down here and became local residents. By night the Muslims withdraw into their section of the city and keep to themselves. Otherwise, they are treated just the same as local inhabitants. Their legal disputes are handled by Chinese magistrates.
>
> (Benedict de Goes. Quoted in Che Muqi, 1989)

Just to the south-west of Jiuquan are the Wenshushan caves. The caves have been vandalised over the years, and what remains is much-restored, but the original influences of Tibet are still apparent in the statuary and paintings at the site.

Jiayuguan

De Goes waited 25 days for permission to enter China at the Jiayu Pass, about 20 km north-west of Jiuquan. Jiayu Pass (Jiayuguan) has been a frontier post since the Han dynasty when the Great Wall reached as far as the Yumen Pass (the 'Jade Gate'), about 90 km north-west of Dunhuang. It has always been regarded as an important strategic location, set between the Mazong ('Horse's Mane') Mountains to the north and the Qilian Mountains to the south. In 1372 the Ming dynasty general, Feng Sheng, defeated the last of the Mongol armies of the Yuan dynasty that had ruled China since 1279 and built a fortress at Jiayuguan, guarding the entrance to the Hexi (Gansu) corridor (Figure 15). The Chinese called the fortress 'The Strongest Pass Under Heaven' and built it with walls 11 m high and 733 m in circumference. Jiayuguan marked the western terminus of the Ming dynasty Great Wall, built in brick and more durable than the earthen walls of its forebears. From the fourteenth century onwards, Jiayuguan was regarded as the limit of the Chinese Empire.

The territory to the west of Jiayuguan was a place of banishment to the Chinese – only those who were exiled, the courageous monks and merchants who travelled the Silk Road, and invading and defending armies would enter it. As late as 1942, Mildred Cable and Francesca French described the sorrowful aspect of Jiayuguan's West Gate and

Figure 15
Jiayuguan fortress, Gansu province. Built in 1372 with later reconstruction.

the inscriptions left by the people who passed through it on their way into exile:

> The most important door was on the farther side of the fortress, and it might be called Traveller's Gate, though some spoke of it as the Gate of Sighs. It was a deep archway tunnelled in the thickness of the wall, where footsteps echoed and re-echoed. Every traveller toward the north-west passed through this gate, and it opened out on that great and always mysterious waste called the Desert of Gobi.
>
> The long archway was covered with writings, and anyone with sufficient knowledge to appreciate Chinese penmanship could see at once that these were the work of men of scholarship, who had fallen on an hour of deep distress [...].
>
> Who then were the writers of this Anthology of Grief? Some were heavy-hearted exiles, others were disgraced officials, and some were criminals no longer tolerated within China's borders. Torn from all they loved on earth and banished with dishonoured name to the dreary regions outside, they stood awhile within the tomb-like vault, to add their moan to the pitiful dirge of the Gate of Sighs.
>
> (Cable and French, 1942)

An old tradition, still practised in Cable and French's day, was for departing travellers to throw a stone at the fortress wall. If it rebounded they would return safely but, if it did not, they would not see China again.

Anxi

> Rain falls at dusk on the frontier town
> Wild geese fly low.
> The new reeds grow,
> Rising high and wild.
> Countless camel bells ring
> Over desolate sands.
> Caravans are travelling
> To Anxi city with silk rolls.
>
> (Zhang Ji, 'A Song of Liangzhou'. Tang dynasty)

Continuing on the main artery of the Silk Road, the route passes through the town of Anxi (ancient Guazhou), known to early travellers in equal measure for its delectable melons and its incessant biting winds. Some 75 km south of Anxi are the Yulin caves, also known as Wanfoxia – 'The Gorge of Ten Thousand Buddhas'. The 42 surviving caves cover a period of more than 1,500 years from the Northern Wei to the Qing dynasty (1644–1911). Caves 2 and 3 are Tangut (Western Xia) period (1032–1227), the latter with magnificent Chinese-style murals. Cave 4 dates to the Yuan period (1279–1368) and its esoteric Tantric iconography reveals the influences from Tibet that we encountered at Khara Khoto. One of the most fascinating of all of the Silk Road artefacts unearthed in China was discovered at the Yulin caves. An ivory carving of a *bodhisattva* riding an elephant, probably Indian and dating to around the seventh century, now resides in the National Museum of Chinese History in Beijing. In a closed position, this ivory carving depicts a *bodhisattva* riding an elephant and carrying a pagoda. When it is opened there are no fewer than 50 squares containing some 300 figures depicting stories from the Buddha's *jatakas* (previous lives). It may have been carried to China by one of the many monks who travelled to India during the Tang dynasty to seek Buddhist scriptures. The likelihood that the carving was brought to China by a monk links neatly to the recent discovery of what is believed to be the earliest portrait of the monk Xuanzang, discovered at the Yulin Cave 3 in 1980. The image is a wall painting, dated to the eleventh or twelfth century, and shows a monk accompanied by a monkey and a white horse and standing by a river. A bundle of what appear to be sutras sits atop a lotus flower on the horse's back, with rays of light emanating in all directions.

Anxi is also the point where the Silk Road splits into its northern and southern routes, the former skirting the Tianshan Mountains and the latter running along the edge of the Kunlun range. In fact, a section of the Silk Road loops back from Dunhuang to Hami to rejoin the northern route and the point of division can therefore also said to be there.

Dunhuang and the Caves of the Thousand Buddhas
(Qianfodong, or Mogao Caves)

It is impossible to overstate the art-historical significance of Dunhuang: 'the art gallery in the desert', 'a cultural treasure house', 'this great museum of the centuries' – none of the superlatives that have been applied to the site succeed in conveying its full importance. The town was established in 111 BC as one of the four Han commanderies (Wuwei, Zhangye and Jiuquan were the others), and a line of watchtowers still stands to the north and west of Dunhuang. The name itself means 'blazing beacon', a reference to these signal towers, used to warn of approaching danger.

The Caves of the Thousand Buddhas lie in a valley to the south-east of the Dunhuang oasis, at the foot of the Mingsha sand dunes (the 'Dunes of the Singing Sands'). Its name derives from the legend of the monk Luo Zun (or Le Zun) who, in 366, is said to have seen a vision of 1,000 Buddhas floating above Mount Sanwei (the 'Mountain of Three Dangers'), on one side of the valley. Another version of the legend relating to Luo Zun concerns his passage through Dunhuang on his way to India with three disciples. One of them, Zhi Qin, was sent to fetch water from the river that runs along the foot of Mount Sanwei. As Zhi Qin rested and admired the sunset,

> the mountain peaks glistening with the sheen of blue satin in the light of dawn became iridescent. In the centre of the golden rays reposed a giant Maitreya, and emerging out of this radiance were thousands of Buddhas – all at perfect ease, smiling and laughing, sweetly conversing. In the golden light, myriads of fairy maidens flitted among them, making music on various instruments.
>
> (Quoted in Chen Yu, 1989)

Zhi Qin was said to have painted a mural on one of the cave walls to record what he had seen, and Master Luo Zun, upon hearing of his pupil's vision, decided that they would go no further on their journey to India and establish a Buddhist settlement at Dunhuang. The collapse of part of the cliff has destroyed the earliest caves of Luo Zun, but his achievements are recorded on a stele, erected at Dunhuang in 698.

Between the fourth century and the Yuan dynasty (1279–1368) the valley became a centre for Buddhist monks and other travellers along the Silk Road. As merchants and pilgrims passed through they would make a donation to improve the site, as a prayer for protection from the dangers they expected to face on their journey west, or as thanks for their safe arrival in China. Documents found at Dunhuang also reveal that the more affluent residents of the town would form clubs to study Buddhism and to sponsor the creation of murals or silk paintings, thereby securing merit for themselves. Cave shrines were carved from the gravel conglomerate of the cliffs and, from the early fifth century of

Figure 16
Exterior
of the
Dunhuang
caves.

the Northern Liang dynasty (421–39) of the Sixteen Kingdoms, many caves were also decorated with wall paintings. Unlike the rock-cut cave temples and sculptures of Yungang and Longmen (see pages 29–32), the statuary at Dunhuang was made of clay, moulded around wooden armatures and then painted. To date, no fewer than 492 caves have been identified containing 45,000 m² of murals and over 2,000 sculptures. It is said that if the walls of all of Dunhuang's caves were to be lined up they would form a display 50 km in length, the longest art gallery in the world. The paintings and sculpture reveal Chinese, Indian, Greco-Roman and Iranian influences.[2]

The oldest caves – caves 268, 272 and 275 – were built during the Northern Dynasties (386–581) and most commonly contain images of the historical Buddha Sakyamuni and Maitreya, the future Buddha. Cave 275 is attributed to the Northern Liang dynasty before 439 (when Dunhuang was conquered and fell under the control of the Northern Wei), and contains the largest of the early images – a painted clay figure of the *bodhisattva* Maitreya (the Future Buddha), seated with crossed ankles and flanked by lions. The upper wall behind the figure of Maitreya is filled with seated figures of *bodhisattvas* with billowing scarves. Influences from the Greco-Buddhist art of Gandhara are apparent in much of the early sculpture at Dunhuang. The early paintings of Kizil are similar in style to the paintings of Cave 275 but the latter are less finely drawn and may have been repainted during succeeding dynasties.

The unification of China under the Sui dynasty (581–618) ended almost four centuries of civil war; it also brought greater freedom of travel and an emperor, Wendi (r.581–604), who actively sponsored the proliferation of Buddhism. The international trade fair at Zhangye, attended by Wendi's son and successor Yangdi in 609, was also attended by representatives from 27 nations and augmented the growing tide of foreigners coming to China. Because of Dunhuang's position on the Silk Road, the increasing level of economic activity brought great prosperity to the area and this is reflected in the splendour of the caves established during this period. A fresh infusion of stylistic influences from India was combined with existing traditions and the result was a fully-fledged mature Chinese style. Sui art at Dunhuang coincided with the growing popularity of the Pure Land Buddhist sect. Depictions of the Pure Land of Amitabha Buddha, where the faithful will be reborn, are painted on a grand scale and are filled with metaphors of a blissful afterworld – sumptuous palaces, lotus ponds and splendid gardens, and heavenly musicians and dancers. Realism and, often, humour, replace the somewhat stylised art of the earlier periods (Figure 17).

Although the Sui dynasty lasted for only 37 years, more than 100 new caves were established. The new interest in Pure Land Buddhism led to the creation of large central images, often of Amitabha Buddha, flanked by attendant *bodhisattvas* and realistically portrayed disciples. This style was refined and perfected during the Tang dynasty when Dunhuang, like the rest of China, enjoyed its 'Golden Age'. Portrayals of foreigners are found in increasing numbers during the early part of the Tang dynasty, a consequence of China's extended borders and its increased contacts with neighbouring countries. The Tang annals contain numerous references to paintings of foreigners but there are few extant today. A rare exception is a painting in Cave 220, dated to 642, and showing foreigners among the audience of a debate between Vimalikirti and Manjusri. The great philosophical debate from the *Vimalakirti-sutra* between the Chinese scholar Vimalikirti and the *bodhisattva* of Wisdom, Manjusri, is a popular subject in Buddhist art and the presence of foreigners in the audience is a statement that the appeal of the new doctrine is universal. Elsewhere in the audience sits the emperor of China himself, resplendent in full ceremonial robes and a signal that Buddhism has the imperial seal of approval. Elsewhere, in

This delightful painting comprises a trio of rabbits, ears joined to form a triangle and running in a circle around the centre of the ceiling. They are surrounded by flying apsaras *(celestial deities). The three rabbits, or three hares, motif has been found at numerous sites along the Silk Road; as well as in Central Asia, the Middle East and on the medieval roof bosses of no fewer than 17 parish churches in Devon.*[3]

Cave 220, on either side of a composition on the north wall, are paradise scenes in which musicians of various nationalities perform on Western and Chinese instruments. Each group of musicians accompanies a pair of dancers with swirling ribbons, performing one of the new dances from the Western Lands – perhaps the 'Dance of Chach' or the 'Western Prancing Dance', two of the most popular. A similar scene occurs in Cave 98 at Dunhuang, dating to the mid tenth century of the Five Dynasties – but by this time there were few foreigners left in China and the participants are Chinese.

Increased levels of commerce along the Silk Road during the Tang dynasty were accompanied by an upsurge in the incidence of highway robbery and a number of murals and inscriptions at Dunhuang reflect the anxieties of merchants (Figure 18).

Figure 18
Wall painting of merchants confronted by brigands. Tang dynasty, first half of the eighth century. Cave 45, Dunhuang, Gansu province.

In this painting the merchants are Tibetan and Central Asian, standing forlornly in front of a man holding a sword, beside the goods they have been obliged to unload from their mules. An alternative interpretation sometimes applied to this painting is that the merchants are being subjected to extortion by avaricious border guards. Whichever way it is interpreted the sentiment is the same – the painting is a reference to the Buddhist legend of the rich merchant who remains safe during a long journey by reciting the Lotus Sutra to invoke the protection of the bodhisattva Avalokitesvara (Guanyin). The sutra is written in a panel above the merchant's heads and reads:

> *'If you all call upon his name, then from the malicious bandits you shall contrive to be delivered; and the multitude of merchants hearing this, speak these words in unison, saying, "Namo bodhisattvaya, He who observes the sounds of the world!" Men, by the mere calling upon his name, they shall forthwith gain deliverance.'*
> *('Scripture of the Lotus Blossom of the Fine Dharma'. Quoted in Knauer, 1998)*

A key function of the Dunhuang caves was to allay the fears of the faithful. Inscriptions found at the site, on paintings and in block-printed manuscripts, seek protection for both the sponsor of the item and for the region as a whole. The following example, a block-printed inscription dated to 947, is typical and was written at a time when the area was controlled by the Cao clan. The sponsor in this instance was no less a figure than Dunhuang's ruler at the time, Cao Yuanzhong (r.946–75), a man of evident piety:

The disciple, Military Controller of the Kuei-i Army, Inspector of Guazhou and Shazhou [Anxi and Dunhuang], and other districts, Commissioner for the distribution of military land-allotments within the sphere of his jurisdiction and for the suppression of Tibetan tribes, specially promoted additional Grand Preceptor, inaugural Baron of the prefecture of Qiao, Cao Yuanzhong carved this printing block and offered it on behalf of the municipal shrines of the city, that they may know no troubles; on behalf of the whole prefecture, that they may be intact and peaceful. That the ways leading east and west may remain open and unimpeded. That the barbarians (?) of north and south may submit and obey. May all severe diseases disappear. May the sound of the war-trumpet no longer be heard; may we have the delight of witnessing and hearing good things and all be wetted by (the dew of) fortune and prosperity.

(Dated 947. From Waley, 1931)

Cao Yuanzhong's exhortation is hardly surprising when we take into account that, by this date, the Tang dynasty had collapsed, China was in chaos and the government's proscription of Buddhism between 842–5 meant that the religion no longer exercised a major influence on Chinese society. During the High Tang period (705–80) these crises were yet to come and Dunhuang was still enjoying its apogee. Cave 45, where the 'brigands mural' was discovered, contains some of the most beautiful of all of Dunhuang's sculpture. In the main niche a seated Buddha, his hand raised in *abhayamudra* (the gesture of dispelling fear), is flanked by six attendants who, despite their divine nature, are remarkably human in appearance. In a typical arrangement from the High Tang period, Cave 45's seated Buddha is flanked by his two most favoured disciples Ananda and Kasyapa, a pair of *bodhisattvas* and two *lokapalas* ('Heavenly Kings'). The Buddha and *bodhisattvas* still retain a somewhat idealised form while the disciples and *lokapala* figures display both physical and emotional idiosyncrasies.

The power and strength of the empire were reflected in the massive images of the High Tang. Two of the largest are the colossal images of the Buddha Maitreya in Cave 96 and Cave 130 – the 'Northern Great' and 'Southern Great' images respectively. The former is 33 m in height and is generally ascribed to the reign of Empress Wu Zetian (690–705); and the latter, 26 m high, to the first half of the eighth century. In Cave 81 is another Buddha of substantial size, this time recumbent as he enters nirvana. Depictions of the moment of the Buddha's final triumph when he finally exits this world and enters nirvana (known as *parinirvana*), are a popular subject for the artists of the High and Middle Tang. A mural in Cave 158 contains a large number of foreigners and forms the backdrop for a massive, 15 m Buddha reclining in nirvana. It is intended, as with other paintings of a multi-ethnic nature, to emphasise the wide appeal of the faith. This painting reveals the funeral customs of various nationalities, or at least the Chinese perception of those customs. One of the mourners cuts off his ear, another falls on his sword while another slashes his chest with knives – the latter a custom followed by Turkic peoples.

Cave 158 was constructed during the Middle Tang when, as a consequence of the turmoil unleashed by the An Lushan Rebellion of 755–63, China lost control of many of her western possessions. Between 781–848 Dunhuang was controlled by Tibetans, a factor which led to the preservation of the caves in spite of the imperially sanctioned suppression of Buddhism in China from 842–5. During the Tibetan occupation Dunhuang was known as Shazou ('City of the Sands') and this was also the name of the prefecture in which the town was situated. The Chinese warlord General Zhang Yichao (d.872) and his private army finally drove out the Tibetans in 848, an event commemorated in a spectacular mural in Cave 156. In the painting Zhang Yichao and his wife, the Lady Song, each move in a stately procession towards the cave's main Buddha image – accompanied by a retinue of cavalry, servants and musicians. At the rear of the procession are camels carrying the possessions of Zhang and his wife. The mural is a declaration of the power and status of the Zhangs, and a number of manuscripts discovered at Dunhuang contain adulatory praise for the great General's accomplishments:

> Our general's triumphant manner embodied grace and martial
>   prowess,
> He so intimidated the barbarian louts that they lost all courage;
> No sooner had the dog barbarians seen that the T'ang armies were
>   victorious,
> Than their retreating troops scattered like stars as they deserted their
>   posts.
>
>   ('Chang I-Ch'ao' (Zhang Yichao), Pelliot ms P2962.
>   From Mair, 1983)

From 848 until the Cao family supplanted them in about 920, members of General Zhang's clan governed Dunhuang. By 857, Zhang Yichao had secured all 11 prefectures of the Gansu corridor and brought them firmly under Tang government control. For the time being at least, the trade routes were secured, although after Zhang's death in 872 much of the territory was lost again. The eminent monk Hong Bian, patriarch of the faith in the area west of the Yellow River, presided over much of Dunhuang's development during this late period of the Tang dynasty and the Zhangs were enthusiastic patrons of the caves. He may, in fact, have been related to the Zhang family through his mother. When Hong Bian died in 862, General Zhang erected a memorial chapel in his honour and a painted stucco statue of the monk seated in meditation was placed there. Behind him is a mural with two attendants – one a female beneath a tree who recalls the *Yakshi* nature spirit images of India, the other the Persian fertility goddess Anahita. In the tree hangs a water bottle and leather satchel – the latter a wonderfully poetic reference to the sutras carried to China by pilgrims travelling the Silk Road. The statue of Hong Bian was originally in what is now known as Cave 17 but was removed sometime during the eleventh century and placed higher up the cliff. It was returned to the cave during this century. Cave 17 was then filled with thousands of manuscripts, paintings on silk, textiles and other objects, and the entrance sealed. It was originally thought that these items were concealed to prevent them from falling into the hands of the Tanguts (Western Xia), who invaded the area in about 1038. However, the careful manner in which the objects were sealed into the cave has led scholars to suggest that the contents may actually represent a ritual deposit of sacred objects. Whatever the reason for their disposal, the contents remained hidden until 1907 when Sir Marc Aurel Stein visited the site. Stein had heard rumours that the custodian of the caves, a Daoist priest called Wang Yuanlu, had discovered a number of manuscripts during restoration work. Stein was refused permission to examine the manuscripts until he and Wang discovered a common interest in the seventh-century monk Xuanzang. After protracted negotiations and a contribution to the upkeep of the caves, Stein acquired about 10,000 manuscripts and paintings from Cave 17 – written mostly in Chinese and Tibetan but with other texts in Khotanese, Tangut, Uyghur, Kok Turkic and even Hebrew. His finds were sent to the British Museum in London and were subsequently divided into three groups: for the British Museum, the India Office and the Archeological Survey in New Delhi.

The French Sinologist Paul Pelliot (1878–1945) arrived a year later and purchased a further group of 6,000 manuscripts for about 90 GBP. They were sent to the Bibliothèque Nationale de France and the Musée Guimet. He was followed in 1911 by the Japanese Zuicho Tachibana – emissary of Count Kozui Otani, abbot of the Honganji Temple in Kyoto. Stein returned in 1913, acquiring more treasures and, as late as

1914, Sergei Oldenberg obtained 600 scrolls and a number of fragments from the site for St Petersburg's Institute for Oriental Studies. By the time Langdon Warner of Harvard's Fogg Art Museum arrived in 1923, many of the caves had been ransacked or vandalised by White Russians fleeing the revolution in Russia. The sheer quantity of material acquired at Dunhuang, and in particular from Cave 17, means that much of it has yet to be studied. There is also the possibility that some of the later finds are forgeries – Islam Akhun, the catering agent for Macartney (the British consul in Kashgar) was discovered by Stein to have faked manuscripts from the Khotan region as early as 1899 – and much work remains to be done.

The treasures of Dunhuang, and especially of Cave 17, are of incalculable value as a source of information about life and religious practice along this section of the Silk Road. There is time for no more than a glimpse of the contents of the manuscripts found in Cave 17 in this book but even the briefest survey provides a cascade of information about the glory days of the Silk Road. Pre-eminent among them is the 'Diamond Sutra', the world's oldest complete printed book, now in the British Library. Dated 868, the Diamond Sutra is a Chinese translation of the *Vajracchedika-prajnaparamita-sutra* by the great fourth-century monk Kumarajiva. The document is a woodblock-printed book in the form of a scroll with an illustrated frontispiece. The scene depicts the Buddha preaching to Subhuti, one of his ten chief disciples. The colophon at the end of text reads: 'reverently [caused to be] made for universal free distribution by Wang Jie on behalf of his two parents on the 13th day of the 4th moon of the 9th year of Xiantong [11 May 868]'. Block-printing techniques had already been in existence for more than 100 years by 868, and the quality of the work suggests that the printer was already an adept craftsman. The document may have been produced in Sichuan, a known centre of printing at this time. The principal idea in the Diamond Sutra is the realisation of the illusory nature of all phenomena.

A concise summary by Lionel Giles (1944) provides a wealth of detail about many of the other documents. In a paper roll, referred to as S.3935, the prayers of a military superintendent are articulated. He vows to read sections of sutras in honour of his deceased parents. He prays that their spirits will travel to the Pure Land, that 'blessings of all kinds may daily descend' upon all of the members of his family and 'that the King's highway may be free and open, and that robbers and thieves may be driven away'.

Narrative ballads figure prominently among the manuscripts. One of the most poignant is 'The Lament of the Lady of Qin', one of several versions in the British Library. It recounts the sack of Changan in 880, by the rebel leader Huang Zhao (see page 57). The ballad concludes with a haunting description of a great city laid waste during the twilight years of the Tang dynasty:

> Ch'ang-an lies in mournful stillness: what does it now contain?
> Ruined markets and desolate streets, in which ears of corn are
>   sprouting.
> Fuel-gatherers have hacked down every flowering plant in the Apricot
>   Gardens;
> Builders of barricades have destroyed the willows along the Imperial
>   Canal...
> All the pomp and magnificence of the olden days are buried and passed
>   away;
> Only a dreary waste meets the eye: the old familiar objects are no
>   more.
> The Inner Treasury is burnt down, its tapestries and embroideries a
>   heap of ashes;
> All along the Street of Heaven one treads on the bones of State
>   officials.
>
>> (Attributed to Wei Chuang, *c.*880. Quoted in Giles, 1944)

One of the versions of the same text in the British Library (S.692), ends with a wistful verse added by the young novice monk who transcribed it:

> Now I have made this copy fair,
> Five pints of good wheat should be mine;
> But wheat's so dear that in despair
> I must my secret hopes resign.
>
>> (Quoted in and translated by Giles, 1944)

The material aspirations of another young man are revealed in one more of the manuscripts from Cave 17:

> Chinese slaves to take charge of treasury and barn,
> Foreign slaves to take care of my cattle and sheep.

Strong-legged slaves to run by saddle and stirrup when I ride,
Powerful slaves to till the fields with might and main,
Handsome slaves to play the harp and hand the wine;
Slim-waisted slaves to sing me songs, and dance;
Dwarfs to hold the candle by my dining couch.

(Translated by Arthur Waley. Quoted in Schafer, 1963)

This traditional prayer, recited by a young bridegroom, indicates that the practice of slavery was still widespread during the Tang dynasty. During the early part of the dynasty most slaves were foreigners: prisoners taken during China's territorial expansion, those given as tribute to the court, or simply kidnapped and sold like any other Silk Road commodity. During the latter part, however, as the economy collapsed and famine threatened, many starving or heavily indebted Chinese sold themselves into slavery.

Among the other documents from Cave 17 are examples of great humour and charm. 'A Debate Between Tea and Wine' (S.406) includes the respective claims of Tea, 'flower of the myriad trees' and Wine, 'drunk by the sovereigns of the Earth', that each is superior to the other. The debate passes back and forth until Water intervenes and tells them they both depend for their existence on him! A letter admonishing a man for his state of inebriation recalls the sort of understated, polite criticism to be found in correspondence between Victorian gentlemen:

Yesterday, Sir, while in your cups, you so far overstepped the observances of polite society as to forfeit the name of gentleman, and made me wish to have nothing more to do with you. But since you now express your shame and regret for what has occurred, I would suggest that we meet again for a friendly talk. Respectfully yours...

(From ms S.5636. Quoted by Giles, 1944)

A final summary might include a request for the return of a donkey (S.5864), a question about rights of irrigation from a canal (S.2103), many notices summoning members of various clubs to attend meetings, and a long treatise on the intricacies of Chinese chequers (S.5574). A project is currently under way to collate all of the Stein manuscripts in the British Library and, as the work continues, more and more fascinating stories of the Silk Road will undoubtedly emerge.[4]

There is room to examine only three of the priceless objects from the hidden library of Cave 17 – two silk embroideries and a painting, all now in the British Museum and each a paragon of Silk Road art. The first, an embroidery on a silk and hemp cloth backing, is one of the largest and finest Chinese examples in existence. Discovered by Sir Marc Aurel Stein and dated to the eighth century, this outstanding, 241 cm high embroidery is on a scale comparable to the majestic cave murals of Dunhuang. Its theme is Buddha Sakyamuni's preaching of the Lotus Sutra at Rajagriha on Mount Grdhrakuta ('Vulture Peak'). His posture – with the right arm extended straight down – is emblematic of the great event. A second embroidery, 92 cm in height and showing flowers and ducks, is secular in style and, when it was found, was folded over and sewn into a bag. It is one of the most perfect examples of Tang dynasty silk embroidery.

As we saw in the documents from Cave 17, the political and religious uncertainties of the late Tang dynasty gave rise to a sense of anxiety among the populace. This is reflected in a greater sense of piety among the town's residents and an increased desire for personal salvation. Depictions of the 'Bodhisattva Avalokitesvara (Guanyin) as Guide of Souls' are found in paintings from the late Tang to the early Song. In a late ninth-century example from Cave 17 the *bodhisattva* leads a finely dressed lady to a paradise in the clouds. In this 80.5 cm high ink and polychrome painting on silk, the *bodhisattva* depicted, despite the absence of an Amitabha Buddha in his headdress, is almost certainly Avalokitesvara. The elegant lady with her elaborate *coiffure* and rich clothes is doubtless a princess or aristocrat and is led towards the celestial palace at the top left of the painting.

The collapse of the Tang dynasty in 907 brought China's 'Golden Age' to an abrupt end. There followed 50 years of black chaos – known as the period of 'Five Dynasties and Ten Kingdoms' – when local military governors declared themselves ruler or even 'emperor' of whatever slice of territory they happened to hold. Dunhuang fell under the control of the Cao family in about 920 and remained so for the next 100 years. The new ruler of Dunhuang, Cao Yijin (d.936) sought to consolidate his grip on power by the arrangement of strategic marriages with the neighbouring rulers of the Uighur kingdom of the north and east, and of Khotan to the west. In a wall painting in Cave 98, dated to around 920 and referred to in an inscription as the 'Cave of the Great King', Cao Yijin and the king of Khotan are shown leading retinues of family members, the two families meshed together by marriage. Behind the king stands his queen, a daughter of Cao Yijin, wearing a necklace and crown of green Khotan jade and carrying a censer (an incense burner). The king himself wears a splendid robe, decorated with sun and moon emblems and embroidered with dragons. Elsewhere in the cave is a mural with leaders of various neighbouring states listening to a sermon by the scholar Vimalikirti.

The Song emperor, Taizu, reunified China in 960 and the country then enjoyed three centuries of relative peace. While trade along the Silk Road never regained the levels it enjoyed during the Tang dynasty, it did not cease and envoys and merchants from other countries still came to the Middle Kingdom. The Northern Song imperial tombs at Gongxian in Henan province demonstrate that China was far from insular during this period. The spirit roads leading to the tombs of the Song emperors are lined with immense figures of foreign ambassadors – including Arabs, Khotanese, Southeast Asians, Uighurs and Koreans. The Song were militarily weak, and peace with rival states such as the Khitan and Jurchen in the north and the Western Xia in the west was maintained by diplomacy and the payment of tribute, rather than by force. The Song were primarily concerned with retaining the territory they held within metropolitan China and were less preoccupied with places such as Dunhuang, situated beyond its borders. As a result of this policy the Liao dynasty of the Khitans (907–1125) was able to flourish and to retain control of a vast area of northern China, including Manchuria and most of modern day Mongolia. The Western Xia (Tangut) kingdom (1032–1227) ruled a similarly large area of Ningxia, Gansu and Inner Mongolia centred around the cities of Xingzhou (modern Yinchuan) and Khara Khoto (see page 99).

The Cao rulers of Dunhuang succeeded in retaining their independence by perpetuating Cao Yijin's strategy of forging matrimonial alliances with the Uighur khans and with the neighbouring king of Khotan. They also sent generous tributes to the Song court. These strategies were successful until about 997 when the Cao clan fractured. Cao Yanlu and Cau Ruibing, two grandsons of Cao Yijin, were murdered by a relative, Cao Zhongshou. By about 1019 Dunhuang had fallen under the control of the Uighurs although the Cao family continued to rule with Uighur consent. Cao loyalties shifted back and forth between the Liao and Song courts and, in

1036, the self-styled 'Prince of Dunhuang' Cao Xianshun (son of Cao Zhongshou) also swore allegiance to the Western Xia. It appears that Dunhuang remained at least nominally independent and under Cao-Uighur control until about 1072, when it fell firmly under the sway of the Western Xia. Motifs from Esoteric Buddhism began to appear in the 80 caves built during the Western Xia period and a number of earlier caves were redecorated. One of the best-known images from the Western Xia period is a portrait of the Western Xia emperor, his young son and a retinue of servants on the east wall of Cave 409. This scene is a fascinating window on a brief phase of the Silk Road's history. The emperor wears the white felt crown and boots of a nomad prince yet his robe carries the coiled dragons of Chinese imperial mythology. His servants stand behind, diminutive and insignificant, stretching upwards to cover the great man with a broad parasol and wielding fans decorated with more dragons. His bow, sword and shield are carried in state to the rear of the painting and he stands on a lavish carpet. A line of seated Buddhas along the top edge of the mural is a reminder that the portraits are of the cave's sponsor, a fervent Buddhist.

The Western Xia's control of Dunhuang was short-lived. In 1227 the armies of Genghis Khan laid waste to the Western Regions, annihilated the populace and began a gradual process of subjugation that would culminate in the establishment of the Yuan dynasty in 1279. Genghis Khan's grandson Khubilai Khan (r.1279–94) permitted religious freedom in China – probably as a result of a tolerance for other faiths learned during childhood from his mother: the redoubtable Sorghaghtani Beki. He was also influenced by his 'Head of the Office of Buddhist Affairs', a Tibetan lama named Phags-Pa (or Baisiba, in Chinese). Under Phags-Pa's guidance, Khubilai and the Mongol population as a whole – hitherto believers in shamanism – were drawn to the sorcery and necromancy of Tibetan Lamaistic Buddhism. Lama temples were built all over China and the survival of Dunhuang was assured. Many of Dunhuang's caves were restored during the Yuan dynasty and the murals are replete with *mandalas* (cosmic diagrams) and deities from Esoteric Buddhism.

The Yuan dynasty proved to be Dunhuang's swansong, however. In 1368 the restoration of Chinese sovereignty occurred and the Ming dynasty was established. China became more inward-looking and the fortunes of the Silk Road and many of its caravan cities fell into decline. When trade revived – as a result of the great European explorations of the fifteenth century onwards – it was via the sea routes and not by land. The cities of the Silk Road receded from history and were, by-and-large, forgotten until the beginning of the twentieth century when the activities of Stein, Pelliot, Albert von Le Coq and others revived the public's interest.

CHAPTER SIX

The Silk Road Through China Beyond Dunhuang: The Northern Silk Road and Southern Silk Road

A section of the Silk Road winds out of Dunhuang, following the course of the Shule River. On the south-western outskirts stand the ruins of a nine-storey structure, the White Horse Pagoda, built during the fourth century by the monk Kumarajiva to memorialise his favourite steed. To the north-west and south-west of Dunhuang, and 86 km apart, are two strategic passes – the Yumenguan and the Yangguan, both located in what used to be Han dynasty sections of the Great Wall.

The Yumenguan (Jade Gate Pass) is situated in the Gobi Desert, 90 km north-west of Dunhuang and is the gateway to the Northern Silk Road. A spur leads from Dunhuang to the main route at Hami. In later years caravans carrying jade would pass through the Yumenguan on their way from Khotan, and it became known as the Jade Gate. It came to be regarded by generations of Chinese as the end of the civilised world:

> For years, to guard the Jade Pass and the River of Gold,
> With our hands on our horse-whips and our sword-hilts,
> We have watched the green graves change to snow
> And the Yellow Stream ring the Black Mountain forever.
> (Liu Zhongyong, eighth century, 'A Trooper's Burden')

> The bright moon lifts from the Mountain of Heaven
> In an infinite haze of cloud and sea,

And the wind, that has come a thousand miles,
Beats at the Jade Pass battlements…
        (Li Po (Li Bai), 701–62, 'The Moon at the Fortified Pass')

The remains of the small fort, with its two portals, and known as the 'Square City' or 'Lesser *Fangpan*' (on account of its shape), is all that remains of Yumenguan (Figure 19). The site is one of the most desolate and remote places on earth and its position was not finally ascertained until 1907, when Sir Marc Aurel Stein discovered inscribed wooden slips on which the site is named. He also explored a network of ancient forts to the north of Dunhuang, built during the Han dynasty along the westernmost extension of the Great Wall. This section extends westwards along the course of the Shule River to the dried up salt lake of Lop Nor, situated less than 300 km from Yumenguan. A line of about 60 beacon towers, each within sight of the other, enabled garrisons to warn of the approach of invading Xiongnu. Stein found bundles of tamarisk ready to be set alight, still scattered near the towers, and legend has it that wolf-dung was also burned because it emitted dark, easily visible smoke. One of the many stories associated with the beacon towers, compared by Stein to the Roman defence roads known as *limes*, is the sad tale of the Lady Baosi. She was the favourite consort of King You of the Zhou dynasty and, during an attack of *ennui*, she persuaded the king to light the beacon signals. The rulers of neighbouring kingdoms rushed to the king's assistance but found the couple enjoying a feast on a local mountainside. When Zhou territory was actually invaded some time later the king's allies ignored the beacon fires: he was killed and Baosi was captured.

Figure 19
Remains of the fort at Yumenguan (Jade Gate Pass). Han dynasty (206 BC– AD 220). Dimensions: 28 x 28 m.

MAP 7
The Northern and Southern Silk Roads through Western China.

The road to the south-east from Yumenguan to Dunhuang is equally desolate. Early travellers must have gazed at a road that stretched endlessly before them and been overwhelmed by a sense of hopelessness.

The gateway to the Southern Silk Road is Yangguan, built during the Han dynasty (206 BC–AD 220) and situated about 70 km south-west of Dunhuang. Yangguan, or the 'Gate of Yang', is said to derive its name from Yang Ming, an official of ancient times who fled through the gate to evade a warrant for his arrest. The remains of a citadel can still be seen at the site and so many artefacts are strewn around the area – coins, arrowheads, pottery shards and even gold jewellery – that the local people call it 'Curio Depot' or 'Relic Bank'. To the Chinese it was a remote, forbidding spot – a place for farewells:

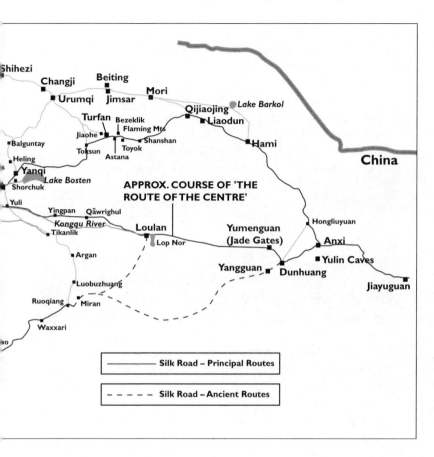

A morning rain has settled the dust in Wei Town,
Willows[1] are green again in the tavern dooryard
Wait till we empty one more cup –
West of Yang Gate there'll be no old friends.

(Wang Wei (701–62), 'A Song at Wei Town')

By the end of the Tang dynasty the incursion of sand and flood had led to the abandonment of the area and Yangguan was forgotten. Yumenguan and Yangguan were gateways to the Western Regions, and Chinese beliefs in the evils that awaited travellers to these areas go right back into antiquity. To the Chinese, the lands to the west were *terra incognita* and were inhabited by monsters:

O Soul, go not to the West
Where level wastes of sand stretch on and on;
And demons rage, swine-headed, hairy-skinned,
With bulging eyes;
Who in wild laughter gnash projecting fangs.
O Soul, go not the West
Where many perils wait!

(Attributed to Qu Yuan, *Ta Chao* ('The Great Summons'),
third century BC. Translated by Arthur Waley, in Waley, 1941)

Another version runs:

O soul, come back! For the west holds many perils:
The Moving Sands stretch on for a hundred leagues.
You will be swept into the Thunder's Chasm, and dashed in pieces,
    unable to help yourself;
And even should you chance to escape from that, beyond is the empty
    desert,
And red ants as huge as elephants, and wasps as big as gourds.
The five grains do not grow there; dry stalks are the only food;
And the earth there scorches men up; there is nowhere to look for
    water.
And you will drift there for ever, with nowhere to go in
    that vastness.

(Attributed to Qu Yuan,[2] *Chao Hun* ('The Great Summons'),
third century BC)

The northern and southern routes of the Silk Road skirt the rim of the Tarim basin. This extends over an area of 530,000 km^2 (about 15 times the size of Taiwan), across Xinjiang, China's largest and westernmost province. The basin is almost completely enclosed by mountains: the Tianshan to the north, the Kunlun to the south and the Pamirs to the west. Within the Tarim basin is the Taklamakan, China's largest desert and some 337,000 km^2 in extent. In Turkic, Taklamakan means 'the place from which no living thing returns' or 'the desert of certain death'. The Chinese called it 'Liu Sha', or 'Shifting Sands', because of the constant movement of its dunes. A modern day traveller, Sir Clarmont Skrine, British consul-general at Kashgar in the 1920s, has captured the overwhelming desolation of the place:

To the north in the clear dawn the view is inexpressively awe-inspiring and sinister. The yellow dunes of the Taklamakan, like the giant waves of a petrified ocean, extend in countless myriads to a far horizon with here and there an extra large sand-hill, a king dune as it were, towering above his fellows. They seem to clamour silently, those dunes, for travellers to engulf, for whole caravans to swallow up as they have swallowed up so many in the past.

(Skrine, 1926)

The cities of the oases along the fringes of the Tarim basin were sometimes abandoned because of invasion or because of the drying up of glacier-fed streams. If a proportion of the population left the town, there was often not enough manpower to maintain the *kariz*, the system of irrigation canals and wells. The amount of cultivable land would soon become insufficient to support the remaining population and the town would eventually be left for the desert to reclaim.

The Northern Silk Road

The desert which lies between Ansi [Anxi] and Hami is a howling wilderness, and the first thing which strikes the wayfarer is the dismalness of its uniform, black, pebble-strewn surface [...] The twelve hard stages between Ansi and Hami offered many new varieties of objectionable water. Sometimes it ran from beneath boulders in a limpid stream, sometimes it lay in a sluggish pool, its surface covered with a repulsive scum; at other times it burst through the soil, and sometimes it was drawn from a well with bucket and rope; but whatever its immediate source, it was always brackish and thirst-creating.

(Cable and French, 1942)

This description of the Northern Silk Road between Anxi and Hami is not the complaint of some ancient traveller. It was written in 1942 when the journey from Kashgar to the old Chinese capital of Luoyang – today a two- or three-day train ride – took five months. The Anxi–Hami section has few wells and what little water there was to be found was often brackish or contaminated with sulphur. The journey took about two weeks and crossed a section of desert known as the 'Black Gobi'. This area was where the monk Xuanzang became lost during the seventh century after straying from the main route. One of the

frequent sandstorms, known as *karaburans*, obliterated Xuanzang's path
and he faced disaster when he dropped his water bag. He was saved by
his skinny roan horse, which carried him to a small oasis.

Hami

Hami (ancient Yiwu or Kamul) is the first of a series of oasis towns
along the foot of the Tianshan or Celestial Mountains. The mountains
act as a barrier between the Dzungarian Plain of southern Mongolia
and the Taklamakan Desert of Xinjiang that extends for 2,000 km from
east to west and 400 km from north to south. The melt water from the
Tianshan is collected in wells linked by underground canals known as
kariz or *kyariz*. Some are 40 km in length and the network of *kariz*
accounts for the fertility of the soil in the Turfan region, an area with
negligible rainfall. The *kariz* were invented in ancient Persia and are still
used in many parts of Central Asia.

Hami is renowned for its melons although 'Hami' melons are
actually grown throughout Xinjiang. There are more than 30 varieties
produced around Hami. They have been a delicacy for centuries and
Hami honeydew melons were sent as tribute to the Chinese court
from ancient times until the Qing dynasty. Preserved remains of Hami
melons, found in the Astana necropolis at Turfan, indicate that they
have been cultivated for at least 1,300 years.

The residents of Hami were hospitable to outsiders to an extraordinary degree: Marco Polo describes how the man of the house
would share all of his possessions, including his wife, with a guest:

> When strangers arrive, and desire to have lodging and accommoda-
> tion at their houses, it affords them the highest gratification. They
> give positive orders to their wives, daughters, sisters, and other
> female relations, to indulge their guests in every wish, whilst they
> themselves leave their homes, and retire in the city, and the stranger
> lives in the house with the females as if they were his own wives [...]
> The women are in truth very handsome, very sensual, and fully dis-
> posed to conform in this respect to the injunction of their husbands.
> (From *The Travels of Marco Polo the Venetian*. Translated by William
> Marsden, in Polo, 1948)

A spur of the Silk Road runs north-west from Hami through the
Tianshan Mountains to the ancient trade post at Lake Barkol. Barkol

was known as the state of Pulei during ancient times and was populated by nomads who raised fine horses, cattle and camels. Lake Barkol (once known as the Pulei Sea) is west of the town of the same name and was the site of numerous battles with the Xiongnu. In AD 73 and AD 74, the Han emperor, Mingdi, sent large expeditions against the ruling Xiongnu clan, the Huyan, and the area was secured. A memorial tablet, 1.4 m high, once stood on the shores of Lake Barkol but has now been removed to a museum. It commemorates the achievements of Pei Cen, prefect of Dunhuang during the Eastern Han dynasty (AD 25–220). The inscription is dated 137 and celebrates Pei Cen's rout of the Xiongnu that was said to have brought peace to the border regions. There are still signal towers lining the route westwards from Lake Barkol and this strand of the Northern Silk Road is said to have run along the northern foothills of the Tianshan, to the kingdom of Jushi, during the Han dynasty; and to Beiting during the Tang dynasty. The Jushi were the original nomadic peoples of the area but were progressively displaced, from about 60 BC, by successive waves of Chinese settlers. By the sixth century AD, when the Gaochang kingdom was established in the area, there were few indigenous Jushi left.

Turfan

Lonely, silent old Kaochang [Gaochang], crumbling back to dust and wholly undisturbed by the hand of any restorer.

(Cable and French, 1942)

The main Northern Silk Road runs directly from Hami to Turfan, across the southern foothills of the Tianshan Mountains. A route also existed to the north, between Turfan and Jimusa (Beshbalik or Beiting) where it joined the northern Tianshan route. Turfan is situated some 150 m below sea level, the lowest elevation on earth after the Dead Sea. Its old name, 'Land of Fire' or 'Oasis of Fire', is a reference to its searing heat: summer temperatures can reach 45 degrees Celsius and annual rainfall is seldom more than 16 mm. Because of the aridity of the area an astonishing array of artefacts has survived in near pristine condition. The early inhabitants of the Turfan oasis were the Jushi nomadic peoples, their capital at Jiaohe (Yarkhoto) just to the west of the modern city. The Chinese and Xiongnu fought each other for possession of the Turfan oasis throughout the Han dynasty but the Chinese eventually prevailed. Large numbers of Chinese settlers arrived during the period of turmoil that followed the collapse of the Han dynasty and, by the end of the fifth century, Turfan was a thriving centre on the Silk Road with a well-integrated community of Chinese and Central Asians. In 499 the Qu family – with the joint support of the Han, the remaining Jushi nomads and other nationalities – established the independent kingdom of Gaochang. The capital of Gaochang state was at the city of Gaochang (Khocho or Karakhoja), about 45 km south-east of modern Turfan. The rulers of the Gaochang state survived for nine generations by simultaneously ingratiating themselves with the northern nomads and paying tribute to the Chinese court. The men of Gaochang wore local attire but the women adopted Chinese dress and hairstyles. After the Sui dynasty reunified China in 589 the Qu rulers maintained good relations with the new government. The ruler at the time, Qu Boya, attended the Sui emperor Yangdi's grand Silk Road 'summit' at Zhangye in 609 (see page 98). He joined the party of rulers who escorted the emperor back to Changan and later married a princess from the Sui royal house.

Qu Boya's son, Qu Wendai, was a somewhat Machiavellian individual who is remembered for his desire to appoint Xuanzang as Buddhist patriarch of the kingdom when the venerable monk passed through in 630. Xuanzang refused and was forced to go on a hunger strike before Qu Wendai would release him and permit him to continue his journey. Qu inadvertently brought about the demise of the Gaochang kingdom when he attempted to exploit its status as a Silk Road entrepôt. He attempted to levy exorbitant taxes on passing merchants and frequently detained the caravans which carried goods to Changan. The Tang government was enraged by Qu's behaviour and Emperor Taizong sent troops to attack Gaochang in 640. As the army approached, Qu Wendai is said to have died of fright and his son quickly submitted to the control of the central government. The Tang renamed the area Xizhou (Western prefecture) and the Qu clan were exiled to Luoyang. For the following one-and-a-half centuries the area enjoyed a period of peace and prosperity when the production of, and trade in, silk flourished. Central Asian merchants, particularly Sogdians, set up trading centres along this section of the Silk Road and their artisans worked side-by-side with Chinese craftsmen. Artistic motifs from the empires of Persia and Gandhara flowed freely into the region (Figure 20).

A population census was conducted in 640 when Tang China regained control of Turfan: officials recorded a population of 37,000 in 8,000

Figure 20
Silk fragment with hunting motif.
Tang dynasty
(618–907).
Length 44 cm,
width 29 cm.
From Tomb 191,
Astana cemetery,
Turfan, Xinjiang
province

Note the use of the 'Parthian Shot' motif on this textile in which a hunter shoots backwards from a galloping horse. The 'Parthian Shot' is said to have been one of the strategies used to defeat the Roman armies of Crassus at the battle of Carrhae (see pages 48–9).

households. The Tang were great administrators and record-keepers, and a large quantity of documents of various types has been unearthed in the Turfan region. Inscribed wooden slips and documents on bone, terracotta and paper in Chinese, Kharosthi, Kuchean, Sogdian, Tibetan, Uighur and Kharakhanid have been found and testify to the cosmopolitan nature of the region at that time. Many of these documents can be seen in the Turfan and Urumqi museums and provide fascinating glimpses into the everyday life and economic conditions of the Silk Road. Among the documents found at Turfan's Astana cemetery is a terracotta epitaph concerning Liang Yanhui, the occupant of Tomb 183. Liang was a resident of Gaochang and served as treasurer to the Qu family, rulers of the Gaochang kingdom. After Tang China regained control of Turfan in 640, Liang served as cavalry commander of the garrison and subsequently worked for the governor's office in Xizhou prefecture, the new name for Gaochang. His tenure therefore covers the periods of both the Qu family and Tang rule.

A second document, also discovered at the Astana cemetery, illustrates both the economic conditions and the diverse nationalities present at the time. It is a deed in Sogdian, found in Tomb 135 and concerning the purchase of a slave girl. This ink-on-paper document, written with exquisite neatness, is dated 639, just before the end of the Gaochang kingdom. It states that Yanasena, son of Uta of the state of Shi, is paying 120 'drachmas of the Sasanian King Peroz' (r.459–84) in Gaochang market to a man with the name of Uhusufert, for the purchase of a slave girl born in the region of the Turks.

The Astana Cemetery

The Astana cemetery, 40 km south-east of Turfan, has already been mentioned several times in this book. It contains over 400 tombs, built in the Chinese style and accessed by walkways. The cemetery contains the dead of Gaochang, both Han Chinese and other ethnic groups, and documents found at the site indicate that it was in use at least as early as the late third century. However, it had fallen into disuse by the end of the eighth century. The arid climate has preserved both the bodies and many of the artefacts interred there, and the contents of the graves provide a fascinating window on the history of a town thriving on the largesse of Silk Road trade. Several of the mummies removed from Astana are now in the Turfan museum. One, a female, has long hair held in place by a wooden comb; and a second, a young non-Chinese man, has long brown hair.

Expeditions by the Japanese explorer Count Kozui Otani in 1902 and 1910, by Sir Marc Aurel Stein in 1914, and by Chinese archeologists from 1959 onwards, have unearthed more than 10,000 objects. A number of silk funeral banners from Astana contain the figures of Fu Xi and Nu Wa, ancestors of humankind in Chinese mythology. Such banners were typically hung on the ceiling or back wall of a tomb and prove that the residents of this remote outpost of the Chinese empire still clung to the legends of the Central Plains. The scarcity of paper in the Western Regions meant that documents were often recycled for other purposes when they were no longer required. The residents of Turfan also followed the practice of burying their dead with paper hats, belts and shoes – i.e., reusing this scarce commodity – and many of the documents discovered from this period have thus been found in graves. A beautiful female tomb figure from Astana has arms made from recycled pawnshop tickets! This figure of wood, paper and silk – found in Tomb 206 – is now housed in Urumqi Museum. It dates to the Tang dynasty (618–907) and features the woman wearing an elaborate suit of clothes made from silk. The motifs on the upper part of her dress are typical Persian pearl roundels, and the details of her face are superbly rendered. The rolled up pawnshop tickets that make up her arms indicate that she was manufactured in Changan (Xian).

Motifs on Turfan Silks

Many of the surviving early Chinese silks have been found in the arid western regions of Gansu and Xinjiang, and large numbers were recovered from the Astana necropolis. During the Tang dynasty woven brocades and embroideries, as well as simple printed silks, were produced. Among the many motifs found on silk textiles excavated at Turfan sites are 'tree-leaf' and 'chess-board' patterns – hexagons, leaf-like hearts, diamonds composed of dots, winged horses and sacred birds. Many of these motifs have filtered through from India and Persia, and the medium through which they came is known to us. During the sixth century, increasing numbers of Central Asian settlers arrived in the Turfan area and by the seventh century they had established a community at the Turfan oasis, in the village of Chonghua. The most populous were the Sogdians, and documents found at Turfan indicate that Sogdian and Chinese weavers worked together and exchanged ideas. The security and stability of traffic along the Silk Road also facilitated the importation of silk textiles from elsewhere in China. Patterned Sichuan silks have been found at Turfan, for example, and are generally finer than locally produced fabrics. One of the most marvellous silk artefacts found at Astana was not a piece of fabric at all but an exquisite posy of artificial flowers made from silk gauze.

Sogdian merchants introduced two important religions from Persia to the Turfan area; namely Zoroastrianism and Manichaeism. The latter did not flourish in China until after the An Lushan Rebellion of 755–63. The Uighurs, a tribe related to the eastern Turks, were asked to assist the Tang to put down the rebellion and in 762 their ruler, Bogu Khagan, converted to Manichaeism and declared it to be the Uighur state religion. The Tibetans took advantage of the weakened state of the Tang to seize control of the Kuqa and Turfan regions. From about 790–840 Turfan remained in Tibetan hands, a situation that persisted until control of the whole area was wrested by the Uighurs. During the ninth and tenth centuries, while much of Chinese Central Asia was under Uighur control, Buddhism, Nestorian Christianity, Zoroastrianism and Manichaeism all appear to have flourished to differing extents. Turfan retained its religious diversity until the tenth century when the Uighur ruler of Kashgar converted to Islam. This conversion began an irreversible process of submission to Islam that would eventually encompass the whole of central Asia and would endure until the present day.

The Turfan area remained under Uighur domination until 1283, when the Mongols arrived, and did not return to full Chinese control until the Qing dynasty campaigns of the mid-eighteenth century. During the earliest period of Uighur control the Turfan area enjoyed its greatest cultural and religious diversity and many of its most fascinating works of art were produced. Examples include the Manichaean paintings – discovered in the city walls of Gaochang by Albert von Le Coq, and now housed in the Museum of Asian Art in Berlin – concealed behind later Buddhist paintings. Until they were discovered it was thought that all of the sacred texts of the Manichaeans had been lost.

Little trace of the Zoroastrian religion has been found at Gaochang except for a few documents relating to animal sacrifice. Nestorianism, which arrived in China around the seventh century, is better represented. The Nestorian temple at Gaochang, discovered and excavated by von Le Coq from 1904–5, was situated north-east of the city walls. A wall painting, removed from the temple by von Le Coq and now in the Berlin Museum, dates to the first half of the seventh century and shows a contemplative figure in long robes and turned up shoes – perhaps part of a solemn procession. One of the most astonishing finds from Gaochang's Nestorian temple is a wall painting thought to be a depiction of Palm Sunday. In this painting, also in the Berlin Museum, a Nestorian priest sprinkles consecrated water over his congregation, who stand before him with heads bowed. Above them a horse's leg can be seen; this has been interpreted as a reference to Christ's entry into Jerusalem.

Among the many Buddhist sculptures discovered at Gaochang by Albert Grünwedel are serene Buddha images, smiling *devatas*, and grotesque demon heads in both Chinese and Indo-Persian styles. A large three-tiered structure at Gaochang – the Buddhist Gamma Temple – resembles the stupas of the Gandhara kingdom to the west. Each of its tiers would have contained sculptures, a technique found in Gandhara temples and also at Jiaohe.

Jiaohe (Yarkhoto)

One can wander from end to end of these lonely, melancholy, dere-
lict cities, where on stormy nights the howling winds make play,
and the swirls of sand spin down the forgotten avenues like Dancing
Dervishes; and nothing can be too weird or too fantastic for the
imagination to devise after lingering, even only for a few hours, in
such surroundings.

(Cable and French, 1927)

As has already been mentioned, Jiaohe was the capital of the Jushi
people as early as the Han dynasty. The Chinese moved the capital to
Gaochang after seizing control of the area but the administrative capital
of the Turfan oasis alternated back and forth a number of times. The
name Yarkhoto means 'cliff town', a reference to its strategic location
on a plateau surrounded by two deep valleys. The ruined city of Jiaohe
(Yarkhoto), 8 km west of Turfan, dates back to the Han dynasty and was
a fortress intended to protect against raids by the Xiongnu. The ruins
are about 1,600 x 300 m and date mostly to the Tang dynasty, a period
when the city's population numbered in excess of 5,000 and when it was
an important trading and Buddhist centre. Among the ruins of Jiaohe
are the remains of a large Buddhist stupa, dated to the fourth century.
The structure consists of a large central stupa with four groups of 25
small stupas, one group set at each corner, making a total of 101.

Headless stucco figures set in niches adorn the central part of the
5,100 m^2 main temple. They are now worn and damaged but are still
strongly reminiscent of the Gandhara sculptures found in Taxila's Jaulian
monastery.

Tangshu ('History of the Tang') provides us with a brief description of
the kingdom of Gaochang in general, and of Jiaohe in particular:

It numbers in all twenty-one towns. The king has his capital in the
town of Jiaohe which is none other than the former royal court [of
the country] of Jushi at the time of the Han dynasty [...] The kingdom has two thousand crack soldiers. The ground is fertile. Corn
and crops produce two harvests a year. There is a plant there called
baidie [almost certainly cotton]. Its flower is picked so that it can be
woven to make cloth. The custom [of the inhabitants] is to plait their
hair into a coil, which hangs behind the head.

(*Tangshu*, 'History of the Tang'.
Quoted in Drège and Bührer, 1989)

A large amount of information about the changing economic conditions of the Turfan oasis at the time of the Silk Road has been obtained from recent studies of coins found in the area. One such study collates the reign dates of more than 150 silver Sasanian and Arab-Sasanian coins. The coin dates peak during two periods: the late fourth century and the late sixth to seventh centuries. Corresponding documents found in Turfan suggest that during the first period coins were not used as currency: cloth was the principal medium of exchange. During the second period coins were circulated and most often used in commerce involving expensive goods. The Qu rulers of Gaochang appear to have encouraged the circulation of such coins – used in taxation and in payments by the government. One such coin was found in the mouth of a corpse at the Astana necropolis.

To the east of Gaochang, carved into the sides of the Flaming Mountains, are the Toyok caves. Toyok contains a large number of caves honeycombed into the rock – which were first explored by Stein, and later by von Le Coq. In one cave – known as the Manuscript Room – von Le Coq found large numbers of manuscripts, many showing signs of fire damage as if some unknown ancient had tried to destroy them.

Turfan abounds with grapes. There are several varieties but the best are the famous 'mare's teat', grapes that are made into wine. Zhang Qian, emissary of the Han dynasty emperor, Wudi, brought grapes to China from the Ferghana region of Central Asia. They were originally planted in the capital at Changan but were eaten rather than used for making wine. As late as the Tang dynasty, wine was still an exotic drink; it did not become widely popular until the Chinese conquest of Gaochang in 640. 'Mare's teat' grapes were subsequently taken to Changan where vineyards were established. Poems by Li Po and others celebrating the virtues of imbibing wine appear more frequently after this event.

The Flaming Mountains

Fire clouds over the mountain never dispel;
Birds dare not approach within a thousand *li*.

> (Cen Shen (715–70), who served for many years
> as an official on the western frontier)

The Flaming Mountains comprise a line of crenellated red sandstone hills, rising to as much as 850 m above sea level, and extending for 100

km to the north of Gaochang. In the midday sun the hills shimmer and
exude a hot vapour that makes them appear as if they are on fire. Surface
temperatures have reached 80 degrees Celcius and legends about the
mountains are legion. The sixteenth century allegorical novel *Journey to
the West* concerns the adventures of the monk Xuanzang. Xuanzang was
a historical figure but the adventures described in *Journey to the West* are
apocryphal. When Xuanzang passes the mountains he is prevented from
proceeding further by a 'mountain of flame'. His companion, Monkey,
borrows a palm-leaf fan from Princess Iron Fan and uses it to extinguish
the flames. The Uighurs believe that the mountains take their colour
from the blood of a dragon that once ravaged the area but was eventually
slain by a young hero.

Bezeklik

At the western end of the Flaming Mountains, about 55 km north-east
of Turfan, are the caves of Bezeklik (in Turkic, 'the place where there
are paintings and ornaments'). More than 80 caves have survived,
about 40 of which are decorated with paintings.[3] They extend for
about 1 km along the Murtuk River gorge and are protected from
unwelcome visitors by a long winding ascent to the cliff-top. The
caves were first explored by von Le Coq in 1905, by representatives of
Baron Otani in 1908–9, and finally by Sir Marc Aurel Stein at the end
of 1914. The best paintings date to the period of Uighur domination
(ninth to thirteenth centuries). The paintings are in both Indo-Persian
and Chinese styles and represent the Uighur Empire at its height. By
the tenth century the Uighurs controlled an area from the Gansu
(Hexi) corridor to Khotan. The Silk Road brought great wealth to
its rulers and Bezeklik flourished as a centre for Buddhist learning.
The murals of Cave 9 and Cave 20 were painted at around the time
that the imperial family of the Uighur Gaochang kingdom converted
from Manichaeism to Buddhism, and they celebrate the cultural and
economic riches of the epoch.

The Museum of Asian Art in Berlin has a remarkable pair of wall
paintings from Cave 9 depicting Uighur royalty making offerings to
the Buddha. They are dated to the eighth to ninth centuries and show
Uighur royalty carrying flower offerings in a solemn procession. Each
party stands upon a beautifully decorated carpet and is dressed in lavish
clothes. The men wear high crowns, tied under the chin with ribbons,
tall nomads' boots and belts from which daggers, flint-pouches, awls
and knotted kerchiefs are suspended. The ladies wear sandy coloured

*The musicians in this lively painting are of various nationalities and reflect the ethnic diversity
of this part of the Silk Road. The instruments they play include two kinds of flute, a lute
(pipa), a tambourine and a hand-drum. The kingdom of Kuqa (or Qiuci) was renowned for
its musicians and it may well be that Kucheans figure among members of this orchestra. See
Figure 10 for a further example from Cave 20.*

robes with wide collars decorated with spirals. Their *coiffures* are
broad and secured with pins, and they wear elaborate crowns – the
left hand one compared by one scholar to 'a goldfish rising'. To the
right is an inscription that reads: 'This is the picture of Her Highness
Princess Joy.'

Depictions of the *parinirvana*, when the Buddha finally exits this
world and enters nirvana, are usually scenes of grief. Scenes of grieving
mourners do exist at Bezeklik but there are also clusters of figures who,
though they too are onlookers at the *parinirvana*, are full of joy and life
(Figure 21).

Many of the larger paintings from Bezeklik were taken by von Le
Coq to Berlin and installed in the Ethnological Museum. During World

War II the museum was struck several times by Allied bombs and many of the wall paintings were damaged or destroyed. Others disappeared at the end of the war, perhaps to the Soviet Union, leaving us with only a photographic record. Bezeklik itself is in a rather forlorn state today. The walkways have been restored but the remaining paintings are damaged and faded.

The main Northern Silk Road continues west from Turfan and heads through the towns of Toksun, Yanqi (Karashahr) and on to Korla. To the north-west, the road branches off towards Urumqi, across the Dzungarian plateau and then onwards over the Tianshan Mountains to Lake Issyk-Kul. Many travellers used this route to avoid the perilous crossing of the Taklamakan Desert and the Pamir Mountains. The route also joined up with other tracks including the spur that originated in Hami. This route was called the 'Tianshan Bei Lu' ('Road North of the Celestial Mountains') by the Chinese and followed the foothills of the Tianshan and then the Pamirs. The topography of this route made for easier travel than the main Northern Silk Road, the flatter terrain suitable in many parts for the use of higher load-bearing carts. The whole area had been a battleground for centuries, however, and most travellers preferred to take their chances crossing the Tarim basin and the high passes through the Pamirs. Only during the peaceful period of the eighth- and ninth-century High Tang, and the *Pax Mongolica* of the late thirteenth and fourteenth centuries, did the road achieve great popularity. Venetian explorer Marco Polo traversed the entire region during the latter period. The main northern and southern routes of the Silk Road combined at Kashgar. From Kashgar, one of them led westwards over the Pamirs, passed through the city of Balkh in Afghanistan, and then continued on to Merv.

Urumqi, the first stop on the modern road that follows the ancient Tianshan route, is now the capital of Xinjiang province. It was not established as a city until the eighteenth century and thus played no role in the early history of the Silk Road. The protector general's office for the region north of the Tianshan Mountains was, instead, at Beiting (or Beshbaliq) in Jimsar county.

Beiting is situated about 150 km north-east of Urumqi and was a walled garrison town during the Tang dynasty (618–907) that protected the trade caravans on this section of the Northern Silk Road. In 840 Beiting was taken by the Uighurs, former allies of the Tang. The Uighur capital was at Gaochang, renamed Qoco or Khocho, with Beiting as a subsidiary capital. The two cities remained Uighur strongholds until the arrival of the Mongols during the thirteenth century. From 1979 onwards, Chinese archeologists excavated a large ritual mound, some 250 m in circumference. Wall paintings similar to those at Bezeklik were discovered, as well as altars for Buddhist images that recall the art of the Gandhara kingdom. A Uighur prince dressed in gold appears in one of the paintings and it has been suggested that the complex is his tomb.

The Ili River rises in the western Tianshan and flows westward across the frontier region into Lake Balkash in Kazakhstan. The Ili River valley is relatively flat and fertile and is home to 13 or 14 different ethnic groups, including Kazakhs, Mongolians and Khirgiz. The Kazakhs, reputed to be descendants of the Wusun nomads, are the most numerous. The lush pasturelands of the Ili River valley were the source of the 'heavenly horses' of the Wusun and large numbers of horses are still bred there.

West of Urumqi is a stretch of the 'Tianshan Bei Lu' ('Road North of the Celestial Mountains') that early travellers would have described as a 'blank on the map'. The 700 km between Urumqi and Yining contained no settlements of any significance apart from the occasional fortification until the Tang dynasty. The ruins of Yanggabaxun City – west of Shihezi on the banks of the Manas River – are a possible exception, although little now remains of the town except its earthen walls. During the Tang dynasty there was an important transit station at Gongyue ('Crescent') City, about 25 km from Yining in the Ili River valley (see Map 7). Written records and Arab coins found in the area indicate that Gongyue was a centre for the region's silk trade. A branch of the Silk Road appears to have run between Gongyue and Kuqa, connecting the 'Tianshan Bei Lu' ('Road North of the Celestial Mountains') with the main northern route.

Close to the China–Kazakhstan border is Lake Sayram (Sailimu Hu or 'Best Wishes Lake'), situated about 2,000 m above sea level. Sayram is the largest mountain lake in Xinjiang, covering an area of about 450 km². Its waters contain a large quantity of calcium carbonate that turns them to a deep azure blue. In ancient times nomadic herders inhabited the shores of the lake and little has changed since then: today Kazakhs and Mongols predominate. The annual Nadam fair is held every July by the lake, and its horseracing, sheep-tossing and wrestling events honour traditions that have existed since the days when the Silk Road passed through the area. There was once a shrine at Sayram – built in a pine grove on the western shore – though nothing of it now remains. It was called Jinghai Temple and was a place where travellers would invoke the protection of the gods to ensure a safe journey.

Beyond Sayram this section of the Northern Silk Road crosses the border with modern day Kazakhstan near the town of Korgas. The route continues onward, passing both north and south of Lake Issyk-Kul towards Tokmak.

★ ★ ★

Returning to the main Northern Silk Road, travellers heading west from Turfan passed through the small oasis town of Toksun. From Toksun there was a choice of two routes to the town of Karashahr (modern Yanqi). The first involved an ascent westward through the Tianshan Mountains along the course of the Ala (Algu) River. This route rises to more than 3,000 m above sea level and then turns south along the Ulastay River to Karashahr. The route is marked by an ancient beacon tower at the Algu Mountain Pass. This route is thought to have been preferred by camel and horse caravans because of its abundant water and grazing. The other route is more direct but requires a harrowing journey through a 100 km gorge known, with good reason, as Dry Gully (Gan Gou). Throughout this stretch of the journey not a blade of grass can be seen and the only water comes from the occasional flash flood.

Karashahr is about 300 km from Turfan and is situated close to Lake Bosten (Bagrash), the largest lake in Xinjiang. The lake is fed by the Kaidu River, known as the 'River of Flowing Sand' on account of the 100 m thick layer of loose sediment that forms its bed. Lake Bosten is the source of the Kongqu (Peacock) River, named for the intense blue of its waters. The Kongqu, along with the River Tarim, once flowed right across the northern Taklamakan to Lake Lop Nor but their waters now dissipate long before they reach it. During the Wang Mang interregnum of AD 9–23, the Chinese were unable to maintain control of the kingdoms of the Western Regions. Even after the establishment of the Eastern Han dynasty in AD 25, the states of the Northern and Southern Silk Road continued to vie for dominance. In AD 41, the kingdom of Yarkand subjugated the neighbouring states of Khotan, Shanshan (Loulan) and Kuqa (Qiuci) and became the dominant force on the Southern Silk Road. In AD 60 the kingdom of Khotan rebelled against Yarkand control and the domination of the southern route became split between two kingdoms – the area between Kashgar and Niya remaining under Khotanese control, and the area around Lop Nor as far as Cherchen falling under Shanshan control. On the northern route, Karashahr was the dominant kingdom. During much of the first century AD the kingdoms of the northern and southern routes were threatened by Xiongnu attacks and by Chinese attempts to re-establish central control. The formidable General Ban Chao (AD 31–103) began to restore Han rule in the Tarim basin area from AD 73 onwards, and had succeeded in doing so by AD 91.

By the time Xuanzang passed through in 630, Karashahr (ancient Agni) was a prosperous kingdom, raising revenues by levying taxes upon passing merchants. Vines and millet grew in the area and local people traded fish, presumably from Lake Bosten just to the east, as well as salt. The residents, according to Xuanzang, wore woollen clothing and kept their hair cut short.

Karashahr ('Black Town')

Sites at Karashahr (modern day Yanqi), Khora and Shorchuk were excavated by Sir Marc Aurel Stein during his 1906–8 expedition. The site at Shorchuk was visited briefly by Grünwedel and von Le Coq in 1906, and then by Sergei Oldenburg of the Russian Academy of Science in 1909–10. Stein called Shorchuk 'Ming-oi' ('Thousand Dwellings'), a name also applied to other sites in the region. Shorchuk is situated about 60 km south of Karashahr. A series of free-standing shrines along a ridge at the site were all destroyed by fire in antiquity. Fragments of clay figures survived the fires, albeit in a damaged state, but the nearby caves have yielded clay statues, intended to be set in niches, wall paintings of great beauty, and a number of important manuscripts. The sculpture and paintings found in the cave shrines date mostly to the seventh to ninth century. A transition occurs during the later part of the eighth century from a 'western' Indo-Persian style to a more 'eastern' Chinese style. Stein recovered fragments of a wall painting from a temple that had been damaged but not destroyed by some ancient conflagration, in the northwestern part of Shorchuk. The fragments depict monks transcribing sutras, receiving instruction from older monks, kneeling in prayer as *apsaras* (celestial figures) descend from the heavens. These fragments, though beautiful, are not the principal murals of the shrine. Stein appears to have missed two large and sumptuously decorated sections, perhaps from the doorway to the main sanctuary of the temple. Both were recovered by Sergei Oldenburg during his 1909–10 expedition and are now in the State Hermitage Museum in St Petersburg. The larger of the two sections shows a pair of *bodhisattvas* and a group of monks, probably a depiction of the Buddha's First Sermon, in the Deer Park at Sarnath (Benares). The figures are superbly and colourfully drawn with many of the details picked out in gold. The group of monks is flanked, on the left of the mural, by Avalokitesvara wearing his characteristic deerskin robe, and by Maitreya, Buddha of the Future.

A very large number of clay sculptures were found at Shorchuk. As with the sculpture of Gandhara, they must have been set in niches within the monastery walls and were manufactured by building up layers of clay over a reed-bundle core. The final section was moulded and fitted as the final layer and finer details such as jewellery and scarves were also moulded and added at the end. The finished sculpture was then painted. Stein recovered several hundred clay figures from the sanctuary of one of the ruined shrines at Shorchuk, but the statues acquired by von Le Coq at the better-preserved cave temples still retain their vibrant colours. They are sculpted with great humour and vitality and tell us a great deal about the attitude of the local residents to foreigners and to those who eschewed the Buddhist faith. Among them are two clay figures of seated brahmins (Hindu priests), found at the Kirin cave and dating to the seventh to eighth century. Now in the Museum of Asian Art in Berlin, these two ill-tempered and rather comical figures sit in their knee-length stockings – the figure on the left resplendent in a panther skin – engaging in noisy debate over the merits of Buddhism. They are characters from *jataka* stories about the Buddha's prior lives, but such individuals may well have passed through the oasis towns of the Silk Road from time-to-time.

The shrines at Shorchuk – like most of the Buddhist remains along the northern route – are Hinayana ('Lesser Vehicle'), while those of the southern route are mainly Mahayana ('Greater Vehicle'). Scenes of preaching, a characteristically Hinayana theme, are found in many of the paintings around Karashahr. Among the small number of objects found by Stein at Khora, close to Karashahr, was just such a scene, painted on wood and showing the Buddha preaching to disciples. The style is similar to that of the sites around Kuqa, in particularly Kizil, which will be examined later.

The route westward from Karashahr runs along the foot of the Tianshan Mountains to Korla. There is little trace of the Silk Road around Korla except for the Iron Gate Pass just north of the town. The Northern Silk Road once passed through the Iron Gate Pass, a steep ferrous-coloured ravine at the entrance to a 14 km gorge in the upper reaches of the Kongqu River. The Tang dynasty poet Cen Shen (715–70), who spent years as an official on the western frontiers, wrote evocatively of Iron Gate Pass:

> An Iron Pass commands the western border of the sky,
> Where scarcely any travellers pass by…
> A bridge spans the gorge thousands of feet deep.
> Hemmed in between cliffs winds a narrow path.
> I climb up the western tower for the view.
> Just one glance, and my face turns grey.
>
> ('Iron Gate Pass' by Cen Shen (715–70))[4]

The route from Korla to Kuqa continues for about 300 km along the southern foothills of the Tianshan Mountains. To the south is the Tarim River and beyond it the vast wasteland of the Taklamakan.

Kuqa (Kucha or Qiuci)

> This country was above 1,000 *li* from east to west and 600 *li* from north to south; its capital being 17–18 *li* in circuit […] This country yielded millet, wheat, rice, grapes, pomegranates, and plenty of pears, plums, peaches and apricots. It produced also gold, copper, iron, lead, and tin: its climate was temperate and the people had honest ways; their writing was taken from that of India, but has been much altered; they had great skill with wind and stringed instruments.
>
> (Xuanzang. Quoted in Wriggins, 1996)

In addition to the economic conditions described by Xuanzang, silver and sal ammoniac, used in the tanning of leather, were mined in the nearby mountains. He also describes a strange custom among the Kucheans – the habit of flattening the backs of the skulls of their offspring with a wooden board. His observations have been borne out by recent excavations of tombs in the area and such practices may be compared to those of the Hepthalites (see page 209). There is still a market in Kuqa town each Friday, occupying the bed and banks of a dried up river. It is smaller than the great Kashgar market but is boisterous enough, a reminder that the lifeblood of these oasis towns was derived from Silk Road trade.

At the time of Xuanzang's visit in 630, a Buddhist king of Indo-European appearance ruled Kuqa. Xuanzang was unimpressed with the king, saying that he had 'little prudence or ability, and allows himself to be dominated by powerful ministers'. A mural depicting the king and queen of Kuqa, dated to the first half of the seventh century, was discovered in the Maya Cave (Site III) at Kizil. It was destroyed during the Allied bombing of Berlin during World War II but photographs have survived. They reveal a king with pale skin and reddish brown hair, and a finely featured queen dressed elegantly in a wide skirt decorated with brown and blue flowers.

Kizil

In the middle part of the seventh century, not long after Xuanzang's visit, large numbers of Persian émigrés sought and were granted sanctuary in Kuqa as the Sasanian Empire collapsed about them. At about the same time, in 658, the town was brought under Chinese control and became the headquarters for the entire Tarim basin. Kuchean art from the period has therefore absorbed influences from Persia and China but it retains a character of its own. Kuchean wall paintings have a strong affinity with the 'Indo-Persian' style of Bamiyan in Afghanistan. The two sites are both centres for Hinayana Buddhism, and visiting pilgrims from the former may well have brought Persian influences to Kuqa long before the arrival of Sasanian refugees. The oldest of Kuqa's paintings date to around 500 and have been designated as the first in Indo-Persian style. They are characterised by somewhat muted colours – red, browns and yellows – but with bright green (made from powdered malachite) used to highlight drapery, jewellery and other fine detail. The later phase, called the second Indo-Persian style and dating from about 600–750, can be recognised by the presence of bright green (malachite) and vivid blue (lapis lazuli), and by the appearance of complex jewellery and headdresses. These two styles are both apparent in the paintings of Kizil,[5] a large number of which were acquired during the third and fourth expeditions of von Le Coq, in 1906 and 1913 respectively, and transported to the Berlin Museum. The Kizil site is about 70 km north-west of Kuqa on the upper part of the Muzart River. It consists of about 235 cave temples cut into the hillside, many of them barrel-vaulted and with a pedestal or pillar for a devotional image. The most common type has narrow passageways on either side of the main chamber to enable worshippers to circumambulate around the central image (Figure 22).

Figure 22
The Kizil
Grottoes,
Xinjiang
province.

Kizil's paintings are joyously beautiful and, with the exception of Dunhuang, are without equal in Central Asia. Their subject matter includes scenes of the Buddha preaching, flying *devatas*, scenes from the Buddha's life and previous lives (*jatakas*), and depictions of the heroic exploits of *bodhisattvas* (*avadana* tales). The paintings are religious but the participants are often involved in secular activities. Kuchean music and dance were renowned throughout the kingdoms of the Silk Road and it is therefore not surprising that both activities occur with great frequency in the paintings of Kizil. Among the masterpieces in the Berlin Museum is a mural from the Cave of the Statues showing the cowherd Nanda, half-brother and disciple of the Buddha, listening to the Buddha preaching. Radiocarbon dating places it between 406–25 and it depicts Nanda, surrounded by his cattle, leaning upon a gnarled club and listening intently as the Buddha preaches. He is so absorbed in the Buddha's words that he is oblivious to the frog that he crushes with his club. The story relates that the frog declines the opportunity to escape so as not to distract Nanda, and is rewarded with reincarnation as a god.

The Cave of the Seafarers, sometimes called the Cave of the Navigator, contained a small fragment of a painting that was discovered among the rubble. It shows three men swimming among water lilies – perhaps a scene from the Maitrakanyaka *avadana* legend – and is one of Kizil's most splendid paintings. Dated to the sixth or seventh century, the man on the right, clearly the principal protagonist, is larger and swims more confidently than his companions. The style, like the previous two, is of the first Indo-Persian type and the influences of Gandhara are particularly strong. The Maitrakanyaka story concerns a rich merchant from Benares in India who drowns at sea. His son, Maitrakanyaka, grows up unaware of his father's fate and, ignoring the pleas of his mother, decides to follow the same profession. He is soon caught in a storm and shipwrecked. He spends years as the captive of a succession of beautiful sirens until he finally escapes and reaches a city of iron. There, he meets a man condemned to eternal torment for insulting his mother. Maitrakanyaka realises that he is guilty of the same misdeed and agrees to take on the man's punishment as penance. He immediately ascends to heaven as a *bodhisattva*. The whole of the Maitrakanyaka legend once adorned the main wall of the cave, a remarkable subject for a place so far from the sea.

Another example of the first Indo-Persian style – also from the Cave of the Seafarers and radiocarbon dated to 341–417 – shows a monk meditating before a skull *memento mori*. The subject matter is truly astonishing and one that we are more accustomed to seeing in the paintings of European artists like Holbein. The sentiment of the mural is best summarised by a line from a manuscript found in Cave 17 at Dunhuang (quoted in Giles, 1944): 'You may pile up a mountain of riches, but you will only have a coffin when you die.' The notion that human existence is ephemeral is a fundamental tenet of Buddhism. It is one that we encounter repeatedly, both in the perpetual rising and falling of the civilisations of the Silk Road and throughout all of history:

> The boast of heraldry, the pomp of pow'r,
> And all that beauty, all that wealth e'er gave,
> Awaits alike th'inevitable hour:
> The paths of glory lead but to the grave.
> (Thomas Gray (1716–71), 'Elegy Written in a Country Churchyard')

Mention should also be made of one other example of the early style, still to be seen on the ceiling of Cave 17. The entire ceiling is covered in depictions of *jataka* tales from the Buddha's previous incarnations. One scene is of great interest to historians of the Silk Road and is said to show a *bodhisattva* guiding a caravan of merchants through the darkness. His hands are raised aloft and turn into torches to light the way while two of the merchants stand next to him and raise their own hands in gratitude.

The second Indo-Persian style,[6] with its greater use of colour, occurs in the portrait of the Kuchean king and queen referred to at the beginning of this section on Kuqa. There is space for reference to only one other example here and it is one of Kizil's most effulgent paintings. A mural depicting a goddess with a celestial musician, found in the Cave of the Painted Floor (Cave 171), was previously dated to around 600–650 but recent radiocarbon dating has established a date of 410–35.

The female figures, both of them voluptuous and heavily jewelled, stand beneath a tree in blossom as flowers rain down around them. They are each enveloped by wide, sweeping necklaces and trailing drapery, and a sense of great intimacy exists between them. There is a virtual mirror image of this painting, damaged and faded but surely by the same hand, on the end wall of Cave 163 at Kizil. Both paintings may tell the story of the Buddha and the Goddess of Music. The Buddha – who disguises himself as a musician – challenges a woman, proud of her musical skills, to a lute-playing contest. She is shamed by the Buddha's superior playing and becomes his devotee.

Sites around Kuqa

Kumtura

An ancient trail led along the Muzart River to the important Buddhist site at Kumtura. Pack animals are unable to negotiate the route today and Kumtura has been left largely to its own devices, seldom visited and with many of its caves covered in soot from the campfires of hunters and shepherds. Between 2001–9 UNESCO carried out a conservation and restoration project at the site and there is now hope that what remains of its paintings might survive.

Kumtura's aspect, like that of so many such places, is startlingly beautiful. The site is situated 28 km north-west of Kuqa beside the Muzart River and comprises 112 rock-cut temples and shrines as well as free-standing buildings. The work at Kumtura appears to have been started in the fifth century but the majority of the paintings date to the eighth to tenth century of the Tang dynasty. Most therefore encompass the second Indo-Persian style, but a third style is also apparent at Kumtura – one not found at Kizil. Many of the paintings show a marked Buddhist Chinese influence – evident in facial characteristics, jewellery and costume – that we encountered in the art of Shorchuk and at the Turfan oasis. It is remarkable that Kumtura and Kizil, situated in such close proximity, have developed such disparate styles of art. The explanation is most likely to be found in the great political upheavals of the eighth century when Chinese power in the Tarim basin ebbed and flowed with each passing year.

There is room here to mention two examples of Kumtura's art. A richly painted clay figure of a *bodhisattva* in Indo-Persian style, dating to the seventh to eighth centuries and now in the Museum of Asian Art in Berlin, is strongly reminiscent of sculpture from Fondukistan.[7] Among Kumtura's paintings is one found in a new cave, discovered in 1977. Known as New Cave 2, and dated to the fifth or sixth century, it has a domed ceiling decorated with a roundel containing a series of *bodhisattva* figures standing in various poses around a central lotus.

Subashi

Xuanzang, delayed for two months in Kuqa because of severe winter weather, visited the monasteries of Subashi, which he called Zhaohuli. The ruins are about 20 km north of Kuqa and are divided in two by the Kuqa River. They were identified as the ancient city of Subashi by the French Sinologist Paul Pelliot during his 1907 visit. They are the largest group of ruins in the Western Lands with 100 temples that were, according to Xuanzang, 'so beautiful that they seemed to belong to another world'.

Pelliot reached Subashi in June 1907 and began to excavate the site. He found relatively little except for coins, graffiti in Brahmi and Chinese script, and about 15 funerary urns made of clay and wood, cylindrical in shape and with conical lids. The best of the group now resides in the Musée Guimet and is covered with cherub-like figures (or *putti*) dancing and playing musical instruments. The first Otani mission had visited the site four years before and discovered a casket of the same type. The Otani casket, now in the Tokyo National Museum, has similar cherubic figures on the lid and a complete orchestra of Kuchean musicians in mid-performance.

Kuqa's music was the best in the world, according to Xuanzang. Around the outside of the Otani casket, figures wearing masks of animals and bearded Persian kings dance to the music of flutes, drums and harps. This form of dance is believed to have originated in the Western Regions and was extremely popular in the Kuqa area. It entered Japan from China during the seventh century and came to be known as Gigaku dancing (also called *kure-uta* or 'Wu singing'). At the eye-opening ceremony for the Great Buddha at Nara's Todaiji temple in 752 there were reported to have been 60 Gigaku performers and musicians and in the city's Shosoin repository there are no fewer than 170 Gigaku masks (see the section on Shosoin on page 82). The most famous poet of the Middle Tang period,

Bai Juyi, provides a vivid description of a Gigaku performance at the Tang court:

> Skilled dancers from Hsi-liang,
> Persian masks and lion masks.
> The heads are carved of wood,
> The tails are woven with thread.
> Pupils are flecked with gold
> And teeth capped with silver.
> They wave fur costumes
> And flap their ears
> As if from across the drifting sands
> Ten thousand miles away.
>
> (Bai Juyi, 772–846. Quoted in Hayashi, 1975)

The most famous lute player of the day, Po Ming-ta, was a Kuchean. His composition, 'Trill of the Spring Warbler' or 'The Spring Nightingale Sings' is still performed in Japan. Another of the Otani casket musicians plays the harp – the Tang court adored music and was spellbound by the playing skills of the great harpist Li Ping, said to have been a Persian:

> Li Ping strums his harp
> In the Middle Kingdom.
> As jade crumbles on Mount K'un-lin
> And the phoenixes cry,
> As the lotus weeps dew
> And fragrant orchids smile,
> Even the cold glare of light
> Before Ch'ang-an's twelve gates
> Is softened,
> And the sound of twenty-three strings
> Moves the heart of His Celestial Majesty.
>
> (Li He (or Li Ho), 790–816. Quoted in Hayashi, 1975)

Duldur-Aqur is a monastic complex to the west of Kuqa. Its buildings were freestanding and have yielded far fewer wall paintings than the more durable cave structures of Kizil and Kumtura. Adding further to the site's decay are the traces of a great fire that seems to have engulfed the complex during the ninth century. The damage to the monastery at Duldur-Aqur is reminiscent of the conflagration at Shorchuk and was so severe that Pelliot was able to find only fragments of mural and a small number of wooden statues. The wooden figures, together with two life-sized painted clay *bodhisattva* heads, are strongly reminiscent of the art of Gandhara. The paintings date from about 500 to the ninth century: many are in the first Indo-Persian style of the sixth century; with a solitary *devata* head surviving from the second period and many more from the period of Tang Chinese influence during the eighth century. Among the wrecked murals of Duldur-Aqur are glimpses of a wonderful legacy – a pair of Kuchean princes, perhaps portraits of two of the kingdom's rulers but now portrayed as actors in a scene from the Buddha's life; and a large and realistic depiction of a Brahmin, both now in the Musée Guimet in Paris.

Kizil-Qargha, about 15 km north of Kuqa, was successively investigated by Otani's representative, Stein, Pelliot and von Le Coq between 1903– 13, but the paintings discovered there were both few in number and fragmentary. The same was true of the 52 caves at Kirish-Simsin, about 40 km north-east of Kuqa where the murals were, for the most part, heavily coated in soot and defaced by iconoclasts.

One of Kuqa's most famous sons was the monk Kumarajiva (343–413), son of an Indian father and a Kuchean princess. Kumarajiva translated some 300 Mahayana Buddhist texts from Sanskrit into Chinese and expounded the doctrines of the new faith for the Northern Wei rulers of China.

The Road from Kuqa to Aksu

The route from Kuqa to Aksu is about 260 km in length and continues to follow the foothills of the Tianshan. Along the route are the remains of beacon towers built during the Han dynasty. To the north-west of Kuqa the ancient route crossed the Yanshui Gorge ('the Gorge of Salt Waters') and followed the course of the dry riverbed. Only during the summer months, when meltwater flows down from the Tianshan, does the river come to life. At other times it is a bleak moonscape, salt encrusted and flanked by strange rocks whittled by the wind.

The oasis town of Aksu was the centre of the ancient kingdom of Baluka, although there is some dispute over whether the capital was there or at Karayulgun just to the north-east. Baluka was one of the kingdoms of the Western Regions.

A branch of the Northern Silk Road veers north-west from Aksu to cross the Tianshan Mountains through the 4,284 m Bedel Pass to Lake Issyk-Kul and on to Samarkand. Another strand of this route originated in Turfan and passed north of the Tianshan, linking up with the other route near Bishkek (formerly Frunze) in Kyrgyzstan. A number of passes linked the two branches – either between Lake Barkol and Hami, or between Turfan and Jimusa (formerly Beshbalik, the Uighur capital, called Beiting by the Chinese). The route from Aksu was followed by Xuanzang in 630 and required an ascent through the Bedel Pass, passing around the 6,995 m peak of Khan-Tengri (the 'Prince of Spirits'). At the end of a calamitous week-long crossing – during which about a third of the men in his party and many of the pack animals were killed – he reached Issyk-Kul (the 'Warm Lake'), which was kept from freezing year round by volcanic activity beneath its surface. Xuanzang's stark description of the glaciers on the slopes of Mount Khan-Tengri provides a succinct reminder that travellers on the Silk Road were sometimes required, quite literally, to take their life in their hands:

> This mountain is steep and dangerous, and reaches to the clouds [...] hard-frozen and cold sheets of water rise mingling with the clouds; looking at them the eye is blinded with the glare, so that it cannot long gaze at them. The icy peaks fall down sometimes and lie athwart the road, some of them a hundred feet high, and others several tens of feet wide.
>
> (Xuanzang. Quoted in Hui Li, 1911)

The original route of the Silk Road is now partly beneath the surface of Issyk-Kul, probably as a result of volcanic activity, and the southern shore contains the remains of a large number of settlements. Throughout the region are *balbals*, anthropomorphic grave markers erected by the western Turks around the sixth to eighth century to celebrate the men they had slaughtered in battle. Their victims were presumably the Hepthalites, defeated in about 560 by an alliance of western Turks and Sasanians. Piles of stones on western Turk graves are said to represent the number of enemies killed by the warrior lying within – one stone for each man killed – and the fact that some contain 1,000 stones indicates that Xuanzang was living in dangerous times (Figure 23).

West of Issyk-Kul, near Tokmak – the ancient domain of the Wusun nomads – Xuanzang met the khan of the western Turks ensconced in his winter capital at Suye (see Ak-Beshim below). At this time, during the early Tang dynasty, the western Turks were at the height of their power: their domain extended from China to the borders of Persia and from the Altai Mountains in the north to Kashmir in the south. The

Figure 23
Stone
balbals,
or tomb
markers.
Western
Turk, sixth
to eighth
century.
Balasagun,
Kyrgyzstan.

These balbals at Balasagun have been collected from sites all over Kyrgyzstan.

Turki Shahi, who achieved dominance in Afghanistan around this time, may have been the same people, although the historical records of the latter are scant (see pages 214–15). The summer capital of the khan of the western Turks was at Tashkent (Chach); and his winter headquarters were here, in the lush pastures around Issyk-Kul. During the winter months the khan moved his court – including his soldiers and his herds of cattle, sheep and horses – to the shores of the lake. Xuanzang gives an amusingly haughty description of the splendours of the khan's residence:

> The Khan lived in a great tent which was decorated with golden flowers, whose brilliance dazzled the eyes. The official ushers had spread long mats at the entrance, and they sat on these in two rows. They were all wearing bright costumes of silk brocade. The Khan's personal guard stood behind them. Although he was a barbarian prince, living in a felt tent, you couldn't help looking at him (and) experiencing a feeling of admiration and respect.
>
> (Xuanzang. Quoted in Hui Li, 1911)

Buddhism had already made modest inroads to the area by the time of Xuanzang's visit, and the religion became more popular during the ensuing years. At Ak-Beshim in the Chu valley near Bishkek, identified with the Turks' winter capital of Suye or Suyab, two Buddhist temples have been discovered dating to the seventh or eighth century. A Nestorian Christian church was discovered nearby in 1954, also dating to around the eighth century. The coexistence of these two faiths indicates that a strong spirit of religious tolerance existed. Further south, at Kuva in the eastern Ferghana valley, are the ruins of a Buddhist shrine, excavated in 1957–8 and found to contain a massive image of Buddha, more than twice life-size. At Adjina-Tepe, in Tajikistan, the remains of a Buddhist monastery bear testament to the wide reach of this religion.

West of Tokmak, the Silk Road traverses the verdant plain to the north of the Alexandrian Mountains, watered by 19 rivers and known, even today, as the 'Land of a Thousand Springs' (Bing Yul). Travellers heading west would eventually reach Tashkent, now the modern capital of Uzbekistan but once one of the most important caravan cities on the Silk Road.

The Aksu–Kashgar Route on the Northern Silk Road

Tumshuq (Toqquz Sarai) is located on a mountain ridge near Maralbashi on the Northern Silk Road, about 300 km before Kashgar. Both Pelliot and von Le Coq investigated the site, and mural fragments and sculpture were found – the latter in both wood and painted clay. Evidence of a devastating fire was found among the ruins – just as at Toyok, Shorchuk and Duldur-Aqur – part of an apparent sequence of destruction along the oases of the Tarim basin. A surprising number of wooden sculptures have survived by grace of the region's arid climate. Von Le Coq recovered a gilded Buddha head and a complete seated Buddha, both dated to around the fifth century and in distinctly north Indian style. Among Pelliot's finds are three relief panels, dating to the sixth to seventh century and containing clay figures that participate in episodes from the Buddha's present and past lives. The Sanjali-*avadana* (or Sankhacarya-*avadana*) relief is especially engaging and is one of the most delightful of all the Buddhist tales. The historical Buddha, during a past life, was an ascetic by the name of Sankhacarya. One day, as he sat meditating on the stump of a tree, his stance and breathing were so perfect that a bird laid its eggs on top of his head. In order to avoid frightening the mother, Sankhacarya remained motionless until the eggs had hatched. In this relief a pair of celestial *apsaras* peer down approvingly at the bird seated on his head. The style is that of the late Gandhara sculpture of Fondukistan.[8]

Kashgar

Kashgar (Kashi) is 3,700 km from Changan – a year's journey in ancient times. It stands at the eastern foot of the Pamirs, at the junction of the Northern and Southern Silk Roads, and is a quintessential caravan city. Travellers heading for China would pause at Kashgar after descending from the Pamir or Karakorum ranges. They would exchange their yaks and mules for camels in preparation for the perilous crossing of the Taklamakan. Westbound travellers would have reached Kashgar, exhausted but relieved, and rested before exchanging their own beasts in preparation for the ascent of the mountain passes at the fringes of Chinese territory. The Silk Road went westwards over the Terek and Torugart Passes in the Tianshan ('Heavenly') Mountains and on to the kingdoms of Ferghana and Sogdiana, through Tashkent and Samarkand, and across the Oxus River to Merv (present day Mary in Turkmenistan). At Merv the Silk Road joined the more southerly route that had passed through the Wakhan corridor to Balkh in Afghanistan.

Kashgar was known from the earliest times as a fertile and thriving commercial centre and, from the Han to Tang dynasties, it was called Shu-le. It fell under Chinese control during the first century BC and became a protectorate of the Middle Kingdom, although the Yarkand and Khotan states also exercised control during periods of Han political instability. It was not until AD 74 that the Chinese general, Ban Chao, brought Kashgar and Khotan firmly under Chinese control. Chinese dominance of the area was intermittent at best, however, and the city appears to have been invaded by Kushans from the Gandhara kingdom around 107. The Kushan occupation of the city led to the introduction of Buddhism and the remains found around the city are China's oldest and most westerly traces of the new faith. There is evidence that both Mahayana and Hinayana Buddhism were practised in Kashgar; the monk Kumarajiva spent a year in the city during the fourth century and was converted to the former religion; and Xuanzang passed through in 644 to find more than 1,000 monks of the latter school. At the time of Xuanzang's visit Kashgar had accepted the sovereignty of Tang China but in 670 Tibet undertook a campaign of expansion throughout the southern Tarim basin, capturing Kuqa, Khotan, Kashgar and Karashahr.

Old Kashgar can still be found in the bazaar that surrounds the fifteenth-century Id Kah Mosque – China's largest. The Sunday market takes place on the eastern edge of town, just beyond the Tuman River.

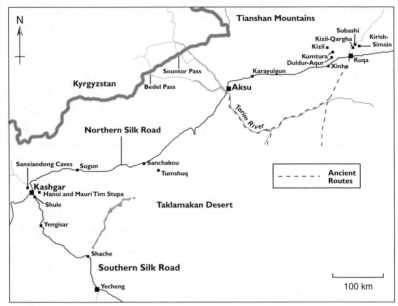

MAP 8
Silk Road sites around Kashgar, Aksu and Kuqa.

The market has been at the centre of Kashgar's commercial life since at least the Tang dynasty:

> Extending over ten *li*, with goods stacked high to the heavens, and visitors like swarms of bees. Precious and rare treasures can easily be found, and there are numerous varieties of fruit and animals.
>
> (From *An Eyewitness Account of the Western Lands*,
> Tang dynasty. Quoted in Yung, 1997)

Today, 100,000 people converge on the town each Sunday (Figure 24). The ethnic diversity of the visitors matches the range of goods on sale – Uighurs, Tajiks, Kyrgyz and Han Chinese predominate. The livestock area is the most vigorous section of the market and gives the best sense of how Kashgar must have been during the Silk Road's heyday. Xuanzang mentioned that the local inhabitants made fine woollen carpets and these are still to be found at the market, but the dazzling lustrous silks of old are almost gone. Khotan and Yarkand (Shache) are still silk-producing centres. In Khotan, the tie-dye method is used with symmetrical patterns and black and white as the main colours; supplemented by reds, yellows

Figure 24 Local merchants at the Kashgar Sunday market, Xinjiang province.

and blues. Yarkand silks are brightly coloured – emerald and jade green, magenta and apricot are favourites. Khotan and Yarkand silks can still be found but imported synthetic textiles are now as likely to be seen in the marketplace.

Kashgar's later history was a direct consequence of the disintegration of the Uighur state after the death of Kutluk Bilge Khan in 805. War erupted between the Uighurs and their Kyrgyz neighbours and in 840, after a bitter winter of famine, the Uighur capital at Karabalghasun on the Orkhon River (in present day Mongolia) was captured and its ruler, or kaghan (khan), was assassinated. The Uighurs fled south and the kingdom fragmented into three groups, centred around the west side of the Yellow River in Gansu and the northern and southern parts of the Tianshan Mountains. The largest group went to the northern Tianshan region, establishing their capital at Karakhoja, modern Turfan, and its descendants still form the most populous Uighur community in China. The southern Tianshan Uighurs allied themselves with other Turkic clans like the Karluks, Turgish and Basmils and established the Kharakhanid kingdom – its capital at Kashgar. In 934 the Kharakhanid ruler of Kashgar, Satuk Bughra Khan, embraced Islam – the first state of the Western Regions to do so. The Kharakhanids waged war against the Buddhist Uighurs of the northern Tianshan and most of the stupas and monasteries around Kashgar were destroyed. Some remains survive, however, mostly to the north of the city. A number of Buddhist stupas were found near the village of Hanoi (Hanoyi or Khan-ui) about 30 km east of Kashgar. The oldest appears to have been the Topa Tim stupa, first explored by Stein in 1900. It was still 100 m round at the base and may date to as early as the first century AD, contemporary with and similar in form to the great Dharmajika stupa at Taxila. A stupa at Kurghan Tim, north-west of Kashgar, is the largest mound in the area and was still 25 m high when Stein first saw it in 1900. Kurghan Tim was built on a square base like many large structures and small reliquary stupas found in Gandhara.

One of the best preserved and most important of Kashgar's stupas is at Mauri Tim, just north of Hanoi. Built and enlarged between the fifth and tenth centuries, Mauri Tim is built on a square base in the manner of Gandhara stupas and sits on a high mound, seeming much taller than its actual height of 11.5 m.

Hanoi itself is the site of a Tang dynasty walled city and may well have been the original site of the capital of the Kashgar city state (or Shu-le as it was then called). The remains of city walls and streets, about 75 x 95 m, have been identified. Hanoi appears to have been abandoned around the eleventh century and traces of fire damage at the site indicate that it was at least partially destroyed in antiquity.

The second- or third-century Sanxiandong ('Three Immortals Caves'), about 20 km north-west of Kashgar, are believed to be the oldest Buddhist caves in China. They are cut into the southern cliff beside the Qiakmakh River but have suffered from 1,000 years of iconoclasm and are in a poor state. Of the three surviving caves, only one has traces of wall paintings and these are no match for the glories of Dunhuang or Kizil. In the middle cave is a headless stone statue of a seated Buddha, and the site itself occupies a beautiful spot above the river.

The Uighur rulers of Kashgar were fully aware of the importance of merchants to the continued prosperity of the state. The Uighur scholar Yusuf Has Hajip was a chancellor to the khan during the eleventh century. His book *Kutatku Bilik* ('The Knowledge Befitting a Ruler') was written around 1070 and describes the social, political and cultural life of the Uighurs. It provides guidance to rulers in order that their reigns might be just. His advice covers the various strata of Uighur society but it is Yusuf's remarks about merchants that are of the greatest interest to historians of the Silk Road:

Deal with them, hold open your gates for them.
Treat them well
so that your good name will spread.

It is these who will carry your name through the world,
who will spread your reputation, good or bad.
If you want to be sure to become famous,
let the merchant have just pay for his goods.
If you want to create a good name for yourself, O Lord,
Treat well the caravan people.

(Yusuf Has Hajip, 'Kutatku Bilik', c.1070.

Quoted in Lattimore, 1950)

By the time of Marco Polo's visit to Kashgar during the thirteenth century, the city state was firmly under the control of the Mongols, as was the rest of the region. Commerce along the Silk Road flourished during the period of the Mongol Empire when travellers could journey unimpeded along its entire length. Kashgar's inhabitants were Muslim although a small community of Nestorian Christians was also tolerated. Polo was impressed with the beauty of the city but was less enthusiastic about the behaviour of its inhabitants:

> They have handsome gardens, orchards, and vineyards. [An] abundance of cotton is produced there, as well as flax and hemp. Merchants from this country travel to all parts of the world; but in truth they are a covetous sordid race, eating badly and drinking worse.

(From The Travels of Marco Polo the Venetian.

Translated by William Marsden, in Polo, 1948)

After the collapse of the Yuan dynasty in 1368, the Tarim basin descended into chaos with only a brief period of stability when Timur took control of the region at the end of the fourteenth century. By this time the Silk Road was already in decline and its cities fading into obscurity.

★ ★ ★

The Southern Silk Road

The Chinese called this route 'Nan Shan Bei Lu' ('The Road North of the Southern Mountains'). It travels in a south-westerly direction from Anxi, via Dunhuang and Yangguan, or the 'Gate of Yang', following the northern foothills of the Kunlun Mountains and skirting the southern edge of the Taklamakan to Loulan, Khotan, Yarkand and Kashgar. At Kashgar the Northern and Southern Silk Roads merge. The southern

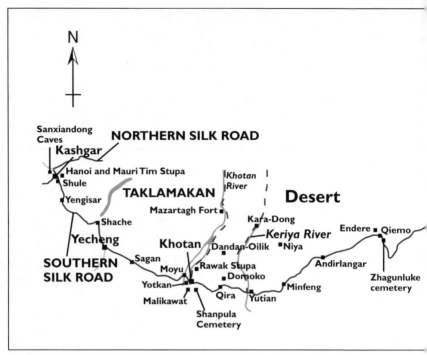

MAP 9
Main sites along the Southern Silk Road.

route was more strenuous because the oases along the route were more widely spaced, but it was more direct and travellers often preferred it because its remoteness meant that there was less likelihood of attack from brigands. Between Dunhuang and Cherchen there were few places to obtain provisions and travellers had to carry their water and food with them. The crossing of the Taklamakan Desert was one of the most dangerous stretches of the Southern Silk Road (see Niya, below).

The lake at Lop Nor, once fed by the Tarim and Kongqu (Peacock) rivers, has a mysterious past. Sven Hedin, Stein and others charted the location of the lake at the beginning of the century and concluded that it was a 'wandering' body of water. More recent Chinese research contradicts this view – the most likely explanation is that the Tarim River has periodically altered its course and formed a new lake. As late as the 1950s Chinese scientists visited the present site and saw a colossal expanse of water from which they were able to catch large fish. By 1973 it was a desiccated salt basin surrounded by marshes, a consequence

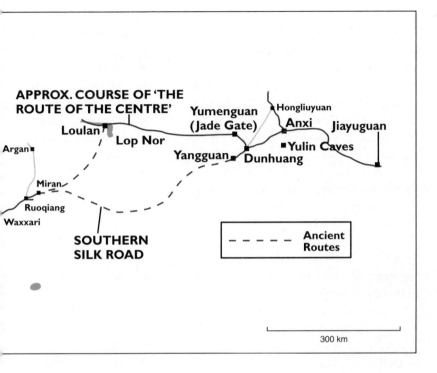

of the Tarim River changing its course in its lower reaches, thereby depriving Lop Nor of its water supply. Lop Nor has always enjoyed a fearsome reputation, a reputation sustained by its current status as China's centre for nuclear testing. West of Lop Nor Lake is Loulan (the Chinese transliteration of 'Kroraina') – a garrison town of the Loulan or Shanshan kingdom, first seen by Hedin in 1900. A shortage of water meant that Hedin was able to make only a cursory examination of the site, but one of his men returned the following day to retrieve a spade and realised its full extent. Hedin returned in 1901 and spent a week exploring but it was not until Stein's visits in 1906 and 1914 that it was examined fully.

Loulan

Loulan marks the eastern edge of the Shanshan kingdom, its capital probably at Miran or possibly Charkhlik (Ruoqiang) – although this is still a matter of debate. The kingdom itself was originally called Loulan and was mentioned in the reports of Emperor Wudi's envoy, Zhang Qian. It was awkwardly placed, trapped between the Xiongnu and the Han, and was subject to a number of bitter power struggles. In 77 BC, a Chinese official assassinated the Loulan king – an appointee of the Xiongnu – during a banquet in his own capital and the kingdom was renamed 'Shanshan'. The king's replacement had been residing as a hostage in the Chinese capital and was sent home to assume the crown. He appears to have been in no doubt about the precariousness of his position:

> For a long time I have been in Han. Now I am returning home deserted and weak at a time when sons of the former king are alive, and I fear that I may be killed by them. There is a town [called] I-hsün ch'eng in the state, whose land is fertile. I would be grateful if Han could send one leader (*chiang*) to set up an agricultural colony there and accumulate a store of field-crops, so that I would be able to rely on the support of Han prestige.
>
> (*Han Shu*, 'History of the Former Han'. Quoted in Rhie, 1999)

The Chinese responded to this request by establishing a post in the Shanshan kingdom, the precise location of which remains unclear. During the Eastern Han dynasty (AD 25–220), the Chinese consolidated their control of the region through the efforts of General Ban Chao. After the death of Ban Chao in 103 the threat to the region from raids by Xiongnu nomads again increased. Ban Chao's son, Ban Yung, the last of the Han generals in Central Asia, responded to the renewed threat by establishing a military post at Loulan in about 124. The post marked the starting point for a third route of the Silk Road. This route was known as the 'Tianshan Nan Lu' ('Road South of the Celestial Mountains'), or the 'Route of the Centre', and ran from Loulan along the course of the Kongqu River through Korla and past Lake Bosten to Yanqi (Karashahr) where it rejoined the Northern Silk Road (see Map 7). The route traverses the desolate wastes of the northern Taklamakan and there is little sign today that there was anywhere en route for travellers to obtain victuals. It appears to have fallen into disuse after Loulan was abandoned sometime during the fourth century, probably because of dwindling water resources.

Stein set off towards Loulan in December 1906, departing from Charkhlik (Ruoqiang) and heading in a north-easterly direction to Loulan. He followed approximately the same route as that followed by

Marco Polo during a harrowing month-long crossing some 650 years earlier. Marco called this part of the eastern Taklamakan the 'Desert of Lop' and describes phantoms who lured men off the paths to their deaths:

> this desert is the abode of many evil spirits, which amuse travellers to their destruction with most extraordinary illusions. If, during the daytime, any persons remain behind on the road [...] they unexpectedly hear themselves called to by their names, and in a tone of voice to which they are accustomed. Supposing the call to proceed from their companions, they are led away by it from the direct road, and not knowing in what direction to advance, are left to perish [...] Marvellous indeed and almost passing belief are the stories related of these spirits of the desert, which are said at times to fill the air with the sounds of all kinds of musical instruments, and also of drums and the clash of arms; obliging the travellers to close their line of march and to proceed in more compact order.
>
> (From *The Travels of Marco Polo the Venetian*.
> Translated by William Marsden, in Polo, 1948)

The monk Xuanzang describes hearing similar voices during his crossing of the Khotan-Niya section of the Taklamakan. Stein's journey was barely less arduous – he carried his water supplies in the form of frozen blocks of ice and was forced to sew pieces of oxhide directly onto the lacerated pads of his camels' feet. Along the route Stein picked up large numbers of Chinese coins, arrowheads and other small objects – the detritus of centuries of travellers. In one such find he discovered a neat line of over 200 Han dynasty copper coins extending about 30 m along the road. Some hapless ancient wayfarer had trudged along Stein's route, centuries before, and had lost them when the string of his purse had come untied.

One of the most important of Stein's discoveries at Loulan was a single bale of yellow silk, 48 cm wide. The discovery of wooden measuring devices and an inscribed fragment of fabric led Stein to conclude that 48 cm was the standard size for the bales of silk that were traded by merchants along the Silk Road. He made further discoveries in an enormous rubbish tip about 30 m across – including wedge-shaped and rectangular documents written on wood; and others on paper and silk in Chinese and in the Kharosthi script of north-west India. A single torn fragment of paper contained writing in Sogdian, the *lingua franca* of Silk Road trade. The documents date from about 260–330 when Loulan and the entire 'Route of the Centre' both appear to have been abandoned. The documents provide an insight into the administration of the Chinese garrison at Loulan and the problems of sustaining it. A number of the documents instruct that food rations to the men of the garrison be reduced. Some reveal the anxieties of men sent to this remote outpost. One letter, presumably never sent, was written by a man named Chao Chi and captures the mood of the place: 'I am living in a far off region and my brothers, sisters and children are all at home. I am afraid the children might not be getting enough to eat.'

Among the larger objects found by Stein at Loulan are wooden architectural fragments, superbly preserved and decorated with Western classical motifs. A Corinthian capital and an Ionic double-bracket capital are among them. Similar fragments were found at Niya, and their existence proves that even remote sections of the Silk Road were susceptible to outside influences. Figural sculpture was also found in and around Loulan – dated to around the third century and comprising Buddha, *bodhisattva* and guardian figures. They draw on elements from both Gandhara and Chinese art to create a uniquely Central Asian style.[9]

Other Sites on the 'Tianshan Nan Lu' or the 'Route of the Centre'

As we have seen, the 'Route of the Centre' followed the course of the Kongqu River through Korla to Yanqi. At Qäwrighul (Gumugou), about 70 km north-west of Loulan, are the remains of an ancient settlement located on the north bank of the river. An ancient necropolis at Qäwrighul was excavated by Chinese archeologists in 1979 and was found to contain several graves enclosed by tight concentric rows of wooden stakes. Excavations of the site have yielded extraordinary human remains, preserved by the region's arid climate. The mummified bodies found at the site are Caucasian in appearance and pose fascinating and as yet unanswered questions as to how they got there. The most famous of all the mummies of Qäwrighul is the 'Beauty of Loulan'. With a height of 152 cm, the woman wore simple clothes of wool and fur, a hat with a goose feather, and fur moccasins. Found with her in the grave were a simple comb, a winnowing tray and a basket containing wheat. Her hair is auburn, parted at the centre, and frames a face that still retains an expression of grace and serenity. She was about 45 years old when she died. Radiocarbon dating of the Qäwrighul graves

Figure 25
Artist's impression of the 'Beauty of Loulan'.

produced the astoundingly early date of around 2,000 BC for some artefacts and an even earlier date for others. If 2,000 BC is accepted as the date for the Qäwrighul mummies it means that they pre-date the similarly Caucasoid, Cherchen mummies of the southern Tarim basin by about 1,000 years; they also precede the arrival of Han Chinese in the region. The second issue is an incredibly important and politically sensitive one. Who these people were and how they came to be living in a remote part of Xinjiang so long before the known beginnings of international travel along the Silk Road has yet to be established. The Beauty of Loulan has become an icon for the Uighur population of Xinjiang – many calling her 'the mother of the nation' – and a local artist has produced a remarkable and credible impression of how she may have appeared (Figure 25).

Continuing westward along the course of the Kongqu River, the 'Route of the Centre' can be made out, even today, by beacon towers that still mark the way. Near the town of Tikanlik are the ruins of Yingpan, a Buddhist settlement of considerable size with the remains of a pagoda still discernible on a northern slope. Yingpan is about 200 km west of Loulan in Yuli county, and recent excavations of the town's

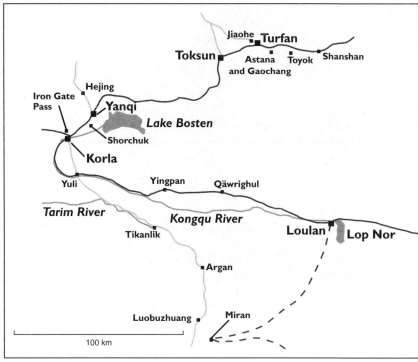

MAP 10
Main sites along the 'Route of the Centre'.

burial grounds have revealed some incredible artefacts. Since 1995, Chinese archeologists have been investigating the tombs and what they have unearthed indicates that Western classical motifs were flowing into the area from the very beginning of the Silk Road's history. Most of the artefacts date to the Han dynasty (206 BC–AD 220) and the Western and Eastern Jin dynasties (265–420). The occupant of Tomb 15 was a fine-looking man of about 30 years old, 1.8 m tall, and dressed in sumptuous silk and woollen garments. A gold leaf mask covers his face and the woollen robe that he wears (in unmistakably Hellenistic style) is covered with yellow designs of paired warriors, animals and trees on a red ground. The robe and the tomb's occupant date to the Han–Jin Dynasties (third century BC to fifth century AD).

A trumpet-shaped Sasanian cup of moulded white glass found at the site testifies to Yingpan's role as a Silk Road entrepôt. Beyond Yingpan,

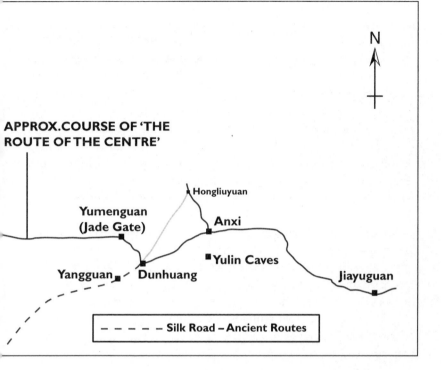

APPROX. COURSE OF 'THE ROUTE OF THE CENTRE'

N

Hongliuyuan

Yumenguan (Jade Gate)

Anxi

Yulin Caves

Yangguan   Dunhuang

Jiayuguan

– – – – – Silk Road – Ancient Routes

however, there are few remains except for the occasional beacon tower, until the northern route is rejoined beyond Korla and Lake Bosten.

★ ★ ★

From Loulan a spur led in a south-westerly direction across the western part of the salt marshes that surrounded Lop Nor. After about 150 km travellers rejoined the Southern Silk Road at Miran, a small remote settlement and one of the jewels of the Silk Road.

Miran

Stein's 1906 discovery of Miran was serendipitous. He had learned of the ruins from his local guide, Tokhta Akhun, and had decided to inspect them en route to his principal objective – the city of Loulan. Stein left Charkhlik (Ruoqiang) in December 1906 en route for Loulan and came upon the ruins about 80 km to the north-east. There was time for no more than a cursory inspection and Stein left the site without realising that he had discovered the most important early Buddhist site in China. He returned the following year and made incredible finds[10] at a site whose art is awash with foreign influences from the Greco-Roman world, Gandhara and India. Mario Bussagli (1963) calls Miran 'an outpost of Gandharan art', and fugitives from the Sasanian invasion of the Kushan Empire during the third century may indeed have populated it. Miran was a fortified town of the Shanshan kingdom – the capital according to some scholars – from the time of the Han dynasty until the fourth century, when it was abandoned. The town's fortunes revived briefly when Tibetans reoccupied it from the eighth to ninth centuries. During the Tibetan occupation a circular fort, still in existence today, was built at Miran – apparently after the rest of the town had been deserted.[11] Stein found mountains of refuse within the fort – much of it of interest only to a scatologist! More than 1,000 documents in Tibetan were also recovered, however, and the dates that they carry suggest that the fort was occupied from about 775–860. Pieces of lacquered leather armour from the Tibetan period are a reminder that the martial function of Miran continued long after its stupas and monasteries had fallen into disuse. During the Tibetan occupation the Tibetans effectively controlled all traffic along the Southern Silk Road, but by this date the 'Route of the Centre' had already ceased to be used – its water sources dried up and the small settlements along its route were progressively abandoned. The northern route was not safe either – its oasis towns were under constant threat from Uighurs and Tibetans – and for a long period China was deprived of a key source of revenue. When the Tibetans were finally expelled from Miran around 860, the desert quickly reclaimed the town's irrigation system and then devoured the town itself. It remained one of the Taklamakan's 'lost cities' until Stein's arrival in 1906.

Miran's apogee occurred around the third to fourth centuries when the town was a flourishing Buddhist and commercial centre. Stein identified 15 buildings including three stupa shrines (M III, M V and M XIV); at least two and possibly three stupas with square bases; several towers and smaller structures; and the Tibetan fort. In Shrines M III and M V, remarkable paintings were discovered that bear witness to the penetration of classical art in a virtually unadulterated form to the remotest regions of Central Asia. The example shown below (Figure 26), and a mural depicting two episodes from the Visvantara-Jataka, have not survived. When Stein returned to Miran in 1914 in the hope of

Figure 26 Mural (no longer extant) depicting a youth in combat with a griffin above a winged angel. Third century. Shrine M V, Miran, Xinjiang province. (After Stein, 1921.)

removing them he discovered that a clumsy attempt by a representative of Baron Otani had destroyed them. We have only Stein's photographs to show how splendid they must have been. Smaller fragments have survived, however, and all but two are now in the National Museum in New Delhi. All of Miran's murals are so similar in style that they must have been painted, if not by the same hand, at least by the same group of artists. A clue is provided by the presence of two Kharosthi inscriptions on the paintings of Shrine M V.

Shrine M V at Miran consisted of a hall and a stupa built of sun dried bricks. The remains of murals were found on the side of the passageway outside the structure's main walls and on the circular passage that surrounded the stupa. The Visvantara-Jataka mural was found on the circular wall and depicts the last of Buddha Sakyamuni's previous incarnations as Prince Visvantara. He is shown leaving the palace with his wife and children and giving away a royal white elephant to a group of brahmins. In the lower section a procession of pensive young men carry a long garland: some dressed in smart tunics and others wearing the Phrygian caps of Asia Minor – motifs found in both classical art and in the art of Gandhara. In the hollows of the garland are figures of the most exquisite beauty in rich colours that can only be imagined from the descriptions left to us by Stein. From the left: a young woman, her hair decorated with white flowers and a crimson cloak trailing across her shoulders, plays a four-stringed lute; a bearded man (perhaps a Parthian) with thick curly hair holds a glass goblet; and a young man, perhaps a Kushan prince, wears a conical cap lined with red and holds an object resembling a pomegranate. A short Kharosthi inscription on the elephant's right thigh reads: 'This fresco is [the work] of Tita, who has received 3,000 Bhammakas [for it].' Stein postulated that Tita was a form of Titus, a Roman name used throughout the Near East. Tita, or Titus, was exceedingly familiar with Western classical motifs and was also skilled in the technique of *chiaroscuro* (treatment of light and shade), used widely in Hellenistic painting and mosaic. Stein (1921) has left us a remarkable description of what kind of person he may have been: 'a sort of Roman Eurasian by blood, brought up in the Hellenistic tradition [...] whom his calling had carried no doubt through the regions of eastern Iran, impregnated with Buddhism, to the confines of China'.

Benjamin Rowland (1938) compares the Miran paintings with the celebrated Romano-Egyptian mummy paintings of Fayum, and the possibility that Tita had been active in both places is an intriguing one.

When Shrine M III was explored by Stein it was found to comprise the remains of a stupa about 2.75 m across and with about 4 m of its original height still remaining. The stupa had been erected within the walls of a rotunda and the surviving wall paintings come mostly from a lower frieze within that part of the structure. A beautiful painting of Buddha and six disciples passing through a forest was removed from M III and now resides in the New Delhi Museum. Both M III and M V had figures of winged male figures akin to Western angels. The 'angels of Miran' are nothing short of amazing and no one was more surprised at their discovery than Stein himself: 'How could I have expected by the desolate shores of Lop-nor, in the very heart of innermost Asia, to come upon such classical representations of cherubim?' (Stein, 1964).

In the outer passage of Shrine M V one of the angels, large-eyed and with a mop of dark curly hair, peers out from beneath a scene of a youth fighting with a griffin. The youth's predicament recalls the tribulations of Herakles (or Hercules) and the Nemean Lion. Stein photographed the painting in 1907 but the original was destroyed during the misguided attempts of Otani's emissary to remove it (Figure 26).

The ruins of a shrine, or *vihara* (a chapel for a sacred image), were excavated in 1907 and again in 1914. Stein designated the site M II and discovered a rectangular platform, measuring 14 x 11 m and with the possible remains of a stupa upon it. The sides of the platform were badly damaged by wind erosion, but on two of them was a series of niches containing the remains of colossal stucco sculptures. Five large, seated figures of Buddha, in the style of Gandhara images of the fourth or fifth century, were among them. A head from the third of the five Buddhas, a full 54 cm in height, was removed by Stein and is now in the British Museum. Other large stucco sculptures, also in Gandhara style, were found when Stein returned to Miran in 1914, at a shrine designated M XV.

This entire section of the Southern Silk Road was brutally difficult for travellers. The route crossed deserts of shifting sands that often obscured the trail, and there was little sustenance to be found. A branch of the road out from Miran turned southwards, over the Kunlun Mountains to Tibet, but the main southern route continued westwards along the foothills of the Altun Mountains to the small town of Charkhlik (Ruoqiang), another caravan centre of the Shanshan kingdom. Chinese historical documents are ambiguous about the location and site of the capital of the Loulan kingdom (i.e. before 77 BC when it was renamed the Shanshan kingdom). The name given in Chinese historical documents was Wu-ni or Chü-mi, and has been pinpointed as either Loulan or Charkhlik. It is therefore possible that Charkhlik was the capital of both the Loulan and, subsequently, the Shanshan kingdom – but the subject is still a matter of dispute. Little else is known about Charkhlik – even the usually reliable observer Xuanzang had little to say when he passed through the town in 644.

The next oasis town, Qiemo (Cherchen) is 340 km to the south-west and sits on the river of the same name. The *Han Shu* ('History of the Former Han') tells us a little about Qiemo:

> Shanshan is situated on the Han communication route; to the west it is connected with Qiemo at a distance of 720 *li* [about 360 km] [...] From Qiemo onwards the states all sow the five crops [rice, two types of millet, wheat and beans].
>
> (*Han Shu* ('History of the Former Han').
> Quoted in Che Muqi, 1989)

Until the 1950s, when the road was built, Qiemo's sole means of contact with the outside world was on camel or donkey. The journey to Korla, a distance of about 800 km, took 40 days. The area is lacerated by sandstorms, known as *karaburans* – sometimes for days at a time. During ancient times Qiemo was a headquarters for the Chinese protector general of the Western Regions; but it was subsequently absorbed into the Shanshan kingdom. In Kharosthi documents found along the Southern Silk Road it is referred to as Calmadana, but few remains have been found other than an ancient stupa.

Marco Polo provides a lucid picture of the knife-edge existence endured by the people of the 'province of Charchan'. He relates that the chief city of the province is 'likewise named Charchan' and passed through a region whose inhabitants were so accustomed to raids by marauding nomads that:

> when they are aware of the approach of any body of troops, they flee, with their families and cattle, into the sandy desert, to the distance of two days' journey, towards some spot where they can find fresh water, and are by that means enabled to subsist.
>
> (From *The Travels of Marco Polo the Venetian*.
> Translated by William Marsden, in Polo, 1948)

The recent discovery of 3,000-year-old mummified remains at the Zhagunluke cemetery near Qiemo has caused great excitement. The mummies, like those of Qäwrighul, appear to be Caucasoid in appearance, suggesting that tribal groups were migrating over vast distances from a very early date (see page 162).

A six-day journey westward from Qiemo, through a region described by Stein as a 'silent uninhabited waste', brought travellers to the town of Endere. This section of the road, Stein observes, is most notable for its infrequent brackish wells, broiling heat and voracious mosquitoes, but there are also patches of vegetation where water from the Kunlun Mountains moistens the parched land. Stein excavated Endere in 1901 and 1906, and discovered a settlement and a large stupa from around the third century and a fort dating to the late seventh or early eighth century. The fort showed signs first of Chinese occupation and then of Tibetan usage – perhaps the result of changing military fortunes. Stein found a small number of Kharosthi documents on wood and leather at Endere, some referring to a place called Saca, which may be the town's ancient name. One of the documents, written in both Kharosthi and Brahmi script, dates to around 230 and is addressed to Vijida Simha, king of Khotan. The use of Brahmi script is fascinating because it gives credence to early accounts that there was a substantial Indian community in Khotan (see the section on Khotan on page 180) and that Indian cultural influence was strong. Stein also found a wooden votive plaque at Endere, painted with a seated figure of the Hindu god Ganesha – additional proof that the area was a willing recipient of motifs from the great country to the south. In the letter to the king of Khotan, he is referred to as *hinajha*, an Iranian title meaning '*generalissimo*'. This suggests that there were also Iranians living in the region.

Niya

> And, little town, thy streets forevermore
> Will silent be; and not a soul to tell
> Why thou art desolate, can e'er return.
> (John Keats, 'Ode on a Grecian Urn')

Niya (referred to as Cadota in a number of documents found at Loulan) is a four-day journey from Endere. It occupies a vast area beside the dried up bed of the Niya River – as much as 30 km north to south and 5 km east to west. To reach it requires a journey by jeep and camel, north from the town of Minfeng (New Niya) across 100 km of lifeless, post-apocalyptic wilderness. During visits in 1901, 1906, 1914 and 1931, Stein unearthed extensive remains at the site, indicating that it was once a major commercial centre on the Southern Silk Road. The town was situated at the western extremity of the Shanshan kingdom, and may even have been one of its capitals. It appears to have been abandoned around 350, perhaps when the Niya River changed course or dried up and deprived the town of its water supply. In contrast to the monasteries and shrines of Miran, most of the buildings are residential. Stein discovered about 40 different buildings at Niya, most built with a strong wooden framework and, in many cases, with adjacent stalls for livestock. The timber frames of many houses are still standing and the withered stumps of ancient orchards still protrude from the sand. Stein's description captures the desolate appearance of the site:

> Like the open sea the expanse of yellow dunes lay before me, with nothing to break their wavy monotony but the bleached trunks of trees or the rows of splintered posts marking houses which rose here and there above the sand crests.
> (Stein, 1912)

Figure 27
Structure
N 3. The
remains
of a large
timber-
framed
building
c. fourth
century.
Niya, north
of Minfeng,
Xinjiang
province.

This building, thought to have contained government offices, is the largest such structure at Niya. The walls are shattered by wind and time but the wooden frame still stands and the remains of wattle walls can still be seen. It was from this structure that Stein unearthed a wooden altar, or table, that now graces the collections of the British Museum.[12] It was also here that, during his last visit in 1914, Stein recovered manuscripts of the type described below.

A single ruined stupa of modest size stands at the centre of the site, to the north of building N 3. It was built of mud-brick before 300 and consists of a cylindrical dome on a square base. The style is similar to many other stupas of the Shanshan kingdom – Endere and Loulan in particular – and also resembles early Gandhara examples. This is not surprising when the large numbers of documents discovered at Niya are examined. They reveal that the majority of foreign travellers passing through Niya, until the time it was abandoned around 350, were Kushans (Yuezhi) from Gandhara, and there appears to have been a community of them residing in the town. The remains of a Buddhist temple were excavated by a Chinese expedition in 1995. The main hall of the temple is about 25 m² and a number of fragmentary wall paintings were recovered.

All over the site there is a pervasive sense, similar to the atmosphere at Pompeii, of time being frozen. An old pond, extinct for almost two millennia, is still hemmed by the dead stumps of fruit trees – planted for shade by the town's occupants. The dwellings at Niya almost all contain the remains of large red terracotta pots and it may be that the inhabitants were forced to use them to store water as the river receded. Fruit stones, wooden implements such as bobbins, and the occasional manuscript still lie scattered about the ruins and archeologists have quite literally only scratched Niya's surface. The buildings visible above the constantly moving sands are widely spaced, sometimes kilometres apart, and there can be little doubt that there are dozens or even hundreds of structures still to be unearthed.

Large numbers of documents were discovered at Niya. During his first visit in 1901, Stein unearthed more than 250 from a rubbish tip attached to dwelling N 5, situated about 3 km north of the stupa. The documents are on sheepskin and wood and written mainly in Chinese and Kharosthi. The wooden examples are of two types – large rectangular documents that tended to involve official and legal issues; and wedge-shaped tablets that were generally concerned with day-to-day matters. The ingenious construction of the square-type ensured that an unauthorised person could not read the contents without either breaking the seal or cutting the strings. Stein found no paper documents at Niya although Chinese researchers discovered a few fragments in 1959. This is significant, given that the site was not abandoned until around the mid-fourth century and paper is thought to have been invented by the court eunuch, Cai Lun, in 105 – more than 200 years earlier. It seems that the new technology was slow to reach these remote parts of Central Asia. Clay seals on the Stein documents show Persian, Indian and classical motifs – themes that are repeated on the wooden architecture of the site. Figures of Athena, Herakles, Zeus, helmeted busts and winged horses are common. The contents of these documents have provided a wealth of information about the social, economic and military life of the Silk Road during the third and fourth centuries. A large number of the Chinese documents are concerned with customs control and with regulating the passage of foreigners (especially Kushans) through Shanshan state. There are also numerous references to other cities in the region – Dunhuang is mentioned frequently and was quite clearly a city of great importance at this time.

Samplings from the Kharosthi documents of Niya and Loulan are a window on the vanished life of the Shanshan kingdom. The following are all from Stein's excavations and are, to borrow a phrase from American poet Archibald MacLeish, 'shard of broken memories':

At present there are no merchants from China, so that the debt of silk is not to be investigated now. As regards the matter of the camel

Tamcina is to be pestered. When the merchants arrive from China, the debt of silk is to be investigated. If there is a dispute, there will be a decision in our presence in the royal court.

(No. 35)

His majesty the king writes, he instructs the *cozbo* [function-ary] [...] as follows: [...] Liýipeya reports that they took out three witch-women. They killed only the woman belonging to him, the remaining women they released. About this matter you received a command from Apgeya that recompense was to be made to Liýipeya for this woman.

(No. 63)

His majesty, etc. [...] Lýimsu informs us that a female camel belongs to them and Simasriae in common. A man called Sugika and her daughter Smagasae rode off on this camel from Simasriae's farm and fled away. He and his father went after them with the frontier guards and brought this camel back. [As a result] two parts of this camel belonged to these two, the father and son, and two parts to the guards [for their services].

(No. 71)

His majesty, etc. [...] Liýipeya informs us that he has a slave called Kacana. Sagana beat him. As a result of that beating the man Kacana died on the eighth day. Here you, the *cozbo* Somjaka received an oral command that the witnesses had to swear an oath and if Kacana had died as a result of Sagana's beating, a man was to be awarded as recompense.

(No. 144)

Concerning the son of Tsina, a novice, and an adopted child, to be carefully preserved by Simema [...] In the 7th year of his majesty Citughi Mahiriya, the son of heaven, in the 3rd month, 5th day, at this date. When the Khotanese plundered the kingdom of Cadota [Niya], at that time three young men of Khotan carried off the woman Tsinae. They came and gave her as a present to the mother of *cozbo* [functionary] Somjaka in the house of the *kitsayitsa* Luthu. They gave that woman Tsinae along with her sons and daughters [...] That woman Tsina[e] gave her son, a novice, five *distis* high, as an adopted child to the man Kacana. As milk payment a *vito* horse was given. This transaction was made in the presence of the *cozbo* Somjaka.

(No. 415)

In the 10th year of his majesty the great king, Jitugha Mahagiri, son of heaven, in the 12th month, 10th day [...] the community of monks in the capital laid down regulations for the community of monks in Cadota [Niya]. It is heard that the novices do not pay attention to an elder, they disobey the old monks. Concerning this these regulations have been laid down by his majesty in front of the order of monks [...] Whichever monk does not partake in the activities of the community of monks shall pay a fine of one roll of silk [...] Whichever monk strikes another monk, [in the case of] a light [blow the fine is] five rolls of silk, [in the case of] a moderate [blow] ten rolls of silk, [in the case of] an excessive [blow] fifteen rolls of silk.

(No. 489)

His majesty, etc. [...] Sagamovi complains to this effect. He is a native of Yave Avana. There is a potter (*kulala*) called Camca and this Sagamovi is his son. A member of the *kilme* [district] of the *ogu* [administrative officer] Asoka, he used to dwell when young next door to Cato. At that time Cato took to wife the daughter of the *sramana* Sundara, called Supriya. After that this Sagamovi and Supriya[e] fled from the house of Cato to the kingdom of Kuci [presumably Kuqa]. They stayed a long time in the kingdom of Kuci. Then they came back to their own country through the influence of me the great king. [...] Whatever this Sagamovi had in the way of wives, sons, daughters, and slaves, this Sagamovi abandoned all claim to them. Now the *sramana* Sundara and Lýipana are causing trouble in Yave Avana about the woman Supriya[e]. They are demanding a ransom (*lode*). When this sealed wedge-tablet reaches you, forthwith careful inquiry is to be made, whether it is true that the *sramana* Sundara and Lýipana are causing trouble to this Sagamovi about a ransom for Supriya[e]. They are to be stopped. They are not to make claims to Supriya[e] against Sagamovi.

(No. 621)

(All the above documents are abridged from
Burrow, 1940. For more examples of manuscripts from
Niya and Loulan, see pp. 133–68, in Whitfield, 2004a)

Such documents continue to be found in the area. One example, written in Kharosthi and unearthed in 1981, provides a clue to the reasons for Niya's abandonment. It is dated to around the middle of the fourth century, a time when the town's water supply was apparently becoming erratic: 'At the time when the river water dried up, Kampila abandoned his wife Ui' (Quoted in Rhie, 1999).

Another recently discovered document from the area refers to a transaction involving a slave. The currency involved, a camel, appears to have been one of the units of choice at the time – camels, bolts of silk and lengths of carpet are mentioned in this regard again and again (Figure 28).

A group of 40 documents were discovered about 2 km north of old Niya in 1959, as well as two grave sites. One of the tombs contained the remains of a man and a woman and yielded a beautiful group of textiles, including a brocade in the shape of a rooster and what is thought to be one of the earliest examples of Batik. The Batik – a wax-resist dyed cotton – is in dark indigo blue and contains designs of a goddess holding a cornucopia ('horn of plenty') and the remains of what appears to have been a Herakles figure with a lion. The richness of the textiles found at Niya demonstrate that the town was a flourishing centre for trade and also show, once again, that motifs from the classical world penetrated to the furthest extremities of Chinese Central Asia.

As we have mentioned, the classical themes of the clay document seals are repeated on Niya's wooden architecture. The absence of moisture in the region has meant that many wooden objects have survived and they bear a strong resemblance to the architecture of Loulan. Pillars with acanthus decoration, Corinthian capitals, amazing griffin-like creatures and the *purnaghata* ('vase of plenty') are all found. Most splendid of all is a table or altar, found by Stein during his 1901 visit and originally identified by him as a chair. This piece of furniture, made of carved poplar and dating to the first to fourth century AD, is probably a table or altar. Unearthed in 1901 from Structure N 3 at Niya, it is decorated with lotus flower motifs, which suggest that it had some sort of ritual function in Buddhism. Items of furniture from such an early date are extraordinarily rare.

Beginning in 1988, a series of Sino-Japanese expeditions have visited Niya and made new discoveries about the town and its inhabitants. The culmination of this work was the discovery, in 1995, of a necropolis serving the town's rulers. Artefacts found in the graves included shells, coral and glass from the countries to the west, and fine silks imported from metropolitan China. One silk fragment, unearthed from Tomb

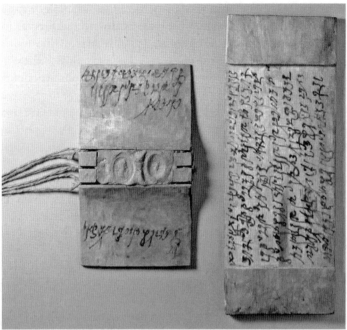

Figure 28
Wooden tablet
written in
Kharosthi.
Third to fourth
century.
Length 26.7 cm,
width 10.2 cm.
Probably from
the vicinity of
Niya, Xinjiang
province.

Two clay seals on the upper section are both in classical style – the left one depicting a king and the right one a winged horse. As far as the content is concerned, the upper section (the cover tablet) is addressed to a monk called Sronasena and states that the document concerns a woman named Ramasria from the Catisa Devi estate. The inscription below the seals on the cover identifies them as the seals of the ogu (administrative officer) Pideyalya and the cozbo (functionary) Punasena. The main inscription on the inside is dated as Year 2 of King Vasmana (around 315) and concerns a woman named Sacgia, the slave of Ramasria who is the sister of the monk Sronasena. The document requests that Sacgia be sent to work on the Catisa estate and that payment for her services will be a four-year old camel, given by Ramasria to Sronasena. The last two lines record the name and titles of the witness and the scribe, Nandasena. Some of the names contained in this document also occur in the Stein documents translated by Burrow (see Burrow, 1940).

3 and dating to the seconnd or third century AD, is inscribed with the phrase 'marriage of the families of the King and Marquis' (*wang hou he hun*). The inscription suggests that strategic marriages were commonplace between the rulers of the Silk Road city states of the Western Regions at this time, and recalls the alliances between the Han and the Xiongnu.

The Chinese monk Fa Xian, who travelled to India between 399–414, visited Shanshan in 399, travelling for 17 days across the desert from Dunhuang. The journey was not a pleasant one:

In the river of sand, there are evil demons in great number and winds so scorching that, when you meet them, all die and not one escapes. Above, no bird flies; below, no beast walks. In whatever direction you look, and as far as you can see, when you seek to know where you must go, you are unable to decide. There are only the relics of the dead to serve as guide.

(Fa Xian. Quoted in Drège and Bührer, 1989)

If the evidence of documents is anything to go by both Niya and Loulan were already abandoned by the time of Fa Xian's visit. It is therefore unclear which towns he is referring to when he describes a kingdom that is ardently Buddhist and is home to more than 4,000 monks following the Hinayana doctrine and using Indian texts.

The Niya–Khotan Section

The road between Niya and Khotan was no more merciful to travellers. Xuanzang travelled the road in the opposite direction in 644 and describes a particularly treacherous expanse of the Taklamakan in which the drifting sands and sandstorms, known as *karaburans*, claimed the lives of innumerable travellers, and sirens lured men to their doom:

There is neither water nor herbage to be found, and hot winds frequently blow. When these winds rise, then both men and beasts become confused and forgetful [...] At times sad and plaintive notes are heard and piteous cries, so that between the sights and sounds of this desert men get confused and know not whither they go. Hence there are so many who perish in the journey. But it is all the work of demons and evil spirits.

(Xuanzang, 1884)

Four days west of Niya, on the Khotan road is Keriya (Yutian), once an important oasis town on the Southern Silk Road and surrounded by the semi-obliterated remains of shrines and settlements. Sites around Keriya, all explored by Stein, include Khadalik, Farhad-beg-yailaki and Darabzan-dong – all apparently abandoned around the end of the eighth century, presumably when water supplies were exhausted. Indian influence was also evident here – at Khadalik Stein found the remains of wall paintings from about the sixth century containing images of Buddha and of Ganesha (the elephant-headed son of the

Hindu god, Siva) holding a basket of his favourite sweetmeats. The area is still yielding its secrets and it seems that many more towns along the old Silk Road are still buried beneath the sands of the Taklamakan. One such place is Kara-dong, about 190 km north of Keriya and visited by both Hedin and Stein. Stein believed Kara-dong to be a stopping place on an ancient communication route that once followed the course of the Keriya River in a north–south direction. The Keriya appears to have once flowed as far as the Tarim River, and the old trail appears to have followed its course until it joined up with the 'Tianshan Nan Lu' or the 'Route of the Centre', thereby creating a more direct route between Khotan and Kuqa. In 1993 a Sino-French expedition found the remains of a large temple and what appears to be a stupa-mound. The site appears to have been occupied from about the second to the fourth century and the delicate paintings of Buddhas discovered on the temple walls are therefore, along with those of Miran, among the earliest in Central Asia.

Stein explored the oasis town of Domoko, just to the north-west of Keriya (Yutian), during his first expedition (1900–1) and attempted to identify the location of the town of 'Pi-mo'. Pi-mo is described at length by Xuanzang and was the site of miraculous events. In Xuanzang's day a sandalwood figure of the Buddha stood in the city, some 6 m high and said to date back to the time of Sakyamuni himself. It emitted a constant bright light and possessed the ability to cure diseases and grant wishes. After the Buddha's departure from the world the statue was said to have ascended into the skies and flown north where it alighted in the town of Ho-lo-lo-kia. The residents of the town were atheistic and paid no respect to the statue. An *arhat* (a monk who has attained enlightenment) arrived in the town and warned the residents that, seven days hence, the city would be destroyed by a deluge of sand and earth. His warnings were ignored and, on the evening of the seventh day, the city was obliterated. The only survivor was the *arhat*, who escaped through a tunnel. Xuanzang relates that the town of Ho-lo-lo-kia is now no more than a great sand-mound, and Stein set out to find it. About 50 km west of Keriya, Stein came across a ruined town to which the locals had attached a legend – almost identical to the one attributed to Ho-lo-lo-kia. Further research at the site convinced Stein that he had discovered not Ho-lo-lo-kia but Pi-mo, the earlier home of the statue and the place where Xuanzang had heard the legend. Pi-mo was still occupied when Marco Polo – who called the town 'Pein' – passed through during the thirteenth century.

Khotan

The Khotan–Kashgar section of the Southern Silk Road skirts the lower margins of the Taklamakan. Khotan (known as Yutian or Hetian in Chinese, and Kustana in Sanskrit) was perhaps the greatest of the kingdoms of the Southern Silk Road.[13] The town of Khotan, and the kingdom of the same name, were famous for nephrite jade – both supplied China for at least 2,000 years. The town is situated between two rivers – the Karakash ('Black Jade River') and the Kurungkash ('White Jade River') – and boulders are washed down from the Kunlun Mountains to the south and harvested from the riverbeds. Khotan was once a source of both dark green and white jade, but only a relatively small amount of the latter is still obtained from the bed of the Kurungkash River. The travels of the legendary Emperor Mu during the third century BC took him as far as the Kunlun Mountains and, as early as the Western Han dynasty, there are references to Khotan as a source of jade. Sima Qian's annals, 'Records of the Grand Historian' (*Shi Ji*, 1993) relate that:

> The emperor [Wudi] also sent envoys to trace the Yellow River to its source. They found that it rises in the land of Yutian among mountains rich in precious stones, many of which they brought back with them. The emperor studied the old maps and books and decided to name these mountains, where the Yellow River has its source, the Kunlun Mountains.

The Tang annals (*Xin Tang Shu*) refer to the ease with which precious jade could be gathered during ancient times: 'There is a jade river in Yutian State. People find exquisite jade in the river whenever the moon shines the brightest.'

Legends about the founding of Khotan, gleaned from both Tibetan sources and in the accounts of Chinese pilgrims, relate that the city was founded by a group of Indian nobles from Taxila – banished from the court of Ashoka during the third century BC for blinding Kunala, the great king's son. Ashoka was known to have been an ardent Buddhist, suggesting that Khotan may have been one of the first kingdoms of the Tarim basin to adopt the new religion. The kingdom fell to the Chinese around the first century BC and was the headquarters of General Ban Chao between AD 77–91, but it continued to prosper as a centre for trade and for the study and practice of Hinayana, and later Mahayana Buddhism.

Yotkan, situated about 10 km west of Khotan, is thought to have been the ancient capital of the Khotan kingdom. Stein explored many sites – too many to mention here – in and around Khotan during all three of his expeditions. His discoveries at Yotkan concur with early Chinese records, which state that the town was a thriving commercial and religious centre.[14] There were no surviving structures at Yotkan – it has been submerged beneath paddy fields – but local treasure seekers have dug down to a depth of about 5 m, revealing strata containing pottery fragments, terracotta figures, jade, seals, coins and manuscripts. The coins found by Stein at Yotkan fall into two broad types – copper examples from the first or second century AD, and square-holed examples from the Tang dynasty (618–907). The earlier coins bear legends in both Chinese and Kharosthi, evidence that there was already a substantial Indian community in Khotan during the time of the Han dynasty, and that it coexisted with the Chinese settlers in the area. He also found extensive traces of gold leaf, suggesting that the faithful applied the precious material to buildings and images during worship. This is borne out by the observations of the monk Fa Xian, a visitor to the kingdom in 401:

Seven or eight *le* (*li*) to the west of the city there is what is called the King's New Monastery, the building of which took eighty years, and extended over three reigns. It may be 250 cubits in height, rich in elegant carving and inlaid work, covered with gold and silver, and finished throughout with a combination of all the precious substances.

(Fa Xian, in Fâ-Hien, 1886)

By the time of Fa Xian's visit, the kingdom was firmly dominated by the Mahayanists. He tells us that the kingdom had four great monasteries (or 14, depending on the translation) and many smaller ones. The greatest of them was the Gomati Monastery – its patron the king himself – and Fa Xian describes a procession in which a large image of the Buddha flanked by two *bodhisattvas* is carried on an immense four-wheeled carriage from the monastery to the city gates. Upon arrival at the gates, the king of Khotan and his entourage would dress in simple clothes to greet the procession and pay homage by scattering flowers and burning incense.

Khotan's prosperity also depended on sericulture and on the production of fine carpets. Khotan carpets are referred to in many of the Kharosthi documents unearthed by Stein at Loulan and Niya, and appear to have been a popular barter commodity. According to the Tibetan annals, sericulture reached Khotan around the second century AD, during the reign of King Vijaya Jaya. The Chinese jealously guarded the secret of silk production and it was not until King Vijaya Jaya married a Chinese princess that the Khotanese acquired the technology to produce it. The story of the Silk Princess is told on a finely painted wood panel from around the sixth century, 46 cm in length and now housed in the British Museum.

Dandan-Oilik

The Silk Princess panel was recovered by Stein at the monastery complex of Dandan-Oilik, on the eastern edge of the Khotan oasis.[15] Dandan-Oilik (in Uighur, 'the place of houses with ivory') is located to the north of the Southern Silk Road and, based on information gleaned from coins and documents, the town appears to have flourished from the fourth to the eighth century. It was abandoned towards the end of the eighth century – a consequence of invasions by Tibetans – and was quickly inundated by the sands of the Taklamakan. On the panel, an attendant on the left points to the cocoons concealed in the princess's headdress and on the far right a lady holds a beating comb and sits before a loom. To her right sits a four-armed deity – perhaps the god of silk weaving. Xuanzang recounts the legend, current at the time of his visit in 644, about the Silk Princess and her role in the introduction of sericulture[16] to Khotan:

In old time this country knew nothing about mulberry trees or silkworms. Hearing that the eastern country [i.e. China] had them, they sent an embassy to seek for them. At this time the prince of the eastern kingdom kept the secret and would not give the possession of it to any. He kept guard over his territory and would not permit either the seeds of the mulberry or the silkworms' eggs to be carried off.

The king of Kustana [Khotan] sent off to seek a marriage union with a princess of the eastern kingdom [China], in token of his allegiance and submission. The king being well affected to the neighbouring states acceded to his wish. Then the king of Kustana dispatched a messenger to escort the royal princess and gave the following direction: 'Speak thus to the eastern princess, – Our country has neither silk or silken stuffs. You had better bring with you some mulberry seeds and silkworms, then you can make robes for yourself.'

The princess, hearing these words, secretly procured the seed of the mulberry and silkworms' eggs and concealed them in her head-dress. Having arrived at the barrier, the guard searched every-where, but he did not dare to remove the princess's head-dress. Arriving then in the kingdom of Kustana […] they conducted her in great pomp to the royal palace. Here then they left the silkworms and the mulberry seeds. In the spring-time they set the seeds, and when the time for the silkworms had come they gathered leaves for their food; but from their first arrival it was necessary to feed them on different kinds of leaves, but afterwards the mulberry trees began to flourish. Then the queen wrote on a stone the following decree: It is not permitted to kill the silkworm! After the butterfly [silk-moth] has gone then the silk may be twined off [the cocoon]. Whoever offends against this rule may he be deprived of divine protection.

(Xuanzang, 1884)

This story has an interesting and important counterpart in the annals of the eastern Roman Empire. Around 550, a group of monks arrived in the capital, Byzantium, and presented themselves at the court of the Emperor Justinian. They claimed to know the secret of sericulture and offered to bring silkworm eggs to Byzantium. According to one version, that of Procopius, the monks came from 'Serindia' – they may have been Nestorians from Khotan – and Justinian offered to reward them if they could supply the eggs. The monks returned two years later with eggs concealed in their staffs and Byzantium thus acquired the process of silk production.

Other painted wood panels from Dandan-Oilik (also dated to around the sixth century) contain depictions of the Hindu gods Indra and Brahma, and a pair of aristocratic figures of Turkish appearance on camel- and horse-back, carrying libation cups. A further panel contains a beautiful image of Siva seated above two white Nandi bulls on one side and, on the reverse, a bearded figure of Iranian appearance: identified as the God of Silk. The bearded figure on this panel wears a gold crown and is dressed in princely robes. He holds the same objects as the four-armed figure in the Silk Princess panel – namely a goblet, a weaver's comb and a shuttle for a loom.

Khotan is awash with legends like these, and one of the most interesting is the story of the rat-king, represented in another of the British Museum's painted panels from Dandan-Oilik. Xuanzang described a number of small hills to the west of Khotan, which the local people believed were built by a tribe of sacred rats. The legend relates that the king of Khotan was able to fight off an attack by the Xiongnu when the rats consumed the invaders' bowstrings and harnesses. A shrine was erected by the Khotanese to the west of the capital and the rats were worshipped as saviours of the kingdom.

The excellence of Dandan-Oilik's paintings reflects the great skill of the artists of Khotan. A number of Khotanese painters were active in China during the Sui and early Tang dynasties; two of the most distinguished were Weichi Boqina and his son, Weichi Yiseng – members of the Khotan royal family. They specialised in a 'relief' style of painting in which layers of paint were built up on silk until the portrait or subject emerged. Khotanese artists are also recorded as having worked at the Tibetan court during the ninth century, and strongly influenced the development of Tibetan art.

Stein discovered large numbers of stucco images at Dandan-Oilik – seated and standing Buddhas as well as *Gandharvas* (celestial deities, sometimes known as musicians of the gods). These images were produced in moulds and were then fastened to the walls of approximately ten shrines or monasteries identified at the site. They are closely linked to the Greco-Buddhist art of Gandhara, a consequence of the spread of Buddhism along the Silk Road. A pair of large bronze Buddha heads, as well as two moulded clay figures of Harpocrates (the Egyptian god of silence) and a chubby baby Herakles (Hercules) – all found at Yotkan by the Otani Mission of 1910 – are further proof that East–West trade was thriving. The two Buddha heads date to around the third century and may well be the oldest Buddhist sculptures in eastern Central Asia.

Other motifs from the classical world are found on the remains of a pair of trousers from the Shanpula cemetery in Luopu county, about 20 km south-east of Khotan. Shanpula occupies an area of about 20 hectares and contains hundreds of graves dating from the Han dynasty onwards (Figure 29).

Cultural relics recovered from the Shanpula site have revealed much about the cultural and commercial activity of the Silk Road (Figure 30).

Chinese authority was reasserted over the whole of the Tarim basin during the seventh century, and Khotan became one of the key

Figure 29
The Shanpula cemetery,
Luopu county, near Khotan,
Xinjiang province.

garrisons of the Western Regions. Even after Chinese power declined during the eighth century the kingdom continued to be an important commercial centre. A celebrated portrait of the king of Khotan in Cave 98 at Dunhuang, painted around 920, reveals something of the enduring prosperity of the kingdom. His bride, a daughter of the Cao rulers of Dunhuang, wears a crown and necklace of Khotan jade. As late as the thirteenth century, when Marco Polo visited, the inhabitants of Khotan had converted to Islam but trade continued to flourish and the state was still sending embassies to China during the Ming dynasty (1368–1644).

Rawak ('High Mansion'), north-east of Khotan is believed to be one of the largest and most important sites in Central Asia, despite the fact that only the stupa is visible above the sands of the Taklamakan. The stupa at Rawak, about 9.5 m in extant height, is the largest on the Southern Silk Road. Stein discovered the site in April 1901 and worked for eight days in scorching heat and raking sandstorms. He uncovered about 90 sculptures adorning both sides of the walls of the stupa-court – the site and its statuary dating to around the fourth to sixth centuries.

Figure 30
Remains
of a pair
of trousers
with the
design of a
centaur and
a warrior.
Han
dynasty,
c. first
century AD.
Length
116 cm.

Unearthed from Tomb 1 at Shanpula, Luopu county, Xinjiang province, in 1984. This textile fragment is unique among all of the archeological finds of China. The left section depicts a centaur blowing a long horn as his cape billows behind him. The right section shows a warrior of distinctly non-Chinese appearance wearing a colourful tunic and carrying a spear. Its singular design raises intriguing questions about how it arrived at the site. Luopu was a prosperous centre for iron smelting during the Han dynasty and would therefore have attracted foreign visitors in large numbers. The fragment may therefore have been imported from Parthian Iran or western Central Asia, or it may have belonged to some Indo-European migrant who settled in the area during ancient times. We already have evidence that there were Iranians in the Tarim basin area from the contents of the letter to the king of Khotan found at Endere. The motifs on this textile fragment are therefore not entirely surprising. But they are a further sign of the high level of commercial and religious activity that was occurring along this section of the Silk Road.

The base of the stupa consists of a cross-shaped platform with a staircase at each end, a more refined version of the type found in the Gandhara region. The sculptures unearthed by Stein – and those discovered by later Japanese and German expeditions – were mostly life-sized painted stucco images of standing Buddhas, carved in relief, but four guardian figures (*lokapalas*) and a number of exquisitely jewelled *bodhisattvas* were also found. The earliest are strongly reminiscent of Gandhara sculptures, most notably those of the Jaulian Monastery at Taxila (see page 212). They date to around the fourth century, or even, perhaps, a little earlier. Later images, perhaps fifth century in date, are smaller in size and are more closely related to the styles of early Chinese Buddhist art – such as that at Binglingsi, for example (see page 93). Whether Rawak served as a prototype for the early Buddhist art of China, or

Figure 31
Photograph
of painted
stucco
sculptures
of standing
and seated
Buddhas
c. fourth
century.
From
the south
corner of
the Rawak
stupa-court,
Xinjiang
province.
Photograph
by Stein.
(Stein,
1907.)

Visible above and to the right of the seated Buddha is a rare example of painting from Rawak, a depiction of a standing Buddha. The sculptures shown in this photograph have fared badly since Stein's visit. Local authorities removed the sand covering them and they were left exposed for a time. They were then subjected to vandalism and what remained was eventually reburied.

whether it acquired the styles developed there is unclear. The relief sculptures of Rawak were too brittle for Stein to recover intact and were therefore measured, photographed and then recovered with sand. Most examples of Rawak sculpture in Western museums are therefore little more than fragments; Stein's photographs of the sculptures still in situ are far more impressive (Figure 31).

Most of the ruins around Khotan are in poor condition. This is most likely a consequence of the fact that the area fell to the Muslim Karakhanid Turks during the tenth century. The destruction of Buddhist sites that we saw at Kashgar occurred here as well. Given the turbulent history of the region it is miraculous that any artefacts have survived at all.

In early Chinese records, Karghalik (Yecheng) is referred to, first as Tzu-ho and, subsequently, as Chu-chü-po. The town sits on a fertile oasis between Khotan and Yarkand.

The area west of Khotan is now a fertile and populous hinterland, thanks to modern irrigation methods, but during the heyday of the Silk Road it was a different and far more hostile environment. The city of Yarkand (Shache) sits on the Yarkand River and was capital of the kingdom of the same name. By 100 BC it was firmly under Chinese control and became one of the 36 states of the Western Regions. Yarkand flourished as a result of its position at a junction of the caravan routes that led west to Central Asia and south over the Pamirs to Ladakh and on to India. During the Wang Mang interregnum (AD 9–23) China lost control of many of these states and Yarkand seized the opportunity to increase its power. For a brief period, from about AD 33–61, it was the most powerful kingdom of the Western Regions, dominating Khotan, Shanshan and Kuqa. Its power did not last, however, and Khotan soon reasserted control over the area. For a brief period, from about AD 63–73, the Southern Silk Road was dominated by the kingdoms of Khotan and Shanshan. By AD 94, the redoubtable General Ban Chao had seized control of the entire Tarim basin, defeated the Xiongnu, and placed the region firmly under Chinese suzerainty. Yarkand continued to prosper, however. From about the sixth century AD the kingdom became a centre for silk production to rival Khotan, and the town became as rich as Kashgar.

CHAPTER SEVEN
The Silk Road Between China and India Including the Karakorum Highway

Beyond Yarkand, the Southern Silk Road runs north-west along the southern fringes of the Taklamakan, through Yengisar to Kashgar. At Kashgar, the circle is completed and the Northern and Southern Silk Roads merge. From Kashgar begins the long road to India, the ancient route of devotees, traders and conquerors. The modern road – retracing the old highway – rises from the Kashgar plain towards the Pakistani border. It passes through the eastern Pamirs, soon joining and following the course of the Ghez River. At the top of the Ghez Canyon the landscape opens out into a vast plain surrounded by sand dunes. The landscape is bleak and forbidding, a foretaste of what awaited travellers through the high passes to India.

Marco Polo journeyed through the high plains of the Pamirs during the thirteenth century, and he describes a barren landscape, devoid of pasturage and food supplies and occupied by 'a tribe of savage, ill-disposed, and idolatrous people' who lived by hunting. Towering above the road are the massive peaks of the Pamirs – Mount Kongur and Mount Muztagh Ata both exceeding 7,500 m. The lake at Kara Kul, surrounded by verdant pasturelands, offers a brief respite but its elevation is so great – around 3,800 m – that it has been known to freeze even in mid-summer. Further on, the road comes to the small town of Tashkurgan, 3,600 m above sea level and almost 300 km from Kashgar.

MAP 11
The Silk Road between China and India.

Tashkurgan

Tashkurgan ('Stone Tower') was the capital of the Pamir kingdom of Sarikol. The 'Stone Tower' is mentioned in many early chronicles, in particular those of the Alexandrian geographer Ptolemy. Writing in about 140, Ptolemy obtained his information from the reports of a Macedonian Greek merchant named Maes Titianus, active about 50 years earlier. Maes did not make the journey himself but employed a network of agents to reconnoitre a new route between the Mediterranean and China. The intention was to bypass the Parthian merchants of Persia, intermediaries in the lucrative early trade of the Silk Road. Ptolemy utilised the information contained in Maes Titianus' reports, as well as that gleaned from contemporary travellers, and estimated that the distance between Hierapolis (Membij) in Syria and Sera Metropolis (presumably Xian, and referred to as the place where foreign merchants obtained their silk) was about 11,000 km. He records that the halfway point on the journey, and therefore the point midway between China and the West, was the 'Stone Tower'. In fact, a number of Central Asian cities – Tashkent for example – have names which approximate to the 'tower of stone' or 'stone castle', but the most likely location was Tashkurgan on the eastern edge of the Pamirs. Ptolemy also tells us that the journey from the 'Stone Tower' to Sera Metropolis took seven months.

At the time of Xuanzang's visit in 644, the town and state were called 'Qiepantuo' (Persian for 'Mountain Road') and the region was populated by followers of the Buddha. The kingdom seems to have flourished between the fifth and eighth centuries, when it submitted to Tibetan control and, during the latter part of the Tang dynasty, the town was a Chinese military outpost. Xuanzang was impressed with the king, a man he describes as 'upright and honest [...] his external manner is quiet and unassuming; he is of a vigorous mind and loves learning'. He was less impressed with the populace. He describes them as 'without any rules or propriety [...] Their appearance is common and revolting'. The rulers of the Qiepantuo kingdom believed themselves to be descended maternally from the Han Chinese and paternally from the sun god. Xuanzang records a local legend from the time before the founding of the kingdom, when Tashkurgan was a desert valley in the Pamirs. A king of Persia had taken a Han Chinese princess as his bride and had sent an escort to accompany her to his domain. When the party reached Tashkurgan they were prevented from proceeding further by the presence of brigands. The princess was placed on an isolated mountain peak and guarded day and night. When order was restored to the area the party was about to proceed when they discovered that the princess was with child. The officials escorting her to Persia, fearing the wrath of the king, were panic-stricken, but were told by her servant that she had been visited by a god of the sun each day at noon and it was he who was father of the child she carried. Afraid to return to Persia, the party built a palace on top of a nearby mountain from which the princess ruled the area. At length, she bore a son 'of extraordinary beauty and perfect parts [...] able to fly through the air and control the winds and snow'. He came to rule the entire region and even after his death he continued to perform miraculous deeds. He died at a great age and was interred in a great mountain cave about 45 km south-east of Tashkurgan. His remains were seen by Xuanzang and had not decomposed – it appeared as if he were only sleeping. From time to time the people of the kingdom would change his clothes and place incense and flowers at his side. There is still a citadel at Tashkurgan – built of rammed earth and, according to local legend, the old abode of the Han princess. The deserted, silent, 'Princess Castle' is saturated with atmosphere and mystery and there are traces of more ancient remains at the site. But archeological evidence suggests that the date of the present structure is no earlier than the Yuan dynasty (1279–1368).

On the Kashgar side of Tashkurgan is the Tangitar Gorge, identified by Sir Marc Aurel Stein as the place where Xuanzang was set upon by bandits. In the ensuing mêlée Xuanzang's magnificent white elephant, presented to him by the Indian king, Harsha, to carry him and his precious Buddhist relics back to China, was drowned.

To the south of Tashkurgan the modern road follows the approximate course of the old Silk Road. After about 30 km the road divides into two – one route passing into Pakistan between the Pamirs and the Karakorums through the 4,730 m Khunjerab Pass, the other following the Wakhan corridor to Afghanistan. The first route is known today as the Karakorum Highway and is the highest public road in the world. It first follows the course of the Khunjerab and Hunza rivers and finally, south of Gilgit, the great Indus – the 'Father of Rivers'. The highway, known by its familiar title 'the KKH', sticks to the Indus valley right down as far as Thakot, south of Besham, and then makes a gentle descent to the upland plateau of modern day Islamabad. A short distance to the west of Islamabad is the ancient Kushan capital of Taxila, the point from which Buddhism began its spread into China. The route of the KKH therefore approximates one of the two principal 'pilgrim roads' between India and China, although there were many other subsidiary paths across the mountains. The second route, also terminating in Taxila, passed along the Wakhan corridor to Balkh in the ancient Greek kingdom of Bactria, and then turned south to cross the Hindu Kush. It then passed through Bamiyan and continued down through the Khyber Pass into what is now modern Pakistan.

The journeys of two of history's most celebrated Buddhist monks – Fa Xian in about 400, and Sung Yun around 520 – approximately followed the first route. Sung Yun was a monk from Dunhuang who was sent by the Northern Wei rulers of China as an ambassador to the king of the Hepthalites – rulers of north-west India at that time – to obtain Buddhist sutras. The indomitable Xuanzang favoured the second route when he made his way back to China from India in 644. All three record that mischievous dragons and evil spirits populated the mountains between China and India – it seems that the fears of travellers who attempted to cross the mountains engendered these stories. Xuanzang has left us with a particularly colourful description of such creatures. As he headed from Peshawar towards Taxila on his way to India, instead of keeping to the course of today's Grand Trunk Road – the most direct route, even in antiquity – he veered off north to explore the Buner and Swat valleys (the latter known by its ancient name, Uddiyana). At Attock, south of Hund, he crossed the Indus to rejoin the old highway:

> Its waters are pure and clear as a mirror as they roll along with impetuous flow. Poisonous *Nâgas* [water spirits] and hurtful beasts occupy the caverns and clefts along its sides. If a man tries to cross the river carrying with him valuable goods or gems or rare kinds of flowers or fruits, or especially relics of the Buddha, the boat is frequently engulphed by the waves.
>
> (Xuanzang, 1884)

The Karakorum ('Black Mountain') route, as we have seen, passes through the Khunjerab Pass. The Tajik name Khunjerab means 'blood valley', perhaps a reference to the bandits from Hunza and Wakhi who continued to prey on caravans heading to and from Kashgar right up to the end of the nineteenth century. The vistas of the route through the Karakorums must have terrified early travellers. The road passes through a treeless alpine wilderness with little shelter from the brutal weather and few opportunities for travellers to obtain supplies. The only sign of life is the occasional wild yak and the odd glimpse of the rare and elusive Marco Polo sheep. During its passage along the course of the Hunza River the road passes through the Gojal region, a high plateau ravaged by floods, rock and mudslides. Near Passu, the majestic Batura Glacier, 60 km in length, nudges the edge of the highway. The glacier is in a constant state of advance and retreat and, as recently as 1976, it devoured both the road and the bridge that carried the road over the river. Further on is the white expanse of the Passu Glacier, gigantic and awe-inspiring, an utter contrast to the grey ice of the Batura (Figure 32).

All along the Karakorum Highway are inscriptions, pecked or chiselled onto the rocks by the side of the road and along the riverbanks. To date, around 30,000 petroglyphs and 5,000 inscriptions in more than ten different languages or writing systems have been identified. The earliest, usually depicting animals and hunting scenes, date back to prehistoric times; the latest date to around the fifteenth century. These inscriptions record the passage of generation after generation of

Figure 32
The Passu
Glacier,
northern
Pakistan.

travellers, and their distribution has enabled scholars to confirm that today's KKH follows the approximate course of the ancient road. They were also left by local inhabitants, however, and their content tells us who ruled the area at that time, what the prevailing religious beliefs were, and what type of culture existed. From the first to around the ninth century AD, the dominant religion in the area was unquestionably Buddhism. Dedicatory inscriptions and drawings of Buddhas, stupas and Buddhist symbols occur with great frequency.

The Hunza Valley

The first of the major sites containing petroglyphs is situated near Karimabad, a modern town set high above the junction of the Hunza and Nagar Rivers, 50 km from Passu. The historic capital of Hunza was Baltit, and Karimabad has developed as an offshoot of the old town. The medieval forts at Baltit, and the even older one at Altit – each around 2,800 m above sea level – are remarkable examples of early wooden architecture. Baltit Fort was the seat of the Hunzakut royal family until the 1950s and was then abandoned. It was restored between 1992–6 and is now a museum. The earliest parts of the building, according to radiocarbon tests conducted during the restoration work, date back to the first half of the thiteenth century, and it is clear that the structure has presided over the old road for centuries. Its wooden construction, distinctly Tibetan in appearance, has allowed the structure to survive the region's frequent earthquakes and to facilitate the rapid repair of damage inflicted by successive waves of invaders.

About 2 km below Karimabad is the old village of Ganesh, and 2 km beyond that is the Sacred Rock of Hunza, on the banks of the Hunza River. The Sacred Rock of Hunza is known to local people as Haldeikish ('the place of the male ibexes'), a frequent theme of its many petroglyphs. Though much-damaged by centuries of rockfalls and by the hammers of men searching for rubies, the Sacred Rock survives as nothing less than a visitors' book of the centuries. The old road appears to have run right past it to Ganesh. One of the earliest inscriptions at the site, on a second slightly smaller rock, is a Kharosthi reference to the first Kushan emperor: 'The most devout, the great king, steadfast, [Kujula] Kadphises'. This suggests that by the reign of Kujula Kadphises (*c*.AD 30–80), the Kushans were already in firm control of the area.

There are inscriptions in Sogdian, the Silk Road's *lingua franca*, and a remarkable Chinese inscription on the second, smaller boulder at the site. The inscription refers to the passage of an ambassador from the court of the Northern Wei (386–534) and translates as follows: 'Gu Wei-Long, envoy of the Great Wei is despatched to Mi-mi.'[1]

The monk Sung Yun was dispatched by the Wei on a diplomatic mission to the Hepthalite rulers of Gandhara in about 520, and it may be that Gu Wei-Long was his contemporary. There are also Tibetan words among the inscriptions at the site and these may well date to the eighth century when Tibetans dominated the area.

The Hunza valley is lush and fertile – a stark contrast to the arid wilderness of much of the trail from China (Figure 33). Stone irrigation channels have created a verdant landscape of poplars, apricot and walnut trees, and fields of maize and wheat. Early travellers must have experienced a palpable sense of relief as the valley opened up before them. The longevity of the inhabitants of Hunza is renowned and the existence of a green valley high among the Karakorums has led to its identification with the legends of Shangri La. The truth is more prosaic, but the utter isolation of the place, until the opening of the KKH, has ensured that these legends have endured. The Hunza people of today belong predominantly to the Ishmaili sect of Islam – their spiritual leader the Aga Khan – but their physiognomy speaks of blood infused from many countries of the Silk Road (Figure 34).

Many Hunzakuts claim descent from soldiers left behind during Alexander's campaigns through the Swat valley in 327 BC. This belief

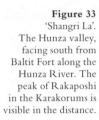

Figure 33
'Shangri La'.
The Hunza valley,
facing south from
Baltit Fort along the
Hunza River. The
peak of Rakaposhi
in the Karakorums is
visible in the distance.

occurs elsewhere in the North-West Frontier areas – most notably the Kalash people of the Hindu Kush valleys south-west of Chitral. The Kalash worship a pantheon of gods, drink wine and sacrifice animals. The evidence is sparse, but blue eyes and fair hair are not uncommon among both Hunzakut and Kalash alike. What is undeniable is that north-west Pakistan's position on an ancient trade route attracted visitors – and surely settlers, too – from many of the countries of the Silk Road.

The road continues southwards along the Hunza River for 105 km from Karimabad towards Gilgit, in sight of the great peaks of the Karakorum Range – Rakaposhi, Diran and Malubiting are all over 7,000 m and dominate the landscape. About 10 km east of Gilgit the Hunza River joins the Gilgit River, just to the west of the town of Danyor. An ancient trade route leads west up the Gilgit River into the Hindu Kush, through the region known today as the Northern Areas – but the main KKH continues southwards. Danyor is an important site on the pilgrims' road to India. In later centuries the riverbank was used as a place for cremation by Hindus (known as a *ghat*), but the large number

Figure 34
A man of
Hunza.

of inscribed boulders in the area suggests that it was also a meeting place for the faithful during the seventh and eighth centuries. Among incised drawings of hunters and animals is a large and clear depiction of a cross, left there by Nestorian Christians. In Danyor town, in the garden of a local man named Yurmaz Khan, is a massive rock about 4 m in length. The rock was inscribed in Sanskrit in about the eighth century and sets out the names of a line of local rulers, perhaps men of Tibetan descent who came to dominate the area.

Some 10 km from Gilgit, at Kargah, a massive figure of the Buddha has been carved on the cliff-face. He has presided over the area since the seventh or eighth century, standing with his right hand raised in *abhayamudra* – the gesture of dispelling fear. The entire aspect and location of this Buddha are quite magical. The spot has clearly been chosen with care – beneath him is a quiet glade with a stream running through it and he faces the setting sun so that only when the last rays fall upon him does the entire figure become illuminated.

Nearby are the masonry remains of four stupas and a Buddhist monastery. During the 1930s, a large number of birch-bark manuscripts were found within the largest of the stupas. Dating to around the fifth century the 'Gilgit Manuscripts' contain the original Sanskrit canon of Buddhism.

Between 730–83 Gilgit and its surrounding area were the scene of sporadic warfare between Tibet and China. The local rulers of the kingdom of Little Balur transferred their loyalties from one side to another with increasing desperation, and were attacked by both sides for their pains.

Some 40 km south of Gilgit is the confluence of the Gilgit and Indus rivers. The point where they meet also marks the point of convergence of three great mountain ranges: the Himalayas, the Karakorums and the Hindu Kush. From here on the Silk Road follows the course of the Indus as it heads south-westwards and then south towards Taxila. In the opposite direction a section of road leads east and south-east along the Indus Gorge to Skardu, headquarters of the Baltistan area. The Baltis' ancestry is a strange mix of Mongol and Tibetan (the latter still spoken there) – a legacy of centuries of conquest. The Indus rises in Tibet and flows through a deep cleft towards Gilgit, dividing the Karakorum from the Himalayas. Dominating the entire area is the eighth highest mountain in the world: Nanga Parbat ('The Naked Mountain') at the western limit of the Himalayas – a colossus of over 8,000 m.

Shatial and Chilas

The largest concentration of petroglyphs and inscriptions is to be found on the rocks beside the Indus at Shatial and Chilas. There is a very logical reason for this – Chilas has been the principal crossing-point of the Indus since time immemorial and is also the junction of routes leading north and south. There are ancient routes leading from Chilas to the Babusar Pass and across the Kaghan valley to Mansehra. Another route leads across the Indus, traversing the Khinnar valley to Gilgit – a distance of about 150 km.

In the Chilas area, gold has been washed from the sand of the Indus River for centuries. During the summer, meltwater from the mountains causes the Indus to flood and gold dust is washed downstream where villagers collect it. Commentators from the Classical world – including Herodotus, Strabo and Megasthenes – describe a large tribe of mountain-dwelling Indians who collected gold dust from giant anthills. The ants, said to be as big as foxes, threw gold-laced sand in the air as they burrowed. A possible explanation for this legend is that the men who conducted the lucrative trade in gold wished to conceal its origin.

Ancient records reveal that Chilas was the name given to the entire district – not just the city. Early travellers called it 'Vira Somonagara' or 'The Heroic City of the Moon', and inscribed the name at Thalpan Bridge just east of Chilas. There are petroglyphs on both sides of the river at Chilas. The earliest date to the first or second century BC and were left by nomads from the northern steppes who travelled the grand old road. The drawings are in 'animal style', with hunting and battle motifs most frequently depicted. Scythians, Parthians and Yuezhi – the latter migrating into the area from China's Gansu province and eventually founding the Kushan Empire – all appear to have left some of these early petroglyphs. At the Chilas I site a modern bridge marks what must have been the ancient crossing-place. Chilas I, like its ancient name, really does resemble a barren rock-strewn moonscape. As the visitor wanders around they can easily imagine themselves as a voyager to some long-deserted other world in which, here and there, ancient travellers have left their traces.

By the first century AD the Silk Road was fully established, and passing merchants and Buddhist pilgrims began to leave their marks on the rocks. There are inscriptions in Brahmi, Sogdian, Iranian, Kharosthi and Sanskrit; and drawings containing motifs from Buddhism, Hinduism and Nestorian Christianity. The fifth to eighth centuries saw domination of the area by Buddhists and the petroglyphs reflect this. Buddhist pictographs in late Gandhara style are to be found in abundance at Chilas but there are also influences from China, from Kashmir and from Tibet. The most popular motifs from this period are seated images of Buddha, standing *bodhisattva* figures, and stupas – the latter often drawn with flying prayer banners. Inscriptions, usually in Brahmi, have been left by generations of passing travellers. They frequently invoke the protection of the Buddha or Avalokitesvara – 'Salutation to the Buddha' and 'Salutation to Lokesvara – The work of Shimadeva, along with his wife' are typical inscriptions. The pilgrim Shimadeva seems to have been especially pious – he has left his name on a number of drawings at Chilas.

These images are not safe from the attentions of modern day iconoclasts. A number of the petroglyphs show signs of recent defacement – a beautiful drawing of a seated Buddha with three smaller attendants, all bearing injuries inflicted during a recent attack with a sharp tool, is but one example.

After the eighth century a strange group of people appeared in the locality. Described by Ahmad Dani as the people of the 'Battle-Axe Culture', they rode and danced on horseback, worshipped Vishnu and Shiva, and wielded large fan-shaped axes. Their language was Brahmi and their art is littered with wheel symbols, horses and axe motifs. They disappeared from history as mysteriously as they emerged.

Just outside Chilas are more large boulders, one with a Kharoshthi inscription referring to the great Parthian king, Gondophares (r.*c*.AD 20–50), for whom St Thomas the Apostle was asked to construct a palace in Taxila:

Vitaspa priyati Guduvharasa raja
[Beloved of Vitaspa, King Gondophares]

It is unsurprising that there should be invocations to the Buddha throughout this region. The landscape is a harsh, treeless wilderness with few places to find food.

Inscriptions in the Sogdian language have been found in large numbers at Shatial Bridge, 30 km from Chilas – like its neighbour, an important crossing point on the Indus. Iranian inscriptions (at the western end of the site), and Brahmi (at the eastern end), have also been identified and it appears that Shatial was some sort of ancient entrepôt where Sogdian traders exchanged their goods for merchandise brought up from India and Gandhara. Research by Karl Jettmar and others indicates that this was indeed the case. Sogdian merchants may have been prevented from continuing further and Shatial therefore seems to have marked an international boundary between two worlds.

There seems to have been little love lost between the Sogdian Zoroastrians of the north and the Brahmi-speaking Buddhists of the south. Graffiti and sexually explicit drawings on the rocks at Shatial, and at the mouth of the Thor valley some 33 km to the east, contain taunts from both sides. In a number of the drawings monkeys are depicted with upper bodies in the shape of phalli; and at Thor (also known as Sthavira – 'the most venerable') an androgynous figure with long Buddha-like earlobes clutches a monk's begging bowl as he is violated by a figure with a large phallus. The second figure has what appears to be a cranial bump (*usnisha*), ordinarily associated with the Buddha. Jettmar (Jettmar *et al.*, 1989–94) proposes that the drawing was left by a Sogdian merchant – a lewd imputation to a supposed predilection for homosexuality among the Buddhists of the lands to the south. To the right is a further drawing of a man in a Persian coat – the dress favoured by Sogdian merchants – sodomising what appears to be a dog. The latter appears to have been added later, perhaps in retaliation to the initial taunt (Figure 35).

The road from Shatial to Besham, a distance of 140 km, passes through a region known as Indus Kohistan. The Indus cuts a deep narrow gorge

Figure 35 Petroglyph depicting an ithyphallic figure assaulting a second figure, *c.* fifth century? Thor, northern Pakistan. (Jettmar *et al.*, 1989–94).

The later addition of the second figure with the dog or goat is visible to the right.

flanked by vertical cliffs devoid of vegetation. Pakistani and Chinese engineers dynamited the modern route through the rock within the past 30 years, at considerable cost in human life. The area is barren and harsh, deprived of sunlight by the high cliffs in places, and prone to rockfalls and flash floods. It is not surprising that travellers on the old route avoided it, preferring instead to head over to Jalkot across the Sapat plateau towards the Harban valley or via the Babusar Pass.

Besham

Just to the south of the town of Besham, the Indus plunges through a steep-sided gorge. Stein believed that this was the site of a harrowing crossing made by the monk Fa Xian. The monk describes a point on the Indus where men had bored through the rock and suspended ladders. After descending the ladders, Fa Xian crossed by a hanging rope-bridge (Figure 36).

Thakot

He wandered on
Till vast Aornos seen from Petra's steep
Hung o'er the low horizon like a cloud;
Through Balk, and where the desolated tombs

Of Parthian kings scatter to every wind
Their wasting dust, wildly he wandered on...
(Percy Bysshe Shelley, 'Alastor, or the Spirit of Solitude')

Shelley's geography is fanciful but the places are real. About 10 km west of Thakot and the Indus is the 2,160 m peak of Pirsar. The far bank, including Pirsar itself, are in Swat region; whereas the near bank, including the town of Thakot, are in Hazara. The Pirsar heights, and the ruins of an ancient fort upon it, were fully explored by Stein in 1904. He identified the peak as the likely site of the 'Rock of Aornos'; a fortress stormed by Alexander the Great during his winter campaigns of 328–327 BC. By the spring of 327 BC Alexander and his army had crossed the Indus and accepted the surrender of Taxila (see page 203).

Just beyond Thakot the road veers away from the Indus and, after a brief climb, begins its slow descent through the Hazara region towards the Peshawar Plain. The road passes through the village of Batagram, with its Kushan-era Buddhist remains, and then continues on south through pine forests – eventually flattening into the Pakhli Plain that surrounds the city of Mansehra.

Figure 36 'Fa Xian's Crossing'. On the Indus near Besham, Swat district, northern Pakistan. The KKH is visible above the far bank of the river.

Mansehra is situated 90 km from Thakot – at the junction of the main road leading north, and a second route leading across to Kashmir. It has evidently been an important city for centuries. The great Mauryan emperor, Ashoka (r.*c.*269–232 BC), left 14 inscriptions on three large rocks at Mansehra during the third century BC. Ashoka was a conqueror who came to regret the suffering caused by his military campaigns. He embraced the concept of non-violence espoused in Buddhism, and his edicts – found in all parts of India except for the extreme south – urge tolerance and restraint. The edicts, now faded almost to the point of illegibility, are written in Prakrit in the local Kharosthi script and reveal a remarkably compassionate side to a man who lived in a time of conflict and invasion:

> That person who does reverence to his own sect and disparages other sects – does all this only out of attachment to his own sect. That person [...] by acting thus injures very greatly his own sect.
> (Rock Edict no. XII, Mansehra. Abridged from Dani, 1983b)

After Mansehra the journey nears its end. About 95 km from Mansehra, after passing through the city of Abbottabad – built by the British as a hill station during the nineteenth century, and the site, in 2011, of Osama bin Laden's demise – the road descends to the Peshawar Plain and arrives at Taxila, among the greatest of all the cities of the Silk Road and the end of this book's journey.

Taxila

Taxila is situated about 30 km north-west of the modern Pakistani capital of Islamabad, just off the Grand Trunk Road. Bactrian Greeks founded a metropolis there during the second century BC, although the Achaemenians and then the Mauryans had occupied the site from the sixth century BC. The Bactrian Greeks were followed, in succession, by Scythians, Parthians, Kushans, Sasanians and finally the Hepthalites (or White Huns), who proved to be the city's nemesis. Greek accounts describe the arrival of Alexander the Great in the spring of 326 BC. Ambhi (Omphis), the king of Taxila, surrendered his kingdom to Alexander and offered an alliance against the Indian king, Porus. Alexander remained at Taxila for a few weeks before marching east to defeat Porus. Following Alexander's premature death in 323 BC, Greek control of the region proved impossible to maintain and the empire fell apart. The Indian empire of the Mauryans under Chandragupta (*c.*311–287 BC) was established, with its capital at Pataliputra (modern Patna, in Bihar). Taxila became the regional seat of government, the Mauryans driving out the Greeks from all of north-west India. Mauryan rule appears to have been despotic and it seems that the embrace of Buddhism by Chandragupta's grandson Ashoka (*c.*269–232 BC) was a reaction to the excesses of the regime. Ashoka carved imperial edicts on rocks and pillars – the latter surmounted by animal capitals – throughout the Mauryan Empire from Afghanistan to Karnataka in southern India[2] (see also the section on Mansehra above). The Greeks did not completely disappear from the region during this period, however. Seleucus, one of Alexander's generals, and his successors, managed to sustain Greek rule north of the Hindu Kush Mountains in Bactria and Sogdiana until about 255 BC, when it became an independent kingdom under the Greek governor Diodotus. During the early second century BC the Greeks of Bactria extended their influence southwards again, establishing capitals at Taxila and Charsadda. Greek rule was maintained, to some degree, until the first century AD but was gradually eroded by influxes of Scythians, Parthians and Yuezhi.

After the Yuezhi's establishment of the Kushan Empire, Taxila became one of its capitals, actually consisting of three separate city sites, these being Bhir Mound (the most ancient), Sirkap and Sirsukh. The capital was moved to Taxila from Peshawar at around the end of the first century AD, first to Sirkap and then, during the second century, to Sirsukh. Sirkap was laid out in a grid pattern, favoured by the city planners of the Hellenistic world. It is not only the streets of Sirkap that owe their appearance to influences from the classical world. The acanthus-topped Corinthian columns of the Stupa of the Double Headed Eagle at Sirkap reveal that such influences also extended to the architecture of some of its buildings.

Like the eastern Kushan capital of Mathura, Taxila owed its prosperity to the trade routes on which it sat. Sir John Marshall, who excavated Taxila between 1913–34, describes how Taxila was situated at the meeting-point of three great highways linking India with China, western and Central Asia, and Europe. Taxila also benefited from sea trade between Alexandria and Barbaricum at the mouth of the Indus, particularly when periods of hostility between Rome and Parthia closed the east–west land route. A famous visitor to Taxila during the Parthian era was St Thomas, who, according to Christian legend, was commissioned by King Gondophares (r.*c.*AD 20–50) to build him a palace. After expending all of the funds provided to him on acts of charity, St Thomas told Gondophares that he had constructed him a palace in heaven. The king's recently deceased brother was miraculously restored to life and confirmed St Thomas' story, leading to the conversion of both men to Christianity. The presence of foreign artisans at Taxila is entirely plausible, given the level of activity along the land and sea routes at this time.

During ancient times, the city would have been dominated by the great Dharmarajika stupa, once over 35 m in height though now reduced by centuries of diggings and seismic activity. It was first built by the Mauryan emperor, Ashoka, during the third century BC – one of the eight principal stupas built to house relics of the Buddha. It was enlarged during the following centuries.

Marshall unearthed a veritable treasure trove of artefacts at the Taxila sites which, because they date to the earliest period of the Gandhara School, are largely unfettered by indigenous styles and show Greco-Roman influence at its most intense. Buddhist statuary was discovered: in bronze, stone and stucco; pottery; gold and silver jewellery; large numbers of coins; and exquisite small items in bone, ivory and shell. Some 30 schist and steatite palette trays were found – possibly used for the application of cosmetics – many with scenes from Greek mythology including bacchanalian themes, amorous couples, and figures astride fabulous beasts. Perhaps the most delightful of all the rich finds of Taxila is a single small bronze figure of Harpocrates, now housed in the Karachi Museum (Figure 37).

Taxila's heyday was brief. The Hepthalite invasions of the fifth century did not immediately put a stop to the production of Gandharan art, but the southern areas were severely affected with considerable devastation wrought by the Hepthalite king, Mihiragula (r.*c.*AD 515–40). When the Chinese pilgrim Xuanzang passed through the region in about 630, Taxila was a deserted ruin. Marshall found graphic evidence of the mayhem wrought by the Hepthalites during his excavations of the Dharmarajika stupa. He unearthed an open courtyard containing a group of six skeletons, several of which had been decapitated, the charred timbers of the building indicating that it had then been burned to the ground.

Figure 37
Bronze figure of Harpocrates.
Probably Roman, first century AD.
Height 13 cm. Found at Sirkap,
Taxila.

Harpocrates, son of Isis, is the Egyptian god of silence. He enjoins quiet by raising his finger to his lips. A number of scholars have suggested that this figure was made in the West, perhaps at the great trading port of Alexandria in Roman Egypt, and imported to Taxila.

THE ART AND HISTORY OF THE GANDHARA REGION AND THE KUSHANS

The Kushans

During the first century AD, a group of nomadic warriors known as the Kushans conquered the ancient region of Gandhara, situated in the Peshawar valley of modern day north-west Pakistan. Most of the information we have on the Kushans comes from Chinese annals – especially those of the Han dynasty historian Sima Qian (*c.*145–90 BC), and from the study of coins. Sima Qian describes how a nomadic tribe called the Yuezhi originally occupied an area in China's Gansu province, between the Tianshan ('Heavenly')

MAP 12
The Kushan Empire: trade routes and main sites.

Mountains and Dunhuang. A once powerful nation, they were attacked and defeated by another nomadic tribe, the Xiongnu. The Xiongnu leader, Maodun, is said to have killed the king of the Yuezhi and made his skull into a drinking vessel. After their defeat they were led westwards by the son of the slain king and conquered the kingdom of Daxia (Bactria), setting up their capital on the north bank of the Oxus on the borders of what we now call Afghanistan and Uzbekistan. The Yuezhi appear to have begun their migration in about 165 BC and arrived in Bactria in about 140 BC, thus migrating over a distance of more than 4,000 km within a single generation. They steadily extended their rule across Bactria and the Kabul region and, during the first century AD, into the Gandhara kingdom and the Punjab. Much of this was accomplished during the reign of Kujula Kadphises (r.c.AD 30–80), ending Parthian rule in the area, unifying the entire region, and establishing the foundations for the Kushan Empire. Kujula issued coins that imitated the styles of the Scythians and Parthians who preceded him. Fascinatingly, some of these coins include depictions of the Roman emperor, Augustus (r. 31 BC–AD 14), with modifications made to the design for his own use.

By the early part of the second century AD the great Kushan king, Kanishka I (r.*c.* 100–126 or 120–146), ruled an empire that extended from the Gangetic Plain of northern India to Sogdiana. Kushan rule brought prosperity and security and led to an increase in trade throughout the region. Kanishka was the greatest of all the Kushan rulers, his empire encompassing part of Central Asia, Bactria (modern Afghanistan), north-west India (modern Pakistan) and northern India as far east as Bihar. Contemporary sources indicate that Kashmir was also part of his empire. The Archeological Museum in Mathura, Uttar Pradesh, India, houses a 1.85 m tall portrait statue of King Kanishka in red sandstone. Another closely related portrait sculpture of Kanishka, from Surkh Khotal, Afghanistan, was once housed in the Kabul museum's collection and was regarded as one of the world's great works of art. It survived the Russian occupation, civil war and looting; only to be destroyed in March 2001 by a Taliban official wielding a sledgehammer. Both images depict Kanishka in the guise of a warrior, but he was also a man of great intellect with eclectic views on religion. His coins include depictions of almost the entire pantheon of Persian, Greek and Indian deities, but it is the appearance of the Buddha image for the first time that has created such excitement among historians. A celebrated gold coin of Kanishka's reign in the British Museum is generally regarded as containing the first firmly dated depiction of the Buddha in human form. Kanishka may not have been a Buddhist himself but there is no doubt that he was a patron of the Buddhist faith. The construction of an immense stupa, now destroyed, at his capital Kanishkapura or Purushapura (modern Peshawar), was accompanied by a surge in the activities of sculptors of Buddhist art.

The last of the great Kushan rulers was Vasudeva I (*c.*164–200 or 184–220). During Vasudeva's reign the Kushan Empire – with its capital at Mathura on the banks of the Yamuna River in modern Uttar Pradesh, northern India – had attained its apogee. Vasudeva's patronage of the Mathura style of art has endowed us with exquisite creations, most notably in the mottled red sandstone sculpture of the period.

The Kushan Empire entered a period of slow decline after Vasudeva's death. The Sasanian king, Ardashir I (r.*c.*224–40), began a campaign to absorb the area into his empire, a campaign completed by his son Shapur I. From about 230–360, the Sasanians ruled this eastern province of their empire through their own princes – governing as Kushan kings. During the rule of the Kushano-Sasanian kings, a small remnant of the Kushan Empire survived in Kashmir and in the Punjab but came under increasing pressure from local tribes and, subsequently, from the Gupta Empire of northern

India. The appearance of various groups of Huns, from the mid-fourth century onwards, brought about the final demise of the Kushans and also led to the decline of Sasanian power in the region. The first of these groups was the Kidarites, who began by seizing Balkh from the Kushano-Sasanians and then invaded Gandhara. At around the same time the Hepthalites or Chionites (also known as the White Huns) moved into Bactria from north-west China. Their empire was enlarged throughout the fifth century, until it threatened the Gupta rulers of the Punjab region. The Hepthalites were essentially nomadic and, as a consequence, did not produce sculptural art. They did produce coins and carved gems, however, and it is within this medium that we discover that they, like their predecessors, were influenced by both Persian and Greco-Roman art. Techniques such as cameo and intaglio carving are clear examples of the importation of Western technology via the Silk Road at this time.

A peculiar aspect of Hepthalite custom was a belief that an artificially deformed head was a symbol of high social status. This disfigurement was achieved by binding the head during infancy. As a result, many Hepthalite coins include extraordinary depictions of their kings with dome-shaped skulls. Hepthalite rule lasted until about 560, when an alliance was formed between the Sasanian king, Khusrau I (r.*c*.531–79), and the western Turks of northern China. They succeeded in gaining control of the Kabul region, and of Gandhara, and ruled the area until the coming of Islam in the late seventh and early eighth centuries.

Gandhara and Mathura Art
By the time of Kanishka I (r.*c*.100–126 or 120–46), the Kushan Empire had two capital cities: Mathura (in modern Uttar Pradesh, northern India) and Peshawar (ancient Purushapur, in what is now north-west Pakistan). Two broad schools of art have been identified: a more Hellenised form in the north-west, and a more 'Indianised' style around Mathura. These styles were far from distinct, however, and numerous common elements have been identified.

The Mathura School of Art
Mathura is located on the right bank of the Yamuna, a tributary of the Ganges some 150 km south of Delhi in Uttar Pradesh. It sits at the junction of India's trade routes and by the first century AD was a thriving religious and commercial centre. Described by Ptolemy as a 'City of Gods', early Indian texts state that the inhabitants lived by trade rather than by agriculture. Hinduism, Buddhism and Jainism all coexisted peacefully – along with the worship of nature spirits – and traders and acolytes brought religious and cultural influences to the city. Mathura's heyday lasted from the first

century AD until the Sasanian incursions of the mid-third century. Despite a partial revival under the Gupta rulers of the fourth to the seventh century, the city never regained its former glory and eventually lost its position as a commercial and religious centre. Mathura sculpture is typically produced from mottled red *sikri* sandstone that is quarried locally. Popular motifs include sensuous young women, nature and water spirits (*yakshis* and *nagas*), architectural elements, flora and fauna, and bacchanalian scenes. Mathura sculpture is often fleshy and full-figured, and its protagonists (both religious and secular) are dressed in diaphanous clothing with multiple folds. While its form is essentially Indian, the influences of Greece and Rome, assimilated via the Silk Road, are also present (Figure 38).

The Gandhara School of Art

> In the entrance-hall stood the larger figures of the Greco-Buddhist sculptures done, savants know how long since, by forgotten workmen whose hands were feeling, and not unskilfully, for the mysteriously transmitted Grecian touch.
>
> (Rudyard Kipling, *Kim*)[3]

The long-destroyed stupa of Kanishka, built at Kanishkapura, near Peshawar in today's north-west Pakistan, measured almost 100 m across and was admired by many early travellers, including the Chinese monk Xuanzang during the seventh century. Peshawar – or Purushapura, as it was called – was the seat of the Kushan Empire, at least during its early period. Other centres were at Taxila, the later capital, the Swat valley, and Hadda and Begram in modern Afghanistan. All of these cities sat astride the ancient routes linking China, Central Asia and the Western world, and were part of a region that modern writers have called 'the crossroads of Asia'. The art of Gandhara – almost exclusively Buddhist in nature – draws its influences from Greek, Roman, Persian and local Indian styles. Grey or blue schist seems to have been the preferred medium, stucco and terracotta were used in areas where stone was unobtainable, and gold and bronze were also used, though much more sparingly. The fully developed Gandhara style was extant by the end of the first century AD. It is generally accepted that stucco and terracotta images are somewhat later than schist sculpture, perhaps because of the depletion of supplies of stone. Early stucco and terracottas have been found, at Taxila for example, but the majority have been attributed to the third to fifth centuries, compared to the first to third for stone.

An extensive repertoire of classical motifs is found in the art of Gandhara. Mythological figures such as Eros (or Cupid) and wingless *Putti* (young boys) with garlands of flowers; figures of Herakles (sometimes transmuted to

Figure 38
Red sandstone Bacchanalian relief with intoxicated courtesan and Vasantasena.
Kushan period, Mathura; late second century. Height 97 cm, width 76 cm.
The sculpture is one of the great masterpieces of Indian art, finding its roots in the Bacchanalian scenes of Greece. The obverse side shows a young courtesan who falls to the floor in a state of intoxication. The reverse side is probably a depiction of the early Sanskrit drama 'The Little Clay Cart', which describes the pursuit of a beautiful courtesan by a foolish and cowardly youth. In this relief she removes a garland from above her head, the aroma of which betrays her presence to her suitor as she conceals herself in the darkness and has pushed her jingling anklets up to her knees to silence them as she runs to hide. The delicate and sensitive way in which this relief has been carved can be compared to depictions of scenes from the Buddha's previous lives (jatakas) that were being produced in Gandhara at this time.

become the Buddhist deity Vajrapani) and Atlas, centaurs and sea monsters; Corinthian columns and capitals with acanthus leaves and floral scrolls (rinceaux). The British Museum even has a schist frieze that tells the story of the Trojan horse!

Images of the Buddha in Gandhara art are devoid of ornament and are formally posed, adhering closely to the designs of Kanishka era coins. Standing Buddha images typically have a high *usnisha* (a raised chignon, indicative of princely origins and superior wisdom), eyes half-closed in meditation, and a heavy monastic robe with multiple pleats. Despite the simplicity of style of these Buddha images, Greco-Roman elements are still to be found and, indeed, it has been suggested that they derive from the figure of the Western philosopher or statesman known as Togatus, found in the classical world.

Gandhara Buddha images were produced in vast numbers. Free-standing (or sitting) images, usually in stone, were produced, as were figures placed in niches against a wall – in common with many stucco or terracotta examples. Very few examples of the latter survive in situ – the Jaulian monastery at Taxila being a rare example. At Jaulian there are tiers of niches containing stucco figures of Buddhas, *bodhisattvas* and devotees in acts of worship or meditation.

Perhaps the most famous examples of the Gandhara ideal were the colossal Buddhas, 55 m and 38 m in height, hewn out of the rock at Bamiyan to the west of the Afghan capital of Kabul. For the 1,500 years that they survived they ranked among the greatest artistic creations on earth, but in March 2001 they were blown up by the country's Taliban rulers. A network of caves adorned with exquisite wall paintings surrounded the Buddhas (Figure 39). Many of the paintings were executed in a style referred to by art historians as 'Indo-Sasanian' but they, like the Buddhas, did not survive the vandalism of the Taliban era.

Images of the *bodhisattva* (those destined for Buddhahood), in the guise of a Kushan prince, are among the most elegant of all Gandhara sculptures. Typically, these images wear a turban diadem that holds in place an elaborate *coiffure*. The hair is sometimes in the form of a top-knot or cockade, sometimes secured by a line of pearls encircling the head. Unrestrained by the austerities associated with the Buddha, *bodhisattva* images are adorned with an abundance of jewellery: heavy earrings (often in the form of lions), *basubands* for the arms, and as many as four necklaces – all in a style which evokes the classical world. The robes, too, follow Greco-Roman models, and the upper torso is generally bare and muscular. Such *bodhisattva* images can be as much as 2 m in height, but even much smaller images can be magnificent and imposing (Figure 40).

The technique of working in stucco, a cheap and readily available substitute for the grey schist stone favoured by the sculptors of Gandhara, attained its zenith around the third century at Hadda, near Jalalabad.

Figure 39
The Great
Buddha,
Bamiyan,
Afghanistan,
c. fifth
century.
Height 55 m.
Destroyed by
the Taliban in
March 2001.

Hadda's numerous monasteries (*viharas*) were still active at the time of a visit by the Chinese pilgrim Fa Xian in around 400, but the city was ruined and desolate when Xuanzang passed through in 630, wrecked by Hepthalite invaders. Sculpting with stucco, a plaster made from calcium oxide or calcium sulphate, seems to have been invented in or near the Roman port of Alexandria in Egypt. It is extremely easy to work, with large figures built up around a core of wood or stone. This enables the sculptor to infuse his creations with a greater degree of naturalism and spontaneity. Hadda stuccos still retain the classical elements seen at Taxila and Begram but the city's

Figure 40
A grey schist figure of a *bodhisattva*. Kushan period, Gandhara, second or third century AD. Height 110 cm. Probably from the vicinity of Takht-I- Bahi, near Sahri Bahlol, north-west Pakistan.

artists have adapted them to produce a unique style that reveals the full flowering of Gandhara art.

Later Buddhist Art of Gandhara

During the seventh and eighth centuries, before the coming of Islam, the Buddhist art of Gandhara entered its final phase. The paintings and sculptures discovered in 1937 by the French at the monastery of Fondukistan, on the Ghorband River to the north-west of Kabul, continue the Indo-Sasanian style that we first saw in the wall paintings of Bamiyan. Figures in similar style were found at Tepe Sardar (near Ghazni), and at Kakrak. The technique of painting unfired clay, sometimes mixed with horse hair and chopped straw and modelled around a wooden framework, is seen for the first time and replaced the old media of schist, limestone stucco and terracotta. It became the method of choice among the artists of the Silk Road, occurring in Kashmir, China, and in parts of Central Asia, and it embodied a refined and somewhat feminine style. The sculptural counterparts of the Fondukistan paintings are equally flamboyant and sensuous and may have their roots in the art of the Gupta dynasty of northern India.

The sudden appearance of the marble figures of the Hindu Shahi dynasty, just before the advent of Islam, was a surprising development in the art of the region. The most important finds were at Khair Khaneh, 15 km north of Kabul. The sun god Surya, and Vishnu, were popular subjects for the Shahi artists and their styles are linked to those of Kashmir. Other sites such as Tagao and Gardez have also yielded sculptures of Hindu deities, including Siva and Durga, although a number of Buddhist images have also been found. When Xuanzang visited the kingdom of Kapisa, north of Kabul, in 630, he recorded that there were 100 monasteries and about 6,000 monks in the city – but that there were also ten Hindu temples. Very little is known about the Hindu Shahi (after the Persian title, 'shah' or 'king'). It appears that they emerged as a result of a palace coup among the Turki Shahi at some point before the ninth century, and they established their capital at Udabhandapura (modern Hund) in Pakistan, to the north-west of Taxila. Although the Hindu Shahi dynasty was established only around the ninth cenury, Hindu sculpture was already being produced in the area – and it has all been labelled 'Hindu Shahi' as a matter of convenience. It seems likely that the western Turks and the Turki Shahi were one and the same tribe, or at least were part of the same confederation – but information about both groups, and particularly the latter, is scarce and contradictory. The Turki Shahi are not even referred to by name until the eleventh century, when they are given mention in Al-Biruni's work 'The History of India' (*Ta'rikh al-Hind*).

The coming of Islam to Central Asia and Afghanistan during the late seventh to eighth century brought monotheism and iconoclasm to the region. Within 100 years of its arrival the activities of artists and monks, Buddhist and Hindu alike, had come to an end, and creativity became the exclusive domain of the new religion.

CHAPTER EIGHT
The End of the Road:
The Silk Road in Decline

The cloud-capp'd towers, the gorgeous palaces,
The solemn temples, the great globe itself,
Ye all which it inherit, shall dissolve...
(William Shakespeare, The Tempest,
Act IV, Scene 1)

The death in 1449 of Ulugh Beg, grandson of Timur, was one of a number of events that brought about the final decline of the Silk Road. After Ulugh Beg's passing the Timurid Empire finally disintegrated as town after town fell to the Uzbeks, and the absence of centralised control in Central Asia meant that the safety of merchants along the trade routes could no longer be guaranteed. Caravans were forced to hire an armed escort, resulting in higher costs. To the west, Constantinople fell to the Ottoman Turks in 1453, bringing the Byzantine Empire to an end and bringing the eastern Mediterranean under Muslim control. All east–west trade was now compelled to pass through Ottoman territory and this resulted in an additional financial burden on merchants in the form of tolls and taxes. The European trading powers began to seek ways to evade the Ottoman monopoly and to reduce these costs, ushering in an era of maritime exploration that would transform the way in which trade would be conducted during the coming centuries. The first voyages had already begun during the early part of the fifteenth century, sponsored by Prince

Henry 'The Navigator' of Portugal, to seek gold, ivory and slaves, and in 1415, the Portuguese captured the Moorish city of Ceuta on the northern coast of Africa. Emboldened by their success they began to explore the African coastline and, in 1487, Bartolomeu Dias became the first European to round the Cape of Good Hope – he was actually blown round it in a storm. He was followed in 1497–8 by Vasco da Gama, discoverer of the maritime route to India, and in 1510 the Portuguese captured Goa, quickly followed in 1511 by the Malay port of Malacca – both becoming important bases for trade with the East. Under the newly founded Mughal Empire the Portuguese were granted trading rights and by the 1540s, they were engaged in commerce with Thailand, Burma, Cambodia and Japan. For more than a century the Portuguese dominated trade with Africa and India, while the Spanish raced to colonise the New World, a process that had begun in 1492 with the voyage of Christopher Columbus. The irony of Columbus' voyage was that, by sailing west, he too hoped to reach Cipangu (Japan) and India. Columbus, believing that the earth was round but miscalculating its circumference, believed until his death that he had reached Asia during his voyage; though in fact he had reached only the Bahamas.

The great age of maritime exploration was not confined to the European powers. During the early years of the Ming dynasty (1368–1644), Chinese emperors launched a number of expeditions led by the incomparable Admiral Zheng He (1371–1434). Zheng, the son of a Muslim from Yunnan province, began his career at the age of 12 as a court eunuch. He distinguished himself in a number of military posts and became a favourite of Emperor Yongle (r.1403–24). Yongle restored China to a position of economic and military strength and selected Zheng to lead a series of maritime expeditions to unite the countries of South and Southeast Asia under Chinese hegemony. Between 1405–33, under the emperors Yongle and Xuande (r.1425–35) – with a brief suspension of operations under Hongxi (r.1424–5) – Zheng led seven different voyages. They were truly epic in both scale and reach: the first, in 1405, involved more than 60 ships – the largest 130 m in length – carrying 27,000 men. The flotilla left Suzhou and travelled for two years, exploring the coastlines of Vietnam, Java, Sumatra, Malacca, Sri Lanka and south-western India. But his subsequent voyages were even more noteworthy. His fourth expedition, from 1413–15, was a round trip of 12,000 km, stopping at Hormuz in the Persian Gulf. Part of the fleet then sailed down the Arabian coast as far as Dhofar and Aden, and went on to explore the east coast of Africa, almost as far south as Mozambique – some 80 years ahead of the Portuguese. Part of the expedition even made a detour by land to visit Mecca and Egypt. When the fleet returned to China in 1415 it brought envoys from more than 30 countries to pay homage to the Chinese court as well as a rich cargo that included a giraffe. His final expeditions all revisited the Persian Gulf and the east African coastline and, although the voyages did not result in the establishment of permanent settlements in the places he visited, they undoubtedly contributed to the diaspora of Chinese to the countries of Southeast Asia that occurred in later years. Zheng's voyages also sought to advance China's commercial interests – his ships carried cargoes that included raw and embroidered silks, porcelain, pearls, musk, camphor, precious metals, rice, millet and beans. He returned to China with spices, gems, medicines, pigments and exotic animals – both as tribute and as the proceeds of barter with the countries along the route.

Zheng died in 1434 and China's status as a great sea power was lost as the country began to fold in on itself. Chinese merchants continued to trade but without official approval. The Portuguese arrived on the coast of southern China in 1517 and, despite being regarded with undisguised contempt by the Chinese, succeeded in establishing a trading port at Macau in 1557. From their bases at Goa and Macau, the Portuguese controlled most of the maritime trade with the East, but the Spanish sought access as well. Their efforts, ironically, were assisted by the Portuguese navigator Ferdinand Magellan. Magellan approached the king of Portugal with a scheme to sail around the coast of South America but, unable to arouse interest in the plan, was eventually commissioned by King Charles I of Spain to sail west in search of spices. After rounding Cape Horn, Magellan traversed the Pacific and reached the Philippines. He was killed in the Philippines in 1521 but this did not prevent the establishment of trading ports at Manila and in the Moluccas Islands in Indonesia. From these bases the Spanish conducted a lucrative trans-Pacific trade via Mexico and Peru to Europe. Goods were carried overland from one side of Mexico to the other where, at the port of Veracruz, they were put on ships bound for Spain. The Portuguese continued to dominate trade across the Indian Ocean, but from 1624 onwards Chinese merchants also traded with the Dutch in Formosa (Taiwan). In 1580 Portugal was annexed by Spain, but Spanish ambitions to dominate trade with the East were short-lived.

Sir Francis Drake's defeat of the Spanish Armada in 1588 put paid to Spanish control of the seas and ushered in the era of the great English and Dutch trading companies. Throughout this period the cities of the Silk Road, starved of revenue from land-based commerce, began to wither and die.

Chronologies

China

NEOLITHIC CULTURES	*c.*6500–1900 BC
EARLY DYNASTIES	
Shang	*c.*1500–1050 BC
Western Zhou	1050–771 BC
Eastern Zhou	
Spring and Autumn	770–475 BC
Warring States	475–221 BC
IMPERIAL CHINA	
Qin	221–207 BC
Han	
Western Han	206 BC–AD 9
Xin (Wang Mang interregnum)	AD 9–23
Eastern Han	AD 25–220
Three Kingdoms	
Shu Han	221–63
Wei	220–65
Wu	222–80
Period of Disunity:	
Southern dynasties (six dynasties)	
Western Jin	265–316
Eastern Jin	317–420
Liu Song	420–79

Southern Qi	479–502
Liang	502–57
Chen	557–89

Sixteen Kingdoms [Chinese appellation for period when a succession of nomadic groups fought for control of northern China] 304–439

Northern dynasties

Northern Wei	386–534
Eastern Wei	534–50
Western Wei	535–57
Northern Qi	550–77
Northern Zhou	557–81

Sui	589–618
Tang	618–907
Five dynasties	907–60
Liao	907–1125

Song

Northern Song	960–1126
Southern Song	1127–1279

Jin	1115–1234
Yuan	1279–1368
Ming	1368–1644
Qing	1644–1911

REPUBLICAN CHINA

Republic	1912–49
People's Republic	1949–current

Pre-Islamic States of Western and Central Asia

Achaemenian Empire	*c.*550–330 BC
Alexander the Great	336–323 BC
Seleucid Empire	*c.*312–64 BC
Parthian Empire	*c.*256 BC–AD 226
Mauryan Empire	*c.* fourth–second century BC
Greco-Bactrian kingdom	*c.* third–second century BC
Scythians	*c.* second–first century BC
Xiongnu confederation	*c.* fourth century BC–*c.* first century AD
Kushan Empire	*c.* first century BC–fourth century AD
Sasanian Empire	224–651
Hepthalites ('White Huns')	*c.* fourth–sixth century AD

| Sogdian states | *c*. second–eighth century AD |
| Western Turks | *c*. fifth–seventh century AD |

Islamic States

Arabian Peninsula
Rule of the Rightly	
Guided Caliphs in Arabia	632–61
Umayyad Caliphate	661–750
Abbasid Caliphate	749–1258

Egypt
Tulunid dynasty	868–904
The Ikhshidids	935–69
The Fatimids	909–1171
The Ayyubids	1168–1260
The Mamluks	1252–1517

Persia and Transoxiana
The Samanids	875–999
The Tahirids	821–73
The Saffarids	867–908
The Seljuks	1037–1194
The Kharakhanids	992–1211
The Kharakhitai (non-Muslim state)	*c*.1124–1210
The Khorezmshahs	1157–1231
The Zangids	1127–77
The (Mongol) Il-Khans	1256–1335
Timurids	1370–1506
The (Uzbek) Shaibanids	1428–1599
The Safavids	1502–1722

Turkey
| Seljuk Sultanate of Rum | 1194–1243 |
| Ottoman Sultanate | 1300–1924 |

Afghanistan and India
Ghaznavids	977–1186
Ghurids	1100–1215
Mughal Empire	1526–1857

Emperors of Byzantium
(Adapted from Kelly, 1987)

Constantine dynasty
| Constantine I | 324–37 |

Constantius II	337–61
Julian	361–3

[Non-dynastic emperors]

Jovian	363–4
Valens	364–78

Theodosian dynasty

Theodosius I	379–95
Arcadius	395–408
Theodosius II	408–50
Pulcheria	450–3
Marcian	450–7

Leonine dynasty

Leo I	457–74
Zeno	474–91
Leo II	474
Anastasius I	491–518

Justinian dynasty

Justin I	518–27
Justinian I	527–65
Justin II	565–78
Tiberius	578–82
Maurice (married Tiberius's daughter)	582–602

[Non-dynastic emperor]

Phocas	602–10

Heraclian dynasty

Heraclius	610–41
Constantine II	641
Constantine III	641–68
Constantine IV	668–85
Justinian II	685–95 and 705–11

[Usurpers during reign of Justinian II]

Leontius	695–8
Tiberius	698–705

[Non-dynastic emperors]

Philippicus Bardanes	711–13
Anastasius II	713–16
Theodosius II	716–17

Syrian dynasty

Leo III	717–41
Constantine V	741–75

Leo IV	775–80
Constantine VI	780–97
Irene (as Regent and then Empress)	780–802

[Non-dynastic emperors]

Nicephorus I	802–11
Stauracius	811
Michael I	811–13
Leo V (the Armenian)	813–20

Phrygian dynasty

Michael II (the Stammerer)	820–9
Theophilus (the Unfortunate)	829–42
Michael III (the Drunkard)	842–67

Macedonian dynasty

Basil I	867–86
Leo VI (the Wise)	886–912
Alexander	886–913
Constantine VII (Porphyrogenitus)	913–59

[Usurpers during and after reign of Constantine VII]

Romanus	919–44
Romanus II	959–63
Nicephorus II	963–9
John Tzimisces	969–76

Macedonian dynasty continued

Basil II (the Bulgar-slayer)	976–1025
Constantine VIII	1025–8
Zoe	1028–50
Romanus III	1028–34
Michael IV	1034–41
Michael V	1041–2
Zoe and Theodora (jointly)	1042
Constantine IX Monomachus	1042–55
Theodora (as sole empress)	1055–6

[Non-dynastic emperors]

Michael VI Stratioticus	1056–7
Isaac I Komnenos	1057–9
Constantine X Dukas	1059–67
Romanus IV Diogenes	1067–71
Michael VII Parapinakes	1071–8
Nicephorus III Botaniates	1078–81

Comnenus dynasty

Alexius I	1081–1118
John II	1118–43
Manuel I	1143–80
Alexius II	1180–3
Andronicus I	1183–5

Angeli dynasty

Isaac II Angelus	1185–95 and 1203–4
Alexius III	1195–1203
Alexius IV	1203–4

[Usurping emperor]

Alexius V Dukas	1204

Latin emperors installed by the Crusaders

Baldwin of Flanders	1204–5
Henry of Flanders	1206–16
Peter de Courtnay (never ruled)	1217
Yolande	1217–19
Robert II of Courtnay	1221–8
Baldwin II	1228–61
John de Brienne (Regent)	1229–37

Byzantine emperors exiled at Nicaea during the Latin occupation of the city

Theodore I Lascaris	1204–22
John III Dukas Vatatzes	1222–54
Theodore II	1254–8
John IV	1258–61

Byzantine emperors restored: Palaeologian dynasty

Michael VIII	1261–82
Andronicus II	1282–1328
Michael IX	1295–1320
Andronicus III	1328–41
John V	1341–91

[Usurping emperor]

John VI Cantacuzenos	1341–54

Palaeologian dynasty continued

Andronicus IV	1376–9
John VII	1390
Manuel II	1391–1425
John VIII	1425–48
Constantine XI	1449–53

Ottoman sultans immediately after the capture of Constantinople in 1453

Mehmet II the Conqueror (Fatih)	1453–81
Beyazit II	1481–1512
Selim I the Grim	1512–20
Süleyman the Magnificent	1520–66
Selim II	1566–74
Murad III	1574–95
Mehmet III	1595–1603

Glossary

abhayamudra	Hand position indicating freedom from fear, or reassurance; the hand raised with the palm pointing towards the viewer.
Amitabha Buddha (Sanskrit; Japanese: Amida)	The Buddha of infinite light, ruler of the pure land known as the Western Paradise.
Ananda	First cousin and devoted companion of the Buddha.
apsaras or *apsara* (Sanskrit)	Female semi-divinity, or celestial nymph.
Aramaic	One of the major systems of writing in the Middle East during the first millennium BC. It derived from Semitic script and became the *lingua franca* of merchants in the region.
arhat (Sanskrit; Chinese: *Lohan*; Japanese: *Rakan*)	A Buddhist holy figure who has gained insight into the true nature of existence and has achieved nirvana.
Ariadne (Greek mythology)	The daughter of Pasiphae and the Cretan king, Minos, *inamorata* of the Athenian hero Theseus.
Athena (Greek mythology)	The goddess of war and city protectress, identified by the Romans with Minerva.
Atlas (Greek mythology)	Son of the titan, Iapetus, and the nymph, Clymene, and brother of Prometheus. In Homer's works he supported the pillars that separated heaven and earth.

avadanas (Sanskrit 'noble deeds')	The Buddha's explanations of events by means of an individual's worthy deeds in a previous life. The most important *avadana* is an account of miraculous events in the life and former lives of the Buddha himself.
Avalokitesvara (Sanskrit)	A celestial *bodhisattva*, the archetype of universal compassion. In his female form, he is associated with Tara and Guanyin.
balbals	Grave-markers, once erected by nomadic Turks above the graves of their companions to designate how many of the enemy the occupant had slain.
bodhisattva	One destined for Buddhahood, eligible to enter nirvana, but who elects to remain a *bodhisattva* in order to help living beings attain salvation.
Brahma	Hindu deity, a member of the puranic trinity (the *Trimurti*), associated with creation.
Brahmins (Hindu priests)	The priestly caste of Hindus (although not all Brahmins are priests).
caitya (Sanskrit 'that which is worthy to be gazed upon')	A sacred place or shrine, especially a Buddhist prayer-hall, often with a votive stupa at one end.
caravanserai	A public building, often fortified, used for sheltering caravans, merchants and other travellers.
cella (central sanctuary chamber)	The main body of a temple containing the image of the deity.
chaikana (or *chaihana*)	A teahouse.
chakra (or *Cakra*) (Sanskrit 'wheel')	A wheel or disc attribute of Vishnu.
chiaroscuro (Italian 'light and shade', or 'dark')	In painting, the modelling of volume by bold contrast of light and shade.
Corinthian	A type of pillar, one of the three classical orders of Greek architecture, characterised by a fluted column, topped by a capital decorated with acanthus leaves.
cozbo (Kharosthi script)	An official or functionary.
Da Qin (Chinese 'Great Qin')	The Chinese name for Rome or the Roman Empire.

deva (Sanskrit 'The Shining One', female: *devata*)	A deity or god, an inhabitant of the heavenly realms.
dharmachakramudra	The gesture signifying the 'turning the wheel of the law', in which both hands are held at chest level. The tips of the thumb and forefinger of the right hand form a circle and are touched by the left hand.
dhyanamudra	The gesture of meditation, where the hands of a seated figure are placed in the lap, one above the other, with palms facing upwards.
Dionysos (Greek mythology)	Known to the Romans as Bacchus – the god of wine and altered states (or religious ecstasy).
Doric	A type of column, one of the three classical orders of Greek architecture. It is characterised by the absence of a base, a simple tapering column and a plain capital.
Durga (Sanskrit 'difficult to penetrate')	A Hindu goddess, the female counterpart of Siva and slayer of the buffalo demon.
dvarapala	Heroic door guardian or keeper of the Buddhist faith, placed in pairs at the entrances to temples.
Eros (Greek mythology)	Known to the Romans as Cupid, the god of love.
gandharvas (Sanskrit)	Male celestial deities, sometimes known as musicians of the gods.
Ganesha	The elephant-headed son of the Hindu god Siva.
Garuda (Sanskrit)	Mythical bird, often depicted in part human form. Garuda is the mortal enemy of the nagas and is also the mount of the Hindu god Vishnu.
ghat (Hindi)	A landing place with steps on the banks of a river. A flat area at the top of the steps, used by Hindus as a place for cremation, is known as a burning ghat.
Gigaku dancing (also called *kure-uta* or 'Wu singing')	Comic dances performed with masks and closely associated with Buddhist temple ritual. *Gigaku* is the earliest form of Japanese theatrical entertainment and was introduced in 612 AD from southern China.

Guanyin (Chinese; Japanese: Kannon)	The *bodhisattva* of compassion, portrayed in female form and identified with the *bodhisattva* Avalokitesvara.
hamsa (Sanskrit)	A mythical semi-divine goose; the mount of the Hindu god Brahma.
Harpocrates (Greek 'Horus the child')	The Greeks' name for the Egyptian sky god Horus, represented as a small boy with his finger held to his lips. Harpocrates was regarded as the god of silence and was popular throughout the Roman Empire.
Herakles (Greek mythology)	Known as Hercules to the Romans, Herakles was the illegitimate offspring of Zeus and Alkmene, granddaughter of Perseus. He was honoured as a hero throughout the Greek world and after his death by poisoning was granted immortality among the gods.
Hinayana (Sanskrit 'lesser path' or 'vehicle')	Older school of Buddhism, popular in Sri Lanka, Thailand and Burma, in which the routes to salvation are more limited than those of the rival, Mahayana school. Also known as the Theravada ('path of the elders') school.
Hu (Chinese, possibly derives from *rou* – 'meat', or *yue* – 'moon')	General name applied in ancient China to the peoples living along the country's northern frontier.
intaglio	A hollow relief carving, commonly used for engraved seals and gems, in which a positive imprint is formed when pressed onto heated wax.
Ionic	A type of column, one of the three classical orders of Greek architecture. Ionic columns generally have a fluted shaft and a capital usually decorated with two scroll-like designs (volutes).
jatakas	Birth stories, episodes from the historical Buddha's prior lives, intended as moral lessons.
karaburan (Turkish)	A strong, warm wind that blows over Central Asia. It often carries fine-grained soil which is deposited as loess.
kariz (Persian – also called *kyariz* or *qanats*)	Underground water conduits for irrigation.

Kasyapa	An Indian ascetic who converted to Budhism late in life and, along with Ananda, became one of the Buddha's key disciples.
khagan (or khan)	King or ruler.
Kharosthi	Writing system used in north-western India before about 500, probably derived from Aramaic script and influenced by another Indian script, Brahmi.
kirttimukha (Sanskrit 'face of glory')	A horned, demon or lion mask used as a decorative device above temple doors and windows.
Kubera	In Hinduism, the king of nature spirits, or *yakshas*, and the god of wealth. Known as Jambhala in Buddhism.
kurgan (Turkish and Russian)	Barrow, artificial burial mound.
lalitasana (Sanskrit)	The position of 'royal ease', in which one leg is placed parallel to the ground and the other is pendent.
li (Chinese)	A *li* is equivalent to about 0.45 km. In Chinese literature, phrases such as 'a hundred thousand *li*' or 'ten thousand *li*' simply mean a distance beyond imagination.
limes (Latin 'path', plural 'limites')	Originally a strip of open land used by Roman troops to advance into hostile territory. The word subsequently came to be used to mean a military road, strengthened with a line of watchtowers and fortifications, or a natural or artificial frontier.
loess	Wind-borne dust from desert or vegetation-free areas at the margins of ice sheets. Loess deposits in north-west China can exceed 150 m in depth and have created vast fertile areas.
lokapala (Sanskrit and Pali)	A 'heavenly king' who protects one of the four cardinal directions.
Mahayana (Sanskrit 'greater vehicle' or 'path')	The school of Buddhism most prevalent from Nepal to Japan, and therefore also known as northern Buddhism – in contrast to the older, 'southern' Hinayana form. Its principal tenet is that salvation is open to all and may be attained rapidly with the assistance of *bodhisattvas*.

Maitreya (Sanskrit 'friendliness'; Japanese: Miroku) — The Buddha of the Future, now residing as a *bodhisattva* in Tushita heaven, but who will become incarnate when the teachings of Sakyamuni have become forgotten.

mandala (Sanskrit 'disk' or 'circle') — In Hinduism and Buddhism, a cosmic diagram, used as an aid for meditation. A *mandala* is essentially a representation of the universe, a collection point of universal forces.

Manichaeism — A religion influenced by both Gnosticism (a religious movement of the early Christian era rooted in paganism and magic), and Christianity itself. It originated in Persia around 230, founded by Mani (216, or 217–76) and spread across Asia and the Roman Empire, surviving in the far west of China until the thirteenth century. It is based on the struggle between the forces of Light (the Spirit) and Darkness (the Flesh).

Manjusri (Sanskrit; Chinese: Wenshu; Japanese: Monju) — In Mahayana Buddhism, the *bodhisattva* personifying supreme wisdom.

mantra (Sanskrit) — A sound expressing the deepest essence of understanding, the recitation of which is believed to evoke a state of enlightenment or intense positive energy.

Mara — The 'Lord of the Senses' who attempted to distract the Buddha as he sat beneath the Bo tree awaiting enlightenment.

mingqi (Chinese 'objects or articles of the spirit') — Objects placed in tombs, deposited in the belief that they would enable the deceased to carry their wealth and their favourite possessions with them to the afterlife.

mise (Chinese 'secret colour') — Green glazed ceramics from the Tang and Five Dynasties periods in China.

Mithra, Mithraism — Pre-Zoroastrian religion in ancient Persia, involving the worship of Mithra, god of light, justice and war. Mithra's slaying of the cosmic bull appears frequently in the art of the classical world. Mithra was associated with the Greek sun god Helios and often appears with Anahita, goddess of the waters.

naga (Sanskrit 'snake')	A snake deity or spirit, often depicted in part-human form.
Nestorius, Nestorianism	Early Christian doctrine, named after Nestorius, Roman Catholic patriarch of Constantinople, who was expelled from the church in 432 for heresy. It held that Christ has two natures – one human and one divine. His followers took Nestorianism eastwards from the sixth century onwards and it survived in parts of China until the fourteenth century.
nirvana (Sanskrit 'blowing out' or 'extinction')	Extinction of the fires of greed, hatred and ignorance, when perfect knowledge is attained and the cycle of earthly rebirths ceases.
pagoda	A brick, stone or wood tower of several storeys, erected to house relics of the Buddha. It evolved from the stupas of India.
parinirvana (Sanskrit)	The moment when the Buddha finally exits this world and enters nirvana.
Parthian Shot	A cavalry tactic, also popular as an artistic motif, in which a hunter shoots backwards from a galloping horse.
Phrygian cap	A conical wool or felt headdress with a pointed crown, originating in Phrygia in Asia Minor.
pipa (Chinese)	A four-stringed lute.
purnaghata	Vase-of-plenty, often used as a decorative element.
putto (plural *putti*)	Chubby, cherub-like young boys, frequently depicted with wings, appearing in paintings and sculpture.
qilin (Chinese 'male' plus 'female')	A Chinese mythical beast resembling a unicorn.
qin (Chinese)	A type of Chinese zither.
Sakyamuni	Title of the historical Buddha.
sancai (Chinese)	Three-coloured, usually lead-glazed earthenware pottery fired at low temperature. Its colours were typically yellow, white, green, brown and blue.
sangharama (or vihara)	A Buddhist monastery.
Seres (Latin 'country of silk')	The name given by the Romans to China.

Serindia	Term deriving from Seres, referring to the region of Chinese Central Asia traversed by the Silk Road and influenced by the cultures of both China and India.
shanyu (Chinese)	High chieftain among the nomads of the Ordos region of China's northern frontier.
Siddhartha	The personal name of the historical Buddha.
Siva (or Shiva, Sanskrit 'beneficent one')	One of the principal Hindu deities, a member of the trinity known as the Trimurti, characterised by a cosmic energy that manifests itself as both a destructive and creative force.
stupa	A Buddhist structure of Indian invention in the form of a mound or dome, built to house relics of the Buddha.
Surya (Sanskrit)	The Hindu god of the sun, often depicted as a charioteer.
sutra (Sanskrit 'thread')	A category of Buddhist scripture, believed to have been the words of the Buddha himself.
Tantric Buddhism (Tantra is Sanskrit for 'loom')	Also called Esoteric or Vajrayana ('Diamond Vehicle') Buddhism; a form of Mahayana Buddhism developed in Tibet and making use of mystic and astrological texts, mantras and mandalas.
Theravada	See Hinayana.
togatus (Latin 'toga wearer')	A Roman philosopher or statesman.
torana (Sanskrit)	In Indian architecture, a gateway, especially to a Buddhist stupa.
Transoxiana (in Arabic *Mawana'an nahr*: 'what is beyond the river')	Important historical region in Central Asia, the lands between the Amu Darya (Oxus) River and the Syr Darya (Jaxartes) River.
urna (Sanskrit)	A tuft of hair between the eyebrows, often represented as a dot, that denotes a great man – particularly with regard to the Buddha.
usnisha (Sanskrit 'that which is on top')	A raised chignon or cranial bump indicative of princely origins and superior wisdom, particularly with regard to the Buddha.

Vairocana (Sanskrit)	The most important of the five cosmic Buddhas, often represented at the centre of a *mandala*.
Vajrapani (Sanskrit 'thunderbolt bearer' or 'diamond bearer')	A celestial *bodhisattva*, the manifestation of Aksobhya, Buddha of the East.
vihara (Sanskrit)	A Buddhist monastery or a hall in a monastery.
Vimalikirti	Indian sage, renowned for his skill in debate.
Vishnu	Along with Siva and Brahma, one of the three members of the Hindu trinity (the Trimurti), who appears as ten different avatars or manifestations, most notably Rama and Krishna.
yaksha (Sanskrit, female: *yakshi*)	Nature or fertility deities found in both Hinduism and Buddhism.
Zeus (Greek mythology)	Supreme god in the Greek pantheon, the protector and ruler of humankind, identified by the Romans with Jupiter.
Zoroastrianism	A pre-Islamic religion, founded in ancient Persia during the sixth century BC by Zoroaster (or Zarathustra). Its basic beliefs concern the struggle between good and evil, light and darkness.

Notes

Introduction: The Early Development of the Silk Road, Principal Routes and Goods Carried

1 Seres ('the country of silk') was the name given by the Romans to China. Their notion of how silk was obtained was patchy at best. Pliny wrote, 'the Seres are famous for the wool of their forests. They remove the down from leaves with the help of water'; and Virgil thought that 'the Chinese comb off leaves their delicate down' (Pliny the Elder, *Natural History*).

1 Precursors of the Silk Road

1 Sima Qian (*c.*145–90 BC) was a descendant of the Qin family of nobles. Both he and his father, Sima Tan, held the post of Grand Historian and Astrologer in the court of Emperor Wudi (r.140–87 BC). He continued the work, begun by his father, of compiling a history of China, and had unquestionably met many of the characters about whom he writes. Sim Qian travelled widely, including journeys to some of the new dominions of Wudi's expanded empire, and appears to have read virtually all the extant Chinese literature – including documents in the Imperial archives. In 99 BC, Sima Qian's life took an appalling turn when an army led by the Chinese general Li Ning was defeated by the Xiongnu. Sima Qian attempted to defend Li Ning's capitulation to the nomads, but Wudi became enraged and ordered that he (Sima Qian) be arrested and castrated. He was subsequently rehabilitated and appointed to the post of palace secretary – a post open only to eunuchs – and this enabled him to complete his history, *Shiji* ('Records of the Grand Historian'). The *Shiji* is a huge work – 130 chapters and more than half a million characters – and is a veritable treasure trove of information about virtually every aspect of ancient Chinese history.

2 Recent genetic research suggests that Turcoman and Caspian horses, and not Arab breeds, may be ancestral to most, if not all forms of oriental horse. See: Firouz, L. *Origins of the Oriental Horse*. Institute for Ancient Equestrian Studies, conference in Petrovpavlovsk, Kazakhstan, 1995.

3 *Equus Przewalski* is the last species of wild horse, first identified by the Russian-Polish explorer Colonel Nikolai Przewalski in the Gobi desert in 1881. Attempts to breed this rare animal in zoos failed and, by 1977, there were only about 300 animals left. A number of concerted campaigns were launched to save the horse and to reintroduce it to the Mongolian steppe. The projects appear to have been a success and, according to the 'IUCN Red List of Threatened Species', in 2008 there were a total of about 1,800 examples, both in the wild and in captivity.

2 The Introduction of Buddhism to China

1 Kipling's description is of another of Asia's great highways – India's Grand Trunk Road, built by the East India Company and running northwestwards from Calcutta across the entire country as far as the Khyber Pass. The road follows the course of ancient trade routes across the country. The presence of columns, erected by the Mauryan emperor, Ashoka, during the third century BC, suggests that the road has been a major route since the earliest times.

4 The Old Capital of Changan (Xian)

1 The city's ancient and modern names – Changan and Xian – will be used interchangeably throughout this section.

2 This song concerns a conscript sent to labour on the Great Wall.

3 For more on this plate, please see *Orientations*, May 2001 issue, pp 52–8.

4 Another instance of the goat-man motif has been identified in a fragment of a woollen skirt from the Shanpula area in the Abegg-Stiftung collection (see Keller and Schorta, 2001). For more on Shanpula see page 186. The goat-man motif is identified and discussed in So and Bunker, 1995.

5 A *li* is equivalent to about 0.45 km. Phrases such as 'a hundred thousand *li*', or 'ten thousand *li*', simply mean a distance beyond imagination.

6 Modern day Xian is still surrounded by moated walls, 12 m high and about 14 km in length. They date to the early Ming dynasty but were built upon the remains of the original Tang dynasty walls.

7 The Taika reform movement sought to change the age-old status of Japan as a nation of loosely affiliated, separate states. Instead, the country would comprise provinces that were governed by a centralised bureaucracy and ruled by the emperor. The reform edicts required that all government officials submit to a Chinese-style civil service examination and drastically curtailed the independence of regional officials – designating the imperial court as a place of appeal and complaint for the people. The overall intention was to bring Japanese society in line with Chinese social practices.

8 Other examples of Li Bai's poetry appear elsewhere in this book.

9 Qinghai Lake – Kokonor, or 'The Blue Lake' – was known as the 'Western Sea' during ancient times and is a remote saline lake situated some 3,200 m above sea level. Qinghai province has been a place of exile since the Han dynasty. It lies on the main route between China and Tibet and throughout the 740s was the scene of fierce fighting between the armies of the two rival countries. Tang poets always regarded war as a cause for sadness because it reflected a failure of government.

5 The Silk Road Between Xian and Dunhuang

1 For travellers heading east, the starting point would have been Baqiao Bridge on the Ba River, east of Changan, where the same willow branch rituals occurred. For a different translation of this poem please see page 125.
2 For a survey of the Dunhuang caves and their works of art see the following link: http://www.art-and-archaeology.com/china/dunhuang/du01.html.
3 For more on this subject see the following website: www.threehares.net
4 For more on the British Library's 'International Dunhuang Project' see: www.idp.bl.uk.

6 The Silk Road Through China Beyond Dunhuang

1 Willows are symbols of farewell for the Chinese.
2 Qu Yuan (*c*.340–278 BC) was a member of the ruling house, a statesman and diplomat. He was eventually banished by the court as a result of slanders by rivals and, in despair, he drowned himself in the Mi-lo – a tributary of the Yangtze. The traditional date of his death is the fifth day of the fifth moon (month). Annual commemoration of the event is said to be the origin of China's Dragon Boat Festival.
3 For a brief survey of Bezeklik's paintings, see the following link: http://www.art-and-archaeology.com/china/turpan/be01.html.
4 There is another Iron Gate Pass on the Silk Road, near Derbent in Uzbekistan. It was also named for the colour of its rock, although the Kushans may have installed an actual gate there of colossal size. Xuanzang passed through it on his way to Balkh.
5 The practice of dividing Kizil's paintings (and therefore the paintings of the Kuqa area as a whole) into first and second Indo-Persian styles has been thrown into question by recent research by Professor Marianne Yaldiz at the Berlin Museum. Samples of straw taken from the back of a number of the museum's wall paintings have been subjected to radiocarbon testing and the preliminary results indicate that the dates are spread far more widely than was previously thought – ranging from 237–650. The two styles also appear to be mixed, not distinct from each other. The dates given in the descriptions on pages 146–7 are the radiocarbon age, where this is known, and the generally accepted date where it is not. For images of these wonderful paintings, see the following link: http://depts.washington.edu/silkroad/museums/mia/kizil.html.
6 See note 5 above.

7   For a survey of works of art from Kumtura in the Museum of Asian Art, Berlin – including this *bodhisattva* – see the following link: http://depts.washington.edu/silkroad/museums/mia/kumtura.html.

8   For a survey of works of art from Tumshuq in the Musée Guimet, Paris (including the Sanjali-*avadana* relief), see the following link: http://depts.washington.edu/silkroad/museums/mg/tumshuq.html.

9   For a survey of the objects discovered by Stein at Loulan, and now housed in the British Museum, see the following link: http://tinyurl.com/3hb9zlm.

10 For a survey of the objects discovered by Stein at Miran, and now housed in the British Museum, see the following link: http://tinyurl.com/3f7sm8q.

11 There was also an important Tibetan fort, the ruins of which still exist, at Mazartagh, beside the Khotan River on the ancient route that leads north from Khotan.

12 For a survey of the objects discovered by Stein at Niya, and now in the British Museum, see the following link: http://tinyurl.com/437co9z.

13 For a survey of the objects discovered by Stein at Khotan, and now housed in the British Museum, see the following link: http://tinyurl.com/3bntl9d.

14 For a survey of the objects discovered by Stein at Yotkan, and now housed in the British Museum, see the following link: http://tinyurl.com/3gu8odf.

15 For a survey of the British Museum objects discovered by Stein at Dandan-Oilik (including the Silk Princess and God of Silk panels), see the following link: http://tinyurl.com/3r33d8k.

16 One of the cruel ironies of Khotan's sericulture industry is that it flourished until the modern age and, only in recent years, has it fallen into decline. As recently as 1959 there were 7 million mulberry trees in Khotan prefecture and the annual output of silkworm cocoons reached a peak of 1,200 tons. During the 1960s China suffered the excesses of the Cultural Revolution, during which widespread and arbitrary deforestation occurred. By 1979 there were only 2 million mulberry trees in Khotan and annual cocoon output had fallen to 400 tons (figures from Che Muqi, 1989). The Chinese government is now making a concerted effort to revive the industry and production is again rising.

7 The Silk Road Between China and India Including the Karakorum Highway

1   The inscription is discussed at length by Ma Yong in Jettmar *et al.*, 1989–94. Ma Yong identifies Mi-mi as the region known to Arab geographers as 'Maymurgh', situated to the south-east of Samarkand. However, Jettmar disagrees and suggests that the place was an as yet unidentified town in the Gandhara region.

2   See also the note on India's Grand Trunk Road (Chapter 2, note 1). Ashokan columns are to be found along the road, indicating that it has been used as an arterial highway since the earliest times.

3   Kipling describes the Gandhara sculpture of the Lahore Museum, 'The Wonder House', at which his father, Lockwood, was curator.

Bibliography

General

Beckwith, C. *Empires of the Silk Road: A History of Central Eurasia from the Bronze Age to the Present*. Princeton, NJ, and Oxford: Princeton University Press, 2009.

Boisselier, Jean. *The Wisdom of the Buddha*. Trans. by Carey Lovelace. London: Thames and Hudson, 1994.

Boulnois, Luce. *The Silk Road*. Trans. by Dennis Chamberlain. New York: E. P. Dutton and Co., 1966.

Boulnois, L. and Mayhew, B. *Silk Road: Monks, Warriors and Merchants*. Hong Kong: Odyssey Illustrated Guides, 2003.

Che, Muqi. *The Silk Road: Past and Present*. Beijing: Foreign Languages Press, 1989.

Collins, R. *East to Cathay: The Silk Road*. New York: McGraw-Hill, 1968.

Drège, J.-P. and Bührer, E. M. *The Silk Road Saga*. New York and Oxford: Facts on File, 1989.

Elisseeff, V. (ed.). *The Silk Roads: Highways of Culture and Commerce*. New York: Berghahn Books; Paris: UNESCO Pub., 2000.

Fa Xian. *A Record of Buddhistic Kingdoms, Being an Account of the Chinese Monk Fâ-Hien*. Trans. by James Legge. Oxford: Clarendon Press, 1886.

Firouz, L. *Origins of the Oriental Horse*. Institute for Ancient Equestrian Studies, Conference in Petrovpavlovsk, Kazakhstan, 1995.

Franck, Irene and Brownstone, David. *The Silk Road: A History*. New York and Oxford: Facts on File, 1986.

Hui, Li. *The Life of Hiuen-Tsiang*. Trans. by Samuel Beal. London: Kegan Paul *et al.*, 1911.

Kelly, Laurence. *Istanbul: A Traveller's Companion*. London: Constable, 1987.

The Koran. Trans. by N. J. Dawood. London: Penguin, 1999.

Liu, Xinru. *Silk and Religion: An Exploration of Material Life and the Thought of People, AD 600–1200*. Delhi and Oxford: Oxford University Press, 1996.

——— *The Silk Road in World History*. New York and Oxford: Oxford University Press, 2010.

Polo, Marco. *The Travels of Marco Polo the Venetian*. Trans. by William Marsden. New York: Doubleday and Co., 1948.

Sérinde, Terre de Bouddha: dix siècles d'art sur la Route de la Soie. Exhibition catalogue, Galeries nationales du Grand Palais, Paris: Réunion des musées nationaux, 1995.

Shiruku Rodo dai bunmei ten. Shiruku rodo, oashisu to sogen no michi ('The Grand Exhibition of Silk Road civilizations'). 3 vols, Exhibition catalogue. Nara National Museum, Nara: Nara Kokuritsu Hakubutsukan, 1988.

The Silk Road and the World of Xuanzang. Asahi Shimbun 120th Anniversary Commemorative Exhibition. Osaka: Asahi Shimbun, 1999.

Sun, Yifu (ed.). *The Silk Road on Land and Sea*. Beijing: China Pictorial Publications, 1989.

Ting, Joseph (ed.). *The Maritime Silk Route: 2000 Years of Trade on the South China Sea*. Hong Kong: Urban Council, 1996.

Tucker, Jonathan. *The Silk Road: Art and History*. London: Philip Wilson Publishers Ltd, 2003.

——— *The Silk Road – Central Asia, Afghanistan and Iran: A Travel Companion*. London: I.B.Tauris, 2015.

——— *The Ancient Silk Road: An Illustrated Map Featuring the Ancient Network of Routes Between China and Europe*. Hong Kong: Odyssey Publications, 2007.

Vollmer, J. E., Keall, E. J. and Nagai-Berthrong, E. *Silk Road China Ships*. Toronto: Royal Ontario Museum, 1983.

Walker, Annabel. *Stein: Pioneer of the Silk Road*. London: John Murray, 1995.

Whitfield, S. *Life Along the Silk Road*. London: John Murray, 1999.

——— *Aurel Stein on the Silk Road*. London: British Museum, 2004a.

——— *The Silk Road: Trade, Travel, War and Faith*. Exhibition catalogue. London: British Library, 2004b.

Wood, F. *Did Marco Polo Go to China?* London: Secker and Warburg, 1995.

——— *The Silk Road: Two Thousand Years in the Heart of Asia*. London: British Library Publishing Division, 2004.

Wriggins, S. H. *Xuanzang: A Buddhist Pilgrim on the Silk Road*. Boulder, Colorado: Westview Press, 1996.

Xuanzang. *Si-yu-ki: Buddhist Records of the Western World, by Hiuen Tsiang*. Trans. by Samuel Beal. 2 vols in one edition, London: Kegan Paul *et al*., 1884.

China and Japan

Agnew, N. (ed.). *Ancient Sites on the Silk Road: Proceedings of the Second International Conference on the Conservation of Grotto Sites, Mogao Grottoes, Dunhuang, People's Republic of China*. Los Angeles: Getty Publications, 2010.

Akiyama, T. and Matsubara, S. *Arts of China: Buddhist Cave Temples – New Researches*. Vol. 2, Tokyo: Kodansha International, 1969.

Alley, Rewi. *Selected Poems of the Tang and Song Dynasties*. Hong Kong: Hai Feng Publishing Co., 1981.

Andrews, F. H. *Wall Paintings from Ancient Shrines in Central Asia Recovered by Sir Aurel Stein*. London: Oxford University Press, 1948.

Anzhi, Yun and Nanfeng, Jiao. *Daily Life of Aristocrats in Tang China*. Exhibition catalogue. Hong Kong: Regional Council, 1993.

Barber, E. W. *The Mummies of Urumqi*. London: Macmillan, 1999.

Barfield, T. J. *The Perilous Frontier: Nomadic Empires and China*. Oxford: Basil Blackwell, 1989.

Baumer, C. *Southern Silk Road: In the Footsteps of Sir Aurel Stein and Sven Hedin*. Bangkok: Orchid Press, 2000.

Bhattacharya, C. *Art of Central Asia: With Special Reference to Wooden Objects from the Northern Silk Route*. Delhi: Agam Prakashan, 1977.

Birrell, Anne. *Popular Songs and Ballads of Han China*. London: Unwin Hyman Ltd, 1988.

Blunden, C. and Elvin, M. *Cultural Atlas of China*. Oxford: Time Life Books, 1983.

Bonavia, J. *The Silk Road from Xi'an to Kashgar*. Hong Kong: Odyssey Publications, 1988 (reprinted 1999).

Burrow, T. A., *Translation of the Kharosthi Documents from Chinese Turkestan*. London: Royal Asiatic Society, 1940.

Bynner, W. *The Jade Mountain. A Chinese Anthology: Being 300 Poems of the Tang Dynasty*. New York: Alfred A. Knopf, 1930.

Cable, M. and French, F. *Through Jade Gate and Central Asia*. London: Hodder and Stoughton, 1927.

———— *The Gobi Desert*. London: Hodder and Stoughton, 1942.

———— *China: Her Life and Her People*. London: University of London Press, 1946.

Cable, M., French, F. and French, E. *A Desert Journal: Letters from Central Asia*. London: Constable and Co. Ltd, 1934.

Capon, E. *Tang China: Vision and Splendour of a Golden Age*. London: Macdonald Orbis, 1989.

Capon, E. and Macquitty, W. *Princes of Jade*. London: Nelson, 1973.

Chen, Yu. *Tales from Dunhuang*. Trans. by Li Guishan. Beijing: New World Press, 1989.

China Cultural Relics Promotion Center. *Treasures: 300 Best Excavated Antiques from China*. Beijing: New World Press, 1992.

Chuka Jinmin Kyowakoku Shiruku Rodo Bunbutsu Ten; The Exhibition of Ancient Art Treasures of The People's Republic of China: Archaeological Finds of the Han to T'ang Dynasty Unearthed at Sites along the Silk Road. Exhibition catalogue. Tokyo: Yomiuri Shinbumsha, 1979.

Duan, Wenjie (ed.). *The Cream of Dunhuang Art*. Beijing: Polyspring Co. Ltd, 1994.

Dubs, Homer. *History of the Former Han by Pan Ku (Han Shu)*. 3 vols, Baltimore: Waverly Press, 1938.

———— *A Roman City in Ancient China?* London: The China Society, 1957.

Dunhuang Research Inst. (ed.). *The Mogao Grottoes of Dunhuang*. Hong Kong: Polyspring Co., 1993.

Emmerick, R. E. *A Guide to the Literature of Khotan*. Studia Philologica Buddhica, Tokyo: The Reiyukai Library, 1979.

Feng, Fei. *The Nude Art of the Qiuci Grottoes*. Hong Kong: Xinjiang Fine Arts and Photographing Press/Educational and Cultural Press Ltd, 1992.

Feng, Zhao and Zhiyong, Yu (eds). *Legacy of the Desert King: Textiles and Treasures Excavated at Niya on the Silk Road*. Exhibition catalogue. Urumqi: Chinese National Silk Museum, Hangzhou and Xinjiang Institute of Archeology, 2000.

Fong, Weng C. and Watt, James C. Y. *Possessing the Past: Treasures from the National Palace Museum, Taipei*. Exhibition catalogue. New York: Metropolitan Museum of Art, 1996.

Fontein, Jan and Wu, Tung. *Unearthing China's Past*. Boston: Museum of Fine Arts, 1973.

Gao, Feng and Sun, Jianjun. *Zhongguo deng ju jian shi*. Beijing: Beijing gong yi mei shu chu ban she, 1992.

Gernet, Jacques. *Daily Life in China on the Eve of the Mongol Invasion, 1250–1276*. Trans. by H. M. Wright. London: Allen and Unwin, 1962.

———— *A History of Chinese Civilisation*. Trans. by J. R. Foster. Cambridge: Cambridge University Press, 1982.

———— *Buddhism in Chinese Society: An Economic History from the Fifth to the Tenth Centuries*. Trans. by F. Verellen. New York: Columbia University Press, 1995.

Giès, Jacques (ed.). *The Arts of Central Asia: The Pelliot Collection in the Musée Guimet*. 3 vols, London: Serindia Publications, 1994–6.

Giles, Lionel. *Six Centuries at Tunhuang: A Short Account of the Stein Collection of Chinese MSS in the British Museum*. London: China Society, 1944.

Harada, Jiro. *English Catalogue of Treasures in the Imperial Repository Shosoin*. Tokyo: Imperial Household Museum, 1932.

Hayashi, Ryoichi. *The Silk Road and the Shoso-in*. New York and Tokyo: Weatherhill/Heibonsha, 1975.

Hedin, Sven. *My Life as an Explorer*. New York: Garden City Publishing, 1925.

———— *The Silk Road*. Trans. by F. H. Lyon. New York: Dutton, 1938.

Hinton, D. *The Selected Poems of Li Po*. London: Anvil Press, 1996.

Hopkirk, P. *Foreign Devils on the Silk Road: The Search for the Lost Cities and Treasures of Chinese Central Asia*. London: John Murray, 1980.

Huang, Zuan. (ed.). *Die Antike Seidenstrasse*. Beijing: China Im Bild, 1987.

Jenner, W. J. F. *Memories of Loyang: Yang Hsüan-chih and the Lost Capital (493–534)*. Oxford: Clarendon Press, 1981.

Juliano, A. and Lerner, J. *Monks and Merchants: Silk Road Treasures from Northwest China*. New York: Harry N. Abrams Inc. with the Asia Society, 2001.

Karetzky, Patricia. *Arts of the Tang Court*. Hong Kong: Oxford University Press, 1996.

Keller, D. and Schorta, R. (eds). *Fabulous Creatures from the Desert Sands: Central Asian Woolen Textiles from the Second Century BC to the Second Century AD*. Riggisberg: Abegg-Stiftung, 2001.

Knauer, E. R. *The Camel's Load in Life and Death: Iconography and Ideology of Chinese Pottery Figurines from Han to Tang and their Relevance to Trade along the Silk Routes*. Zurich: Akanthus, 1998.

Krahl, R. *Chinese Ceramics from the Meiyintang Collection*. London: Azimuth Editions, 1994.

Lattimore, Owen. *Pivot of Asia: Sinkiang and the Inner Asian Frontiers of China and Russia*. Boston: Little, Brown and Co., 1950.

Le Coq, A. von. *Buried treasures of Chinese Turkestan: An Account of the Activities and Adventures of the Second and Third German Turfan Expeditions*. Trans. by Anna Barwell. London: George Allen & Unwin, 1929.

Lee, Sherman E. *China – 5000 Years: Innovation and Transformation in the Arts*. Exhibition catalogue. New York: Guggenheim Museum, 1998.

Li, Guo and Gao, Guo Xiang (eds). *The Treasure House of Dunhuang.* Dunguang: wen yi chu ban she 1993.

Li, Wei. (ed.). Women of the Tang Dynasty. Exhibition catalogue. Shaanxi History Museum, Hong Kong: Pacific Century, 1995.

Li, Zhengyu (ed.). *Dunhuang Art Relics Collected in the State Hermitage Museum, Russia.* Vols I and II. Shanghai: Shanghai gu ji chu ban she, 1997.

Liao, Jingdan (ed.). *The Great Treasury of Chinese Fine Arts and Crafts.* Vol. 10, Beijing: The People's Fine Arts Publishing House, 1988.

Liu, Wenmin. *The Silk Road: An Ancient Road to Central Asia.* Trans. by Jiang Ying. Beijing: China Three Gorges Publishing House, 1993.

Loewe, M. *Everyday Life in Early Imperial China during the Han Period, 202 BC–AD 220.* London: Carousel Books, 1973.

Ma, Yue and Yan, Zhongyi. (eds). *Xian: Legacies of Ancient Chinese Civilization.* Beijing: Morning Glory Publishers, 1992.

Mair, Victor H. *Tun-huang Popular Narratives.* Cambridge: Cambridge University Press, 1983.

Mallory, J. P. and Mair, V. H. *The Tarim Mummies: Ancient China and the Mystery of the Earliest Peoples from the West.* London: Thames and Hudson, 2000.

Mancheng Han mu fa jue bao gao. 2 vols, Beijing: Wen wu zhu ban she: Xin hua shu dian fa xing, 1980.

Medley, M. *Tang Pottery and Porcelain.* London: Faber and Faber, 1981.

Metropolitan Museum of Art, New York and Museum für Indische Kunst, Berlin. *Along the Ancient Silk Routes: Central Asian Art from the West Berlin State Museums.* Exhibition catalogue. New York: Metropolitan Museum of Art, 1982.

Michaelson, Carol. *Gilded Dragons: Buried Treasures from China's Golden Ages.* London: British Museum, 1999.

Mission Paul Pelliot. I & II (M. Paul-David, M. Hallade and L. Hambis). *Toumchouq.* 2 vols, Paris: Académie des Inscriptions et Belles-Lettres, 1961–4.

Mission Paul Pelliot. III & IV (M. Hallade, S. Gaulier and L. Courtois). *Douldour-Aqour et Soubachi.* 2 vols, Paris: Imprimerie Nationale, 1967–82.

Mission Paul Pelliot. XIII (Krishna Riboud, G. Vial and M. Hallade). *Tissus de Touen-houang conservés au Musée Guimet et á la Bibliothèque nationale.* Paris, 1970.

Mission Paul Pelliot. XIV & XV. *Bannières et peintures de Touen-Houang conservées au Musée Guimet.* 2 vols, Paris, 1974–6.

Mu, Shunying (ed.). *The Ancient Art in Xinjiang, China.* Urumqi: Xinjiang Fine Arts and Photo Publishing House, 1994.

National Museum of Chinese History. *A Journey into China's Antiquity.* 4 vols, Beijing: Morning Glory Publishers, 1997.

——— *Exhibition of Chinese History.* Beijing: Morning Glory Publishers, 1998.

Needham, Joseph. *Science and Civilisation in China. Vol. 1, Introductory Orientations.* Cambridge: Cambridge University Press, 1954.

Paludan, Ann. *Chronicle of the Chinese Emperors: The Reign-by-Reign Record of the Rulers of Imperial China.* London: Thames and Hudson, 1998.

Pelliot, Paul. *Trois Ans dans la Haute Asie.* Paris: Bulletin du Comité de l'Asie française, 1910.

Piotrovsky, M. (ed.). *Lost Empire of the Silk Road: Buddhist Art from Khara Khoto (X-XIIIth century).* Lugano: Thyssen-Bornemisza Foundation, 1993.

Prodan, M. *The Art of the Tang Potter.* London: Thames and Hudson, 1960.

Qi, Xiaoshan and Wang, Bo (eds). *A Collection of Important Historical Sites and Relics in the Western Regions.* Urumqi: Xinjiang People's Publishing Press, 1999.

Qian, Hao, Chen Heyi and Ru Suichu. *Out of China's Earth: Archeological Discoveries in the People's Republic of China.* London: Frederick Muller; Beijing: China Pictorial, 1981.

Rawson, Jessica (ed.). *Mysteries of Ancient China: New Discoveries from the Early Dynasties.* London: British Museum, 1996.

Research Center for Silk Roadology. 'Space Archeology' in *Silk Roadology* 1. Nara, 1995.

Rhie, Marilyn Martin. *Early Buddhist Art of China and Central Asia.* Vol. 1, Leiden and Boston: Brill, 1999.

Rodzinski, Witold. *The Walled Kingdom: A History of China from 2000 BC to the Present.* London: Fontana, 1984.

Roran okoku toyukyu no bijo ('The Kingdom of Loulan and the Eternal Beauty'). Exhibition catalogue. Tokyo: Asahi Shinbunsha, 1992.

Schafer, Edward. *The Golden Peaches of Samarkand: A Study of T'ang Exotics.* Berkeley and London: University of California Press, 1963.

—— *The Vermilion Bird. T'ang Images of the South.* Berkeley and Los Angeles: University of California Press, 1967.

Schloss, Ezekiel. *Foreigners in Ancient Chinese Art.* Exhibition catalogue. New York: China Institute in America, 1969.

—— *Ancient Chinese Ceramic Sculpture. From Han Through Tang.* Vol. I, Stamford: Castle Publishing, 1977.

Seth, Vikram. *Three Chinese Poets.* London: Faber and Faber, 1992.

Shao, Menglong (ed.). *Precious Cultural Relics in the Crypt of Famen Temple.* Xian: Shaanxi People's Fine Arts Publishing House, 1989.

Sickman, Laurence and Soper, Alexander. *The Art and Architecture of China.* Harmondsworth: Penguin, 1988.

Sima, Qian. *Records of the Grand Historian: Shiji.* Trans. by Burton Watson. 2 vols, New York: Columbia University Press, 1993.

Sinor, Denis (ed.). *The Cambridge History of Early Inner Asia.* Cambridge: Cambridge University Press, 1990.

Skrine, Sir Clarmont. *Chinese Central Asia.* London: Methuen, 1926.

So, Jenny F. and Bunker, Emma C. *Traders and Raiders on China's Northern Frontier.* Exhibition catalogue. Seattle: Arthur M. Sackler Gallery in association with the University of Washington Press, 1995.

Stein, M. Aurel. *Sand-Buried Ruins of Khotan.* London: Hurst and Blackett Ltd, 1904.

—— *Ancient Khotan: Detailed Report of Archaeological Explorations in Chinese Turkestan.* 2 vols, Oxford: Clarendon Press, 1907.

—— *Ruins of Desert Cathay.* 2 vols, London: Macmillan, 1912.

—— 'A Third Journey of Exploration in Central Asia, 1913–16' in *The Geographical Journal,* August/September 1916.

—— *Serindia – Detailed Report of Explorations in Central Asia and Westernmost China.* Oxford: Clarendon Press, 1921.

—— *Innermost Asia – Detailed Report of Explorations in Central Asia, Kan-su and Eastern Iran.* Oxford: Clarendon Press, 1928.

——— *On Central Asian Tracks*. New York: Pantheon, 1964.

Sullivan, Michael. *The Cave Temples of Maichishan*. London: Faber and Faber, 1969.

Swann, Peter C. *Chinese Monumental Art*. London: Thames and Hudson, 1963.

Tang, Z. C. *Poems of Tang*. San Rafael, California: T. C. Press, 1969.

Time Life Books. *China's Buried Kingdoms*. Virginia: Time Life Books, 1993.

Tomb Treasures from China: The Buried Art of Ancient Xian. Exhibition catalogue. Asian Art Museum of San Francisco and Kimbell Art Museum, Fort Worth, 1994.

Treasures of Chang'an: Capital of the Silk Road. Exhibition catalogue. Hong Kong Museum of Art and the Overseas Exhibitions Department, Cultural Bureau of Shaanxi. Xian: Xianggang shi zheng ju, 1993.

Treasures of Dunhuang Grottoes. Hong Kong: Polyspering Co. Ltd, 1999.

Turfan Museum Guide. Urumqi: Xinjiang Fine Arts and Photo Publishing House, 1992.

Twitchett, Denis (ed.). *The Cambridge History of China. Vol. 6, Alien Regimes and Border States, 710–1368*. Cambridge: Cambridge University Press, 1993.

Twitchett, Denis and Fairbank, John K. (eds). *The Cambridge History of China. Vol. 3, Sui and T'ang China, 589–906. Part 1*. Cambridge: Cambridge University Press, 1979.

——— *The Cambridge History of China. Vol. 1, The Ch'in and Han Empires, 221 BC–AD 220*. Cambridge: Cambridge University Press, 1986.

Waley, Arthur. *A Catalogue of Paintings Recovered from Tun-huang by Sir Aurel Stein KCIE*. London: British Museum, 1931.

——— *Translations from the Chinese*. New York: Alfred A. Knopf Inc., 1941.

——— *The Real Tripitaka and Other Pieces*. London: Allen and Unwin, 1952.

Wang, Zhongshu. *Han Civilisation*. Trans. by K. C. Chang. New Haven, Connecticut and London: Yale University Press, 1982.

Warner, Langdon. *The Long Old Road in China*. New York: Doubleday, Page & Co., 1926.

Watson, B. *The Columbia Book of Chinese Poetry*. New York: Columbia University Press, 1984.

Watson, W. *The Genius of China*. Exhibition catalogue. Royal Academy of Arts, London: Times Newspapers, 1973.

——— *Tang and Liao Ceramics*. London: Thames and Hudson, 1984.

Watt, J. (ed.). *China: Dawn of a Golden Age, 200–750 AD*. Exhibition catalogue. New York: Metropolitan Museum of Art, 2004.

Wei, Cuiyi and Luckert, K. W. *Uighur Stories from along the Silk Road*. Lanham, Maryland: University Press of America, 1998.

White, J. and Bunker, E. *Adornment for Eternity: Status and Rank in Chinese Ornament*. Exhibition catalogue. Denver: Denver Art Museum, 1994.

Whitfield, R. *The Art of Central Asia: The Stein Collection in the British Museum*. Vols 1–3, Tokyo: Kodansha, 1985.

——— *Dunhuang: Caves of the Singing Sands. Buddhist Art from the Silk Road*. London: Textile & Art Publications, 1996.

Whitfield, R. and Farrer, A. *Caves of the Thousand Buddhas. Chinese Art from the Silk Route*. London: British Museum, 1990.

Wong, Grace. *The Silk Road. Treasures of Tang China*. Exhibition catalogue. Singapore: Landmark Books, 1991.

Wong, How Man and Dajani, Adel A. *Islamic Frontiers of China. Silk Road Images.* London: Scorpion Publishing, 1990.

Xian Forest of Stone Tablets Museum Guide, Xian, 2000.

Xinjiang: The Land and its People. Beijing: New World Press, 1989.

Xu, Huatian, Xie, Yaohua and Che, Hongbo. *A Guide to the Scenic Spots and Historical Sites in Xinjiang China.* Urumqi: Xinjiang People's Publishing House, 2000.

Xu, Yuan Zhong. *300 Tang Poems – A New Translation.* Beijing, 1987.

———— *Golden Treasury of Chinese Poetry from Han to Sui (206 BC–AD 618).* Beijing: Peking University Press, 1996.

Yamanobe, T. *Fabrics from the Silk Road: The Stein Collection, National Museum.* New Delhi and Kyoto: Shikosha, 1979.

Yang, Xiaoneng (ed.). *The Golden Age of Chinese Archaeology.* New Haven and London: Yale University Press, 1999.

Yap, Yong and Cotterell, A. *The Early Civilisation of China.* London: Weidenfeld and Nicolson, 1975.

Yue, Feng (ed.). *A Grand View of Xinjiang's Cultural Relics and Historic Sites.* Urumqi: Xinjiang Meishu Sheying, 1999.

Yung, Peter. *Bazaars of Chinese Turkestan: Life and Trade along the Old Silk Road.* Oxford: Oxford University Press, 1997.

Zhang, Xuerong (ed.). *A Series of Books of Maijishan Grottoes.* Vol. 1, Tianshui: Gansu People's Fine Arts Publishing House, 1997.

Zheng, Zhenduo (ed.). *Bingling si shi ku.* Beijing: Zhongyang ren min zheng fu wen hua bu wen hua si ye guan li ju, 1953.

Zhenghuang, He (ed.). *Xian: An Ancient Capital of China.* Beijing: Foreign Languages Press, 1990.

Zhou, Xuejun and Song, Weimin (eds). *Archaeological Treasures of the Silk Road in Xinjiang Uygur Autonomous Region.* Exhibition catalogue. Shanghai Museum, Shanghai: Shanghai Translation Publishing House, 1998.

Zou, Zongxu. *The Land within the Passes: A History of Xian.* Trans. by Susan Whitfield. London and New York: Viking, 1991.

India, Pakistan and Afghanistan

Czuma, S. J. *Kushan Sculpture: Images from Early India.* Cleveland: Cleveland Museum of Art, 1985.

Dani, Ahmad Hasan. *Chilas: The City of Nanga Parvat (Dyamar).* Islamabad: Quaid-I-Azam University, 1983a.

———— *Guide to the Karakorum Highway.* Islamabad: Quaid-I-Azam University, 1983b.

———— *Human Records on the Karakorum Highway.* Lahore: Sang-e-Meel Publications, 1995.

———— *The Historic City of Taxila.* Lahore: Sang-e-Meel Publications, 1999.

Dupree, A., Dupree, L. and Motamedi, A. A. *A Guide to the Kabul Museum.* Kabul: Afghan Tourist Organization, 1968.

Dupree, N. H. *The Road to Balkh.* Kabul: Afghan Tourist Organization, 1967.

———— *An Historical Guide to Afghanistan.* Kabul: Afghan Tourist Organization, 1977.

Dupree, N. H., Dupree, L. and Motamedi, A. A. *The National Museum of Afghanistan: An Illustrated Guide.* Kabul: Afghan Tourist Organization, 1974.

Errington, E. and Cribb, J. (eds). *The Crossroads of Asia.* Exhibition Catalogue. Cambridge: Ancient India and Iran Trust, 1992.

Hackin, J. *Nouvelles recherches archéologiques à Begram.* 2 vols, Paris: Imprimerie Nationale, 1954.

Hallade, H. *The Gandhara Style and the Evolution of Buddhist Art.* London: Thames and Hudson, 1968.

Ingholt, H. and Lyons, I. *Gandharan Art in Pakistan.* New York: Pantheon Books, 1957.

Jettmar, K. (ed.). *Antiquities of Northern Pakistan: Reports and Studies.* Mainz: Zabern, 1989–94.

Klimburg-Salter, D. *Buddha in Indien: Die frühindische Skulptur von König Aśoka bis zur Guptazeit.* Exhibition Catalogue. Milan and Vienna: Skira editore and Kunsthistorisches Museum, 1995.

Kurita, I. *Gandharan Art.* 2 vols, Tokyo: Nigensha, 1988.

Marshall, Sir John. *A Guide to Taxila.* Calcutta: Superintendent Government Printing, 1918.

—— *Taxila: An Illustrated Account of Archaeological Excavations Carried Out at Taxila under the Orders of the Government of India between the Years 1913 and 1934.* Cambridge: Cambridge University Press, 1951.

Mousavi, S. A. *The Hazaras of Afghanistan: An Historical, Cultural, Economic and Political Study.* Richmond, Surrey: Curzon Press, 1998.

Mukhtarov, Akhror. *Balkh in the Late Middle Ages.* Papers on Inner Asia No. 24. Trans. by R. D. McChesney. Bloomington, Indiana: Research Institute for Inner Asia Studies, Indiana University, 1993.

Rice, F. Mortimer and Rowland, B. *Art in Afghanistan: Objects from the Kabul Museum.* Miami: University of Miami Press, 1971.

Rosenfield, J. M. *The Dynastic Arts of the Kushans.* Berkeley: University of California Press, 1967.

Rowland, Benjamin. *Ancient Art from Afghanistan: Treasures from the Kabul Museum.* Exhibition catalogue. New York: Asia Society, 1976.

Sariandi, V. *Bactrian Gold from the Excavations of the Tillya Tepe Necropolis in Northern Afghanistan.* St Petersburg: Aurora Art Publishers, 1985.

Sharma, R. C. *Buddhist Art: Mathura School.* New Delhi: Wiley Eastern Press, 1995.

Wolfe, N. H. *The Valley of Bamiyan.* Kabul: Afghan Tourist Organization, 1963.

Zwalf, W. *A Catalogue of the Gandhara Sculpture in the British Museum.* London: British Museum Press, 1996.

—— *The Shrines of Gandhara.* London: British Museum Publications, 1979.

Central Asia, Mongolia, Steppe Peoples

Barthold, W. *Turkestan Down to the Mongol Invasion.* Karachi: Indus Publications, 1981 (first published in Russian 1900, first English edition 1928).

Basilov, Vladimir N. (ed.). *The Nomads of Eurasia.* University of Washington Press, 1989.

Berger, P. and Tse Bartholomew, T. *Mongolia: The Legacy of Chingis Khan*. Exhibition catalogue. Asian Art Museum of San Francisco. London: Thames and Hudson, 1995.

British Museum. *Frozen Tombs: The Culture and Art of the Ancient Tribes of Siberia*. London: British Museum Press, 1978.

Buryakov, Y. F., Baipakov, K. M., Tashbaeva, Kh. and Yakubov, Y. *The Cities and Routes of the Great Silk Road (On Central Asian Documents)*. Tashkent: 'SHARQ' Publications, 1999.

Bussagli, Mario. *Painting of Central Asia*. Geneva: Editions d'Art Albert Skira, 1963.

Klimburg-Salter, D. *The Silk Route and the Diamond Path: Esoteric Buddhist Art on the Trans-Himalayan Trade Routes*. Los Angeles: UCLA Art Council, 1982.

Rowland, Benjamin. *The Wall Paintings of India, Central Asia and Ceylon: A Comparative Study*. Boston: Merrymount Press, 1938.

Index

Page numbers in italics are illustrations; in italics with '*m*' are maps; with 'g' are glossary terms; with 'n' are notes.